Wildflowers
of
Western
America

A Chanticleer Press Edition

Wildflowers
of
Western
America

Robert T. Orr
Margaret C. Orr

Alfred A. Knopf, New York

Planned and produced by Chanticleer Press, Inc., New York

Composition by All India Press

Printed and bound by Amilcare Pizzi, S.p.A., Milan, Italy

First Edition 1974

Library of Congress Catalog Card Number: 74-943

ISBN: 0-394-49363-X

Contents

Preface

By learning to identify native flowering plants one appreciates them more and begins to see how each relates to its environment. That is one of the main purposes of this book. It is also our hope that the reader will enjoy the challenge of trying to identify new species in the wild.

In many areas species of wildflowers are disappearing or becoming difficult to find because of human activity. Subdivisions, industrial expansion, freeways, agricultural development, valleys flooded by dams—all mean fewer plants. Many of the species affected by these activities are widespread and will continue to survive but must be sought in more remote areas. Some, however, are restricted and may become extinct if their habitat is disturbed. Fortunately, conservationists are now watching many of the species whose survival is in a precarious state.

Although quite a few of the pictures used here are our own, we wish to thank the many other persons whose excellent photography adds so much to this volume. Their contributions are listed in the back of the book. We thank Rachel Speiser, formerly illustrator for the New York Botanical Garden, for the drawings of flower parts and types of leaves. We also wish to thank many others who aided our botanical searches, both in the herbarium and in the field. These include Dr. Ira L. Wiggins, Emeritus Professor of Biology, Stanford University, who critically read the manuscript, Dr. Elizabeth McClintock, Chairman of the Department of Botany, California Academy of Sciences, Dr. George E. Lindsay, Director, California Academy of Sciences, many colleagues, friends, and members of our family. We are indebted to Milton Rugoff and his staff at Chanticleer Press, especially Celeste Targum, who guided us in this project, and to Charlotte Dorsey, whose meticulous editing, typing, and proofreading were invaluable.

ROBERT T. ORR
MARGARET C. ORR

San Francisco, California

Introduction

Man started classifying flowers thousands of years ago, but the systematic arrangement we use today was begun in the mid-18th century by the great Swedish botanist, Linnaeus. He presented a system which gave two Latin names, the first the genus and the second the species, to each kind of living organism. The genus name may be used for one or a group of species that have many characters in common and are therefore closely related. The species name applies to a group of plants or animals that are alike, apart from individual variation. For example, most Buttercups are of the genus *Ranunculus*, but there are many different species of Buttercups within the genus.

Some species show differences in different regions and are described as separate varieties or subspecies. Likewise, genera are combined into families which have broad general characters in common. The various families of plants included in this book are described in the back in a special section.

For the specific identification of a plant, botanists rely largely on the reproductive parts which comprise the flower or inflorescence. This is difficult for the novice since it entails a knowledge of plant structure, called morphology, and sometimes microscopic dissection. To avoid these problems we have used certain simple key characteristics as identification aids. First, the various species are arranged in color groups. Under color they are separated by the habitat in which they occur, then by growth characteristic (whether herb or shrub). Finally they are segregated by flower shape.

Segregation by color is an artificial classification since great color variation is shown by some closely related species and even occurs within species. It is a practical system, however, for most flowers, and one readily understood by a person with little or no knowledge of botany. After much consideration five color groups were selected. These are: (1) White-Green (including cream), (2) Yellow-Orange (including salmon), (3) Red-Pink (including rose and coral), (4) Blue-Violet (including lavender, violet, magenta, and orchid), and (5) Brown (various shades of dark purplish-brown and reddish-brown). In instances where several color variants occur within a species, the flower is placed in the most frequently encountered color and reference is made to the others. Arbitrary segregation had to be made between the Blue-Purple and Red-Pink groups, since a few flowers are in an intermediate category between Purple and Pink and some show a range from one to the other on the same inflorescence or at different stages of maturity. With these few flowers it may be necessary to go through both color groups.

Since most flowering plants are associated principally with one major natural community, this has been indicated insofar as possible for each species. A few have an extremely broad range of tolerance, occurring from sea coast to desert, but these are exceptions. For practical purposes most plants can be classified in one or two of the following biotic communities, which are dominated by certain conspicuous plants, especially trees: (1) Alpine and Subalpine, (2) Coniferous Forests, (3) Woodland, (4) Pinyon-Juniper-Sagebrush, (5) Chaparral, (6) Grassland, (7) Desert, (8) Sea Coast, (9) Aquatic, (10) Widespread. These habitats are described below.

After we have placed a plant with a flower of a particular color in the most likely community, the next decision is whether it is an herb or a shrub. The former lacks a woody stem above ground and may be an annual (surviving only for the season) or a perennial (living for several years or more). A shrub has a woody stem, which usually has branches, and is smaller than a tree.

The last key character is based upon the shape of the flower. While flowers vary greatly in form, generally they may be placed in one of three different groups—*regular, irregular,* or *composite* (see drawings following Introduction). *Regular* flowers are radially symmetrical with sepals, petals, and stamens radiating from the center, as, for example, in a buttercup or a rose. *Irregular* flowers have bilateral symmetry. They can be separated into similar halves only in one plane; the parts are not of the same size and shape, as, for example, a snapdragon. *Composite* flowers are made up of a number of flowers joined together to form a compound head, surrounded by bracts, known collectively as the involucre, on a receptacle. Usually the central flowers are tiny and have tubular corollas forming what is called the disc, while the marginal flowers have a limb- or strap-shaped corolla which extends outward and appears to be the petal, as, for example, in a daisy.

Major Habitats

1. *Alpine and Subalpine.* Areas at or above timberline in the higher mountains where the snow leaves the ground late in spring, temperatures are low, and the growing season is short. Heathers, Alpine Willow, Alpine Columbine, certain species of Buttercups, and *Potentilla* are among the dominant plants. In the lower margins conifers such as Whitebark Pine, Limber Pine, stunted Lodgepole Pine, and dwarfed Mountain Hemlock occur sparingly.
2. *Coniferous Forests.* These include the montane forests, principally of pine, fir, spruce, hemlock, and cedar, in the Cascade range, Sierra Nevada, Rocky Mountains, intermountain ranges of the Great Basin, higher mountains scattered over the Southwest, and Pacific coast coniferous forests of redwood, spruce, beach pine, and cedar.
3. *Woodland.* Primarily nonconiferous forests of evergreen and deciduous trees, especially oaks, madrone, buckeye, maples, and black walnut.
4. *Pinyon-Juniper-Sagebrush.* An extensive plant community occupying much of the Great Basin intermontane region between the Sierra–Cascade axis and the Rocky Mountains as well as certain adjacent areas.
5. *Chaparral.* A term used in parts of the West for brushland, some of it coastal but much of it occurring in dry, arid or semi-arid interior regions below the coniferous forests and woodlands. Characteristic species are Chamise *(Adenostoma fasciculatum),* Yerba Santa *(Eriodictyon),* Wild Lilac *(Ceanothus* spp.*),* Bush Poppy *(Dendromecon rigida),* Manzanita *(Arctostaphylos* spp.*),* Toyon *(Photinia arbutifolia),* Coyote Brush *(Baccharis pilularis),* and Coffeeberry *(Rhamnus californica).*
6. *Grassland.* Prairie grasslands east of the Rocky Mountains, desert grasslands of the Southwest, the Palouse Prairie of the Columbia River drainage east of the Cascade Range, much of the lowlands of California, and parts of western Oregon and Washington.
7. *Desert.* The great desert that extends from east of the Rio Grande in Texas to southern California and from northern Mexico to southern Utah.
8. *Sea Coast.* Including beaches, dunes, and coastal bluffs where we find salt-tolerant species that can also withstand wind.
9. *Aquatic.* Those few species of flowering plants that live in or partly in ponds and

lakes or along streams and must be at least partly in water to survive, such as water lilies.

10. *Widespread.* This category covers the few plants that may not be restricted to one or two plant communities.

Parts of a Plant

Flower (see drawings following Introduction). The flower is the reproductive part of the plant, which produces the seeds that produce new plants. Sometimes it is small and inconspicuous, but more often its showy nature insures its fertilization by insects attracted to it for nectar or pollen.

A flower consists of a base or *receptacle* to which the other elements are attached. On the outside generally two sets of *perianth* segments are arranged in whorls, the outer, composed of sepals, called the *calyx* and the inner, made up of petals, the *corolla*. Both calyx and corolla may be similar and petal-like, as in most lilies; then the term perianth alone is used. In flowering plants other than lilies they generally differ, with the calyx usually green like the herbage and the petals mostly a contrasting color. Sometimes the sepals are joined together to form a tubular calyx, and the petals may be joined to form a tubular corolla. In some flowers the upper and lower lips of the calyx, corolla, or both differ, so the flower is irregular, with bilateral symmetry, rather than regular with radical symmetry.

Usually rising from the center of the flower is the *pistil*, consisting of an *ovary* containing embryonic seeds, surrounded by a *style* which terminates in the *stigma*, an organ receptive to pollen. A tube grows from the pollen grain down the center of the style and enters the ovary, where fertilization takes place. Surrounding the pistil are the *stamens*, each consisting of an elongate *filament* on the tip of which is an *anther* that bears pollen. The stem on which a flower grows is known as a *pedicel*. Where the pedicel arises there may be a modified leaf or *bract*.

Flower Arrangement (see drawings following Introduction). Flowers may be *terminal*, occurring singly at the end of a stem, or *axillary*, emerging from the axil of a leaf where the leaf joins the stem.

Flowers often occur in clusters which vary in arrangement and have been given different names. A *raceme* is composed of a long axis on which flowers with pedicels or stems are distributed. A *spike* is similar, but the flowers lack pedicels. A *corymb* is like a raceme, with pedicels of differing length so that those of the lower flowers are much longer than the upper ones. A *panicle* is a compound inflorescence that may consist of a cluster of racemes, spikes, or corymbs. An *umbel* is a flat-topped cluster of flowers without a central axis. A *cyme* is an inflorescence in which the terminal bud is the first to open. It differs from the raceme, spike, corymb, and panicle, in which the lowest bud opens first and the terminal buds continue growth for an indefinite period. The latter are referred to as *indeterminate* inflorescences as opposed to cymes and umbels, which are *determinate* inflorescences.

The most important function of the flower is to produce a fruit, which may either be dry like a pod or fleshy like a tomato, on or inside of which are the seeds for the growth of future plants. Since we are not using fruits as a primary feature of identification they will not be described here, but they are many and varied.

Leaves (see drawings following Introduction). Leaves are the most conspicuous parts of most plants, and their shape and arrangement provide important clues for identification. They are divided into simple and compound types. A *simple* leaf is undivided; a *compound* leaf is divided into sections called *leaflets*. If the leaflets radiate from one point on the end of the leaf stem, known as a *petiole*, it is a *palmate* leaf or one shaped like a hand with extended fingers. If they are arranged along either side of the main axis, the leaf is *pinnate* or feather-shaped. The leaflets of a pinnate leaf may in turn be divided into secondary leaflets, forming a *bipinnate* leaf. Even further subdivisions may occur.

Leaves have many different shapes apart from being simple or compound. They may be *elliptic* or oblong, *ovate* or egg-shaped, *cordate* or heart-shaped, *sagittate* or arrow-shaped, *spatulate* or spade-shaped, *lanceolate* or lance-shaped, *reniform* or kidney-shaped, *linear* or narrow elongate, to mention a few. The margin of the leaf may be *entire* or smooth, *undulate* or wavy, *serrate* with sawtooth-like edges, or *dentate* with spiny edges. Many leaves are *lobed* or with deep, rounded indentations, as in some oaks. Others are *trifoliate* or divided into three parts, such as a clover leaf. Most leaves are attached to a stem or branch by means of a petiole, but if this is absent the leaf is *sessile*. In some plants, especially herbs, the leaves all arise at ground level and are *basal*. If these are arranged in a circle or *whorl* they form a basal *rosette*. The leaves farther up the stem are the *cauline* leaves. When a leaf is directly underneath a flower or cluster of flowers it is called a *bract*. Leaves may be *opposite* each other on a stem, *alternate* (only one at a stem joint), or whorled (3 or more attached to a stem at the same joint).

Although these terms may seem a bit confusing at first, they can be learned in a short time and will prove most valuable as an aid in plant identification.

Major Floral Regions

Western North America is a region of diverse geographical conditions ranging from desert to alpine tundra. From the Mississippi River westward for hundreds of miles the land rises gradually to the Rocky Mountains, forming the prairie grasslands of the Great Plains. To the south these short-grass prairies merge into the desert grasslands of western Texas and New Mexico. West of the Rocky Mountains and extending over to the next great mountain systems, the Sierra Nevada–Cascade ranges, is the Great Basin or Intermountain Region, marked by sagebrush-covered valleys separated by isolated mountain ranges. To the south is the great Sonoran Desert. West of the Sierra Nevada and Cascades are valleys separating them from the Coast Ranges that extend from the Mexican border to British Columbia.

Within this diversified geographic area botanists have distinguished many floral regions which have certain characteristic plants. Following are some of the more important of these regions, a number of whose plants are described in this book.

Pacific Northwest. This is a region dominated by conifers. It extends south from western British Columbia to northwestern California. Rainfall is high in some regions, especially near the Pacific Ocean, decreasing farther inland. It is proper to divide the Pacific Northwest into several subregions. The western part of the Olympic Peninsula, especially in the Hoh River drainage, is a true northern rain forest characterized by dense stands of White Cedar *(Thuja plicata)*. Western Hemlock *(Tsuga heterophylla)* and Douglas Fir *(Pseudotsuga menziesii)* are also important components of this forest, along with some Sitka Spruce *(Picea sitchensis)* and Lowland Fir *(Abies grandis)*. The Sitka Spruce, Lowland Fir, and Western Hemlock extend southward to north-western California and are intermixed locally with Beach Pine *(Pinus contorta)*; the Douglas Fir is widespread over the western mountains east to the Rockies. From southern Oregon to central California the Coast Redwood *(Sequoia sempervirens)* becomes dominant just inland from the coast. In places it shares dominance with the Douglas Fir. Oaks of various species replace these conifers in the lower interior coastal mountains. Flowering plants characteristic of the Pacific Northwest Coastal Region include Salal *(Gaultheria shallon)*, Huckleberry *(Vaccinium ovatum)*, Redwood Sorrel *(Oxalis oregana)*, Vanilla Leaf *(Achlys triphylla)*, Pacific Rhododendron *(Rhododendron macrophyllum)*, and Salmon Berry *(Rubus spectabilis)*.

East of the coastal forests of the Pacific Northwest is the Cascade range, a series of volcanic peaks extending from British Columbia to northern California. The western slopes, covered with a mantle of conifers, receive a much higher rainfall than the eastern side. In the lower western parts Douglas Fir, Western Hemlock and White Fir *(Abies concolor)* are among the most conspicuous. Higher up these give way to Lodgepole Pine *(Pinus murrayana)*, Red Fir *(Abies magnifica)*, and Silver Fir *(Abies amabilis)*, with subalpine forests of Mountain Hemlock *(Tsuga mertensiana)* and Subalpine Fir *(Abies lasiocarpa)*. On the eastern slopes, where it is more arid, Ponderosa Pine *(Pinus ponderosa)*, Sagebrush *(Artemisia tridentata)*, and Antelope Brush *(Purshia tridentata)* dominate the flora. The Cascades are rich in flowers. Common species are Oregon Grape *(Berberis nervosa)*, several kinds of Windflowers or Anemones including *Anemone oregana, A. delloidea,* and *A. lyallii,* Starflower *(Trientalis latifolia)*, Washington Lily *(Lilium washingtonianum)*, Drummond's Cinquefoil *(Potentilla drummondii)*, Bleeding Heart *(Dicentra formosa)*, Common Gentian *(Gentiana sceptrum)*, and Avalanche Lily *(Erythronium montanum)*.

Californian Region. Excluding the northwest coast and the southeastern desert areas, the Californian Region comprises the sea coast and Coast Ranges, the great Central Valley, and the Sierra Nevada. The region is one of dry summers, with precipitation almost entirely restricted to the winter months. The climate is temperate along the coast, hot in summer inland, with heavy winter snows in the Sierra Nevada and high inner Coast Ranges and cross ranges. Along the coast scattered closed-cone pines such as Bishop Pine *(Pinus muricata)*, Monterey Pine *(Pinus radiata)*, Knobcone Pine *(Pinus attenuata)*, and cypresses of several species occur, along with Douglas Fir, on headlands or back from the coastal plain on ridges. On the higher Coast Ranges some Ponderosa Pine and Sugar Pine *(Pinus lambertiana)* occur, as well as White Fir. Where it is warmer and dryer, including the lower western slopes of the Sierra Nevada, Digger Pine *(Pinus sabiniana)* grows. Considerable grassland is interspersed with these forests, and brushland dominates extensive areas. Along the coast the dominant vegetation consists in part of various kinds of Wild Lilac *(Ceanothus)*, Coyote Bush *(Baccharis pilularis)*, Chaparral Pea *(Pickeringia montana)*, and Coastal Sage *(Artemisia californica)*, while in dryer, more inland situations Chamise *(Adenostoma fasciculatum)*, many kinds of Manzanita *(Arctostaphylos)* and Scrub Oak *(Quercus dumosa)* are found. Numerous endemic flowering plants are associated with this chaparral as well as with the coastal coniferous forests.

The Great Valley of California has undergone much change from its original condition because of its use for agriculture. However, in the spring certain areas along the margin and in the lower foothills become wildflower gardens with great masses of Goldfields

13

(Baeria chrysostoma), Baby Blue-Eyes *(Nemophila menziesii)*, California Poppies *(Eschscholtzia californica)*, Fiddleneck *(Amsinckia intermedia)*, and other common annuals or perennials.

The Sierra Nevada is an extensive north-south range that rises slowly from the west side to over 14,000 feet in places and then drops off abruptly to the east. The chaparral and then the Digger Pine and Blue Oak *(Quercus douglasii)* belts along the lower western slopes give way at middle altitudes to Douglas Fir, Ponderosa Pine, Incense Cedar *(Libocedrus decurrens)*, White Fir *(Abies concolor)*, and Black Oak *(Quercus kelloggii)*, with various kinds of Mountain Lilac *(Ceanothus)* and Manzanita forming an undercover. In places Mountain Misery *(Chamaebatia foliolosa)* forms a solid ground cover. Higher up the Red Fir *(Abies magnifica)*, Sugar Pine *(Pinus lambertiana)*, and Lodgepole Pine are dominant, intermingled with Aspen *(Populus tremuloides)*. In the spring, shrubs such as Service Berry *(Amelanchier)*, Mountain Ash *(Sorbus sitchensis)*, Bitter Cherry *(Prunus emarginata)*, Snowbrush *(Ceanothus cordulatus)*, and Tobacco Brush *(Ceanothus velutinus)* produce a profusion of blooms along with such herbs as Columbine *(Aquilegia formosa)*, Paint Brush *(Castilleja miniata)*, and Mountain Penstemon *(Penstemon newberryi)*. Higher up Western White Pine *(Pinus monticola)* and Mountain Hemlock become abundant, and at timberline Whitebark Pine *(Pinus albicaulis)*.

Rocky Mountain Region. The Rocky Mountains of the United States, bordered on the west by the Great Basin and the Columbian Plateau and on the east by the high Great Plains, have a montane flora somewhat resembling that of the Sierra Nevada. In addition to such conifers as Ponderosa Pine, Douglas Fir, Lodgepole Pine, and White Fir there are Engelmann Spruce *(Picea engelmannii)* and Subalpine Fir *(Abies lasiocarpa)*, with Limber Pine *(Pinus flexilis)* near timberline. Western Larch *(Larix occidentalis)* extends down from Canada into northern Idaho and western Montana, and White Cedar also grows there in areas of higher rainfall. Many annual and perennial plants grow in the Rocky Mountain region. Some of the conspicuous and common ones like Skyrocket Gilia *(Gilia aggregata)*, Mertensia *(Mertensia ciliata)*, Groundsel *(Senecio triangularis)*, Cinquefoil *(Potentilla gracilis)*, Yellow Monkey Flower *(Mimulus guttatus)*, Elephant's Head *(Pedicularis groenlandica)*, and Corn Lily *(Veratrum californicum)* are also common to other western mountain ranges, while others such as Mariposa *(Calochortus gunnisonii)*, Rocky Mountain Beeplant *(Cleome serrulata)*, and Whipple Beard Tongue *(Penstemon whippleanus)* are restricted largely to the Rockies.

Great Basin. The extensive intermontane region between the Rocky Mountains and the Sierra Nevada and southern Cascade range is known as the Great Basin because it lacks any drainage outlet to the sea. It includes parts of eastern California, all except the extreme southern end of Nevada, western Utah, extreme southern Idaho, and parts of southeastern Oregon. It is a land of extreme temperatures, hot during the short summer, with long, cold winters, but relatively little precipitation since the Sierra Nevada to the west forms a rain shadow, taking most of the available moisture out of the atmosphere coming from the west and northwest. It is a moderately high plateau, sloping downward toward the south and marked by arid valleys separated by numerous north-south mountain ranges. Vegetation in the valleys is dominated by Sagebrush *(Artemisia tridentata)*, but many other kinds of plants are associated with it, especially where there is some moisture. These include Rabbit Brush *(Chrysothamus nauseosus)*,

Desert Poppy or Chicalote *(Argemone platyceras)*, Saltbush *(Atriplex confertifolia)*, Prince's Plume *(Stanleya pinnata)*, and Purple Sage *(Salvia carnosa)*. Loose, pygmy forests of Pinyon Pines *(Pinus cembroides* vars. *monophylla* and *edulis)* grow on the mountains with many annual or perennial plants appearing in spring and summer. Antelope Brush, Arrowleaf Balsam Root *(Balsamorhiza sagittata)*, Spurred Lupine *(Lupinus caudatus)*, and Sego Lily *(Calochortus nuttallii)* are among the conspicuous species.

Northwest of the Great Basin Region on the Columbian Plateau of eastern Washington and north central Oregon is an area known as the Palouse Region. It is semi-desert with low rainfall, characterized by grassland, some Sagebrush, and scattered Ponderosa Pine.

Southwestern Desert. This is a vast area of dry land extending from southeastern California east to Texas and south into Mexico as far as the state of Zacatecas. It is frequently divided into the Mohave and Sonoran Deserts. The former is characterized by such plants as the Joshua Tree *(Yucca brevifolia)*, Mohave Sage *(Cassia armata)*, Spiny Senna *(Dalea arborescens)*, Horse Bush *(Tetradymia stenolepis)*, and Parry Saltbush *(Atriplex parryi)*. The Sonoran Desert is perhaps best characterized by the Smoke Tree *(Dalea spinosa)*, such Sages as *Salvia greatai* and *S. eremostachya,* Desert Agave *(Agave desertii)*, and Crucifixion Thorn *(Holocantha emoryi)*. The Creosote Bush *(Larrea divaricata)* is common to all desert regions from California to Texas and is probably the best indicator.

Climatic conditions in the desert are severe with great extremes of dry heat and cold. Strong winds prevail in many areas, and rainfall is low. In southern Arizona there are normally two rainy seasons per year, one in summer and one in winter, hence two flowering seasons. After favorable rains the deserts become flower gardens with numerous annuals suddenly appearing and perennials leafing out and blooming. Many types of Cacti, Evening Primroses *(Oenothera* spp.*)*, Penstemons, Ghost Flowers *(Mohavea* spp.*)*, Golden Yarrow *(Eriophyllum wallacei)*, Panamint Daisy *(Enceliopsis argophylla)*, Desert Blazing Star *(Mentzelia involucrata)*, Desert Dandelion *(Malacothrix glabrata)*, Nolina *(Nolina parryi)*, and Ocotillo *(Fouquieria splendens)* are a few of the numerous colorful plants found there.

Great Plains Region. From about 3500 feet altitude on the west side of the Mississippi Valley to the base of the Rocky Mountains stretches an extensive area of prairie characterized by grass and the absence of trees except along watercourses. Bluestem grasses *(Poa* spp.*)* predominate in the lower-altitude, tall-grass prairies nearer the Mississippi River. Much of the region in the West, however, is higher and dominated by shorter grasses *(Bouteloua)*, Buffalo Grass *(Buchloe dactytoides)*, Scurfpea *(Psoralea)*, certain Cacti, Groundsels *(Senecio* spp.*)*, Sages (*(Salvia)*, Prairie Ground Cherry *(Physalis lanceolata)*, and other grassland species.

The northern part of the Great Plains contains potholes or small prairie ponds which provide the environment for many kinds of moisture-loving plants, especially Willows *(Salix)*, Cattails *(Typha)*, Sedges *(Carex)*, Rushes *(Juncus)*, Pondweed *(Potamogeton)*, and Arrowhead *(Sagittaria)*.

Parts of a Flower

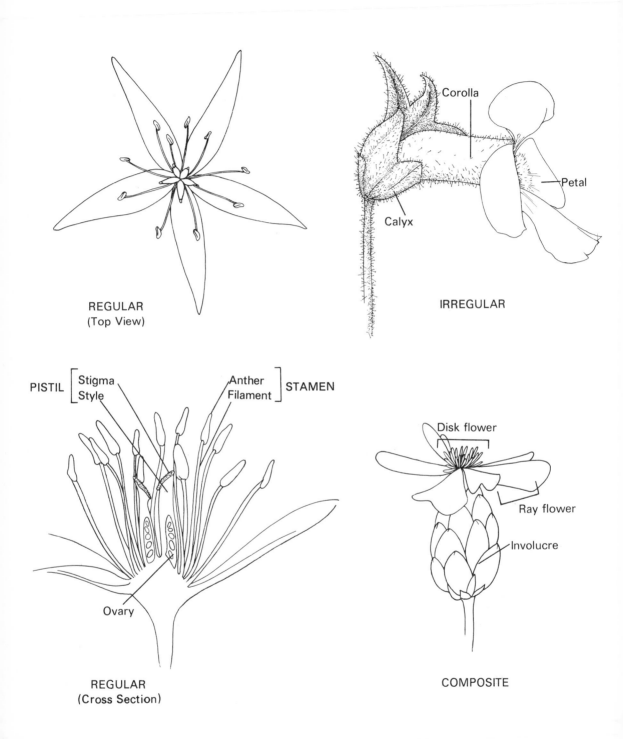

REGULAR
(Top View)

Corolla

Petal

Calyx

IRREGULAR

PISTIL
Stigma
Style

Anther
Filament
STAMEN

Ovary

REGULAR
(Cross Section)

Disk flower

Ray flower

Involucre

COMPOSITE

Flower Clusters

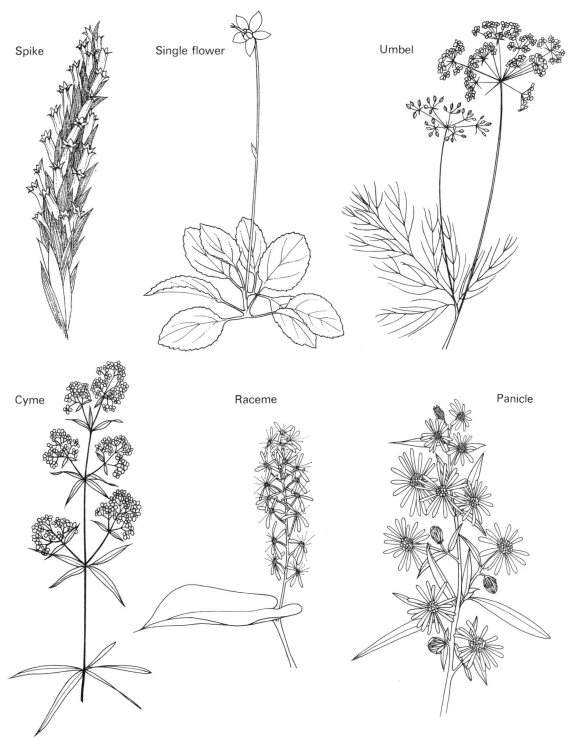

Spike

Single flower

Umbel

Cyme

Raceme

Panicle

Types of Leaves

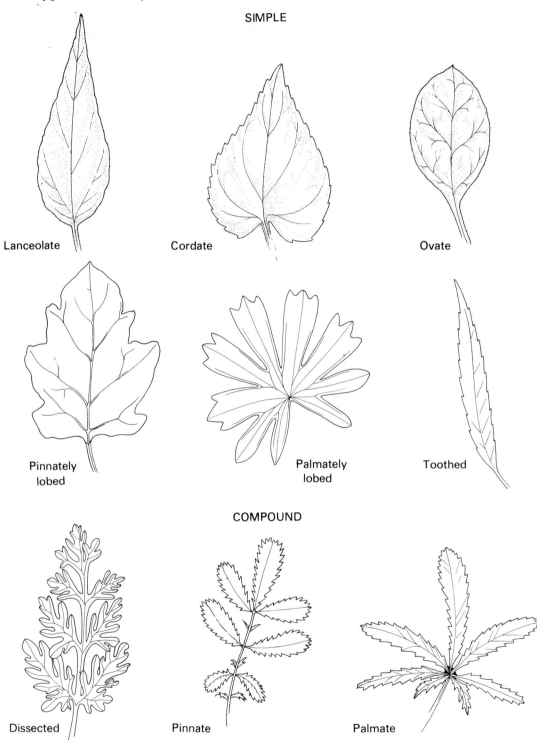

SIMPLE

Lanceolate

Cordate

Ovate

Pinnately lobed

Palmately lobed

Toothed

COMPOUND

Dissected

Pinnate

Palmate

Arrangement of Leaves on Stem

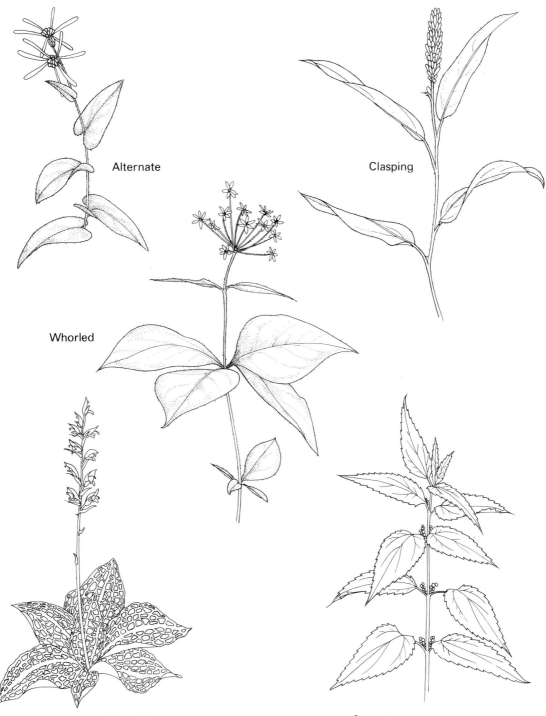

Alternate

Clasping

Whorled

Basal Rosette

Opposite

Glossary

Achene. A small, seedlike fruit containing one seed.

Alternate leaves. Arising singly from the stem, not in pairs.

Anther. The upper portion of a stamen, containing pollen grains.

Axil. The angle between the upper side of a leaf and the stem from which it rises.

Banner. Uppermost petal in a pea flower.

Basal leaves. Leaves at the base of the stem.

Berry. A fleshy fruit developed from a single ovary.

Bipinnate leaf. A compound leaf whose leaflets are divided into secondary leaflets.

Bracts. Modified leaves, usually situated at the base of a flower or inflorescence.

Bulb. A short underground stem, bearing fleshy food-storing scale leaves.

Calyx. Collective term for the leaflike sepals of a flower, usually green.

Campanulate. Bell-shaped.

Capsule. A dry fruit that splits open along several lines.

Cauline. Of or growing on a stem.

Clasping. A description of a leaf that wholly or partly surrounds its stem or petiole.

Claw. Narrowed base of a petal.

Composite flower. A central cluster of tiny regular flowers forming a disk surrounded by a circle of tiny irregular flowers with corollas that appear to be petals.

Compound leaf. A leaf divided into smaller leaflets.

Cordate. Heart-shaped.

Corm. A short, thickened underground stem, upright in position.

Corolla. Collectively, the petals of a flower.

Corymb. A form of inflorescence in which the lower pedicels or stems are longer, so that the flowers form a flat-topped or convex cluster.

Cross-pollination. The transfer of pollen from the anther of one plant to the stigma of a flower of another plant.

Cuneate leaf. Triangular and tapering to a point at the base.

Cyme. A type of inflorescence in which a terminal flower develops first, followed by secondary, tertiary, and other axes. The result is a flat or convex cluster.

Dioecious. Bearing male and female flowers on different plants of the same species.

Disc flower. The tubular flowers that compose the central part of a head of flowers in most Compositae.

Dissected leaf. Deeply cut into numerous segments.

Elliptic. Having the form of an ellipse.

Embryo. The small plant within the seed.

Entire leaf margin. Without divisions or teeth.

Exserted. Extending beyond, such as stamens protruding from a corolla.

Fascicle. A small bundle or cluster of fibers, leaves or flowers.

Filament. A thread; the stalk supporting an anther of a stamen.

Fimbriate. Fringed.

Glabrous. Bald.

Gland. A small secreting structure usually producing oil or nectar.

Glandular. Bearing glands that produce a sticky liquid.

Glaucous. A whitish powdery coating on the surface of leaves or fruit.

Head. A crowded cluster of sessile or nearly sessile flowers.

Herb. A nonwoody plant; usually remaining soft and succulent.

Indistinguishable flower. Lacking recognizable petals or sepals or with petals or sepals too small to be easily identified.

Inflorescence. A flower cluster; flowers collectively.

Involucre. A circle of bracts around a flower or flower cluster.

Irregular flower. With petals and/or sepals that are not uniform in shape but are usually grouped to form upper and lower "lips" that may be lobed

Keel. A ridge or rib; in a pea flower, the two lowest petals united along their lower margins.

Lanceolate leaf. Lance-shaped; much longer than wide; the widest portion below the middle.

Leaflet. One of the parts of a compound leaf.

Linear leaf. Long and narrow, with the margins essentially parallel.

Lobed. Indented at the margins not more than half way to the center.

Monoecious. Having both staminate and pistillate flowers borne on the same plant.

Node. The region of the stem where leaves or branches are attached.

Oblanceolate leaf. Shaped like a lance head; broadest toward the apex.

Obovate leaf. Egg-shaped, with narrow end at the base.

Opposite leaves. Leaves occurring in pairs at a node.

Ovary. The swollen basal portion of a pistil, within which seeds develop.

Ovate leaf. Egg-shaped, with broader end at the base.

Ovule. The immature seed in the ovary.

Palmate. With 3 or more divisions or lobes like outspread fingers of the hand.

Panicle. A compound raceme; elongated diversely branching flower cluster.

Pappus. A feathery tuft of bristles on certain fruits, as on the seeds of the dandelion.

Pedicel. The stalk of a flower.

Peduncle. A flower stalk or stem.

Perianth. The calyx or corolla or both.

Petal. A structural unit of a corolla; usually brightly colored.

Petiole. The stalklike portion of a leaf; attaches leaf to stem.

Pinnate leaf. A compound leaf with the leaflets arranged along the sides of a common petiole; literally like a feather.

Pistil. The female organ of a flower, typically consisting of a stigma, a tubular style, and an ovary at the base.

Pistillate flower. A flower with one or more pistils but no functional stamens.

Pod. Any dry fruit that opens on maturing.

Pollen. Spores produced in the anthers.

Pollination. The transfer of pollen from the anther to the stigma of the same or another flower.

Pubescent. Covered with hairs.

Raceme. An elongate, unbranched inflorescence in which the individual flowers are borne on pedicels along a stalk.

Ray flower. The flowers that encircle the disc flowers in some members of the daisy family.

Receptacle. End of the pedicel on which the flower parts are borne.

Regular flower. With petals and/or sepals arranged symmetrically around the center, like the spokes of a wheel.

Reniform. Kidney-shaped.

Rhizome. A horizontal underground stem, often enlarged by food storage; distinguished from roots by the presence of nodes.

Rootstock. Another term for rhizome.

Rosette. A circular cluster of leaves; usually basal.

Runner. A stem that grows horizontally over the surface of the soil, often developing new plants at the nodes or tip.

Sagittate. Arrow-shaped.

Saprophyte. A plant living on dead organic matter and lacking chlorophyll.

Scape. A leafless flower-bearing stem.

Sepal. A division of the calyx.

Serrated leaf. Having sharp teeth along the margin, resembling a saw.

Sessile. Without a stalk.

Sessile leaf. One lacking a petiole and with the blade attached directly.

Shrub. A branching woody plant.

Simple leaf. A leaf that consists of an undivided blade.

Spadix. A club-shaped spike of tiny flowers, usually enclosed in a spathe.

Spathe. A bract or pair of bracts, often large, enclosing an inflorescence.

Spatulate leaf. Shaped like a spatula; having a broad rounded end and a narrow base.

Species (abbreviation of plural, spp.). A fundamental category of taxonomic classification, ranking after a genus.

Spike. An elongated flower cluster with sessile or nearly sessile flowers.

Spur. A slender, usually hollow projection from some part of a flower.

Stamen. The male organ of a flower; composed of a filament topped with a pollen-producing anther; there are usually several in each flower.

Staminate flower. Bearing anthers and usually without pistils.

Standard. The upper petal or banner of a pea flower; also an iris petal.

Stigma. The tip of the pistil; it receives the pollen grains.

Stipules. Small leaflike appendages on either side of some petioles.

Style. The narrow part of the pistil, usually connecting ovary and stigma.

Succulent. A plant with fleshy, water-storing stems or leaves.

Tap root. A stout vertical root.

Tendril. A slender coiling modified leaf or stem that aids in the support of climbing plants.

Toothed leaf margin. With a sawtooth edge.

Umbel. A flower cluster in which the flower stalks arise from the same point, like the ribs of an umbrella.

Undulate. Having a wavy outer edge.

Whorled leaves. A circle of three or more leaves, branches, or pedicels at a node.

Wing. In plants, a projecting membrane found on margins of a seed, leaf, or leaf stalk; lateral petal of a pea flower.

Flower
Descriptions

Note:

The following descriptions are divided into five color groups: ✳ White·Green, ★ Yellow·Orange, ● Red·Pink, ■ Blue·Violet, and ▲ Brown. Within each color group, flowers have been arranged by habitat, and within each habit according to general visual similarities.

Where several color variants occur within a species, usually the flower with the color most frequently encountered is illustrated; the other color variants are noted in the text.

Only the species descriptions illustrated in color bear a number; this is also the number of the color plate.

The simplified keys preceding the text for each color section will aid in the exact identification of a flower of that color.

The glossary and drawings at the front of the book explain the terms used in this book.

The names of flowers that are relatively rare or endangered by overpicking are marked with a dagger (†) symbol.

White · Green

Simplified Key

	HABITAT	HERB	SHRUB
Regular	ALPINE	2 Western Pasque Flower 3 Marsh Marigold 1 Mountain Dryad Alpine Forget-me-not	4 White Heather 5 Labrador Tea
Regular	CONIFEROUS	16 Mariposa Lily 14 Leichtlin's Mariposa 23 Bride's Bonnet 18 Avalanche Lily 8 False Solomon's Seal 9 Solomon's Seal Corn Lily 27 Bear Grass 11 Alkali Grass 12 Ground Iris Smartweed 22 Southern Lewisia 19 Tweedy's Lewisia 28 Anemone Meadow Rue 17 Inside-out Flower Alum Root Miterwort 15 Grass-of-Parnassus Saxifrage 20 Indian Pipe White Phlox	Serviceberry 13 Mountain Misery 24 Syringa 25/26 Bitter Cherry Granite Gilia
Irregular		7 Spotted Coralroot 21 Lady's Slipper 10 Rein Orchid Yerba Buena	
Composite		6 Western Coltsfoot	
Regular	WOODLAND	32 White Globe Lily 30 Pussy Ears Wood Anemone 39 Milkmaids 34 Vanilla Leaf 35 Woodland Star	Cream Bush 31 Deer Brush 29 Mountain Dogwood 33 Salal 36 Western Azalea
Regular	PINYON-JUNIPER-SAGE	40 Sego Lily 42 Sand Corn 41 Evening Primrose 37 Jimson Weed	38 Apache Plume

Simplified Key

HABITAT		HERB	SHRUB
Regular	**CHAPARRAL**	45 Nolina 47 Matilija Poppy 44 Western Morning Glory	43 Our Lord's Candle Tree Anemone 46 Parry Manzanita 48 Pitcher Sage
Irregular			Joshua Tree Sahuaro
Regular	**DESERT**	55 Desert Lily 58 Desert Lily Sandpaper Plant 50 Sand Blazing Star 53 Pincushion Cactus 49 Desert Evening Primrose Sand Mat 52 Chicalote Canbya 57 Milkweed Desert Tobacco	
Irregular			Wand Sage
Composite		White Tack-stem 54 Fleabane White Tidy Tips 51 Desert Star 56 Desert Chicory Pincushion Flower	
Regular	**GRASS**	59 Wild Onion Soap Plant 60 Lace Pod 62 Meadow Sidalcea 61 Cream Cups	
Regular	**SEA COAST**	64 Ice Plant 63 Beach Strawberry	
Regular	**AQUATIC**	Western Water Hemlock 65 Canadian Dogwood Meadow Foam	
Regular	**WIDESPREAD**	66 Mouse Ear 67 Cow Parsnip Lace Parsnip Five Spot Popcorn Flower	
Composite		Yarrow	

1 MOUNTAIN DRYAD *(Dryas octopetala)* Rose family *(Rosaceae)*

Height: Perennial herb, 4"-6" (10-15cm). **Flowers:** Sepals, petals attached to rim of flower tube; sepals 5; petals 8-10, 1"-2" (2.5-5cm) long, white to cream; styles long, silky at maturity. **Leaves:** Lance-shaped, about 1" (2.5cm) long, with scalloped edges. **In bloom:** June-August. **Habitat-Range:** Alpine slopes and ridges; Oregon to Alaska, east to Rocky Mountains.

This tiny alpine plant is here called an herb, but, despite its diminutive size, its stems are woody and might qualify it as a shrub.

2 WESTERN PASQUE FLOWER Buttercup family *(Ranunculaceae)*
(Anemone occidentalis)

Height: Perennial herb, 4"-15" (10-40cm). **Flowers:** Solitary, without petals; sepals white, showy, 5-8; stamens numerous; pistils numerous, developing into achenes with long plumelike tail. **Leaves:** Basal, 1 1/2"-3" (4-7 1/2cm) wide, silk-haired, twice pinnately divided. **In bloom:** Spring-summer. **Habitat-Range:** Dry rocky alpine slopes; Canada south to California, east to Montana.

The conspicuous flower often appears before the leaves fully open, blooming where the snow has just melted. The stems are stout and very hairy with a whorl of three leaves near the base of the flower. The ripened seeds form a silky, feathery head, curved downward. "Pasque" refers to the Passover or Easter time of blooming and to the purity of the white sepals. It is also called "Wind Flower" because the seeds are wind-borne. A related species, *A. patens*, also known as Pasque Flower, has blue petals and is the state flower of South Dakota.

3 MARSH MARIGOLD Buttercup family *(Ranunculaceae)*
(Caltha leptosepala)

Height: Perennial herb, 4"-8" (10-20cm). **Flowers:** 1 1/4" (3cm) across; sepals white, 5-9, no petals; stamens, pistils many. **Leaves:** Few, smooth, heart-shaped, slightly toothed, often purple-veined on underside. **In bloom:** June-September. **Habitat-Range:** Alpine or subalpine areas along mountain streams, 7000'-10,000' (2150-3050m); Alaska, Canada south to Oregon, Rocky Mountains south to Arizona, New Mexico.

The generic name *Caltha* in ancient Latin referred to the true Marigold, a member of the Sunflower family, which this buttercup superficially resembles. These white flowers are closely related to the common yellow Marsh Marigold of the East (*C. palustris*). Both are found in wet places, often blooming as the snow melts at altitudes up to 12,000' (3650m).

ALPINE FORGET-ME-NOT Borage family *(Boraginaceae)*
(Cryptantha humilis)

Height: Perennial herb, 4"-12" (10-30cm). **Flowers:** White, tubular, tiny, expanding to 1/2" (1cm) broad; calyx lobes lance-shaped, twice as long as tube; borne on scorpioid (curled like the tail of a scorpion) spikes. **Leaves:** Silky, hairy, lance-shaped, 1"-2" (2.5-5cm) long, dense on several stems. **In bloom:** June-August. **Habitat-Range:** High alpine mountain ridges, 6000'-14,000' (1800-3470m); Sierra Nevada, east to Nevada, north to southern Idaho.

Cryptantha comes from the Greek *cryptos,* meaning hidden, and *anthos,* flower. Some of the first species described had such minute flowers that they appeared hidden. The blossoms are all on one side of the stalk. In some places the multitude of these plants produces a white carpet in summer.

4 WHITE HEATHER *(Cassiope mertensiana)* Heather family *(Ericaceae)*

Height: Perennial shrub, 2″-12″ (5-30cm). **Flowers:** Solitary, bell-shaped, nodding on slender pedicels; calyx, corolla 4-5 lobed. **Leaves:** Small, densely overlapping, enclosing stem. **In bloom:** July-August. **Habitat-Range:** Rocky alpine ledges up to 12,000′ (3650m); Sierra Nevada, Coast Ranges of California north to Alaska; Rockies.

This plant appears as a thick mat when not in bloom, with the scalelike leaves covering the stems. The waxy white flowers bloom thickly in the manner of Lily-of-the-valley. Their starlike appearance no doubt inspired the name Cassiope, who, in Greek mythology, was set among the stars as a constellation.

5 LABRADOR TEA *(Ledum glandulosum)* Heath family *(Ericaceae)*

Height: Perennial shrub, 2′-5′ (.6-1.5m). **Flowers:** Small in umbel-like clusters; sepals 5, small; petals 5, separate, white; stamens 10. **Leaves:** Fragrant, opposite, oblong, glandular, often lighter underneath; 1″-2 1/2″ (2.5-6.5cm) long. **In bloom:** June-August. **Habitat-Range:** Borders of wet meadows; alpine Sierra Nevada, Oregon, east to Rocky Mountains.

This plant has several subspecies at lower elevations, with the main differences in the leaves. Some have more glands and hairs with leaf edges curled under. All grow in moist, boggy places and are considered poisonous to sheep. Some species are called Rosemary flowers and have been used as a medicinal tea, although the taste is bitter and the odor unpleasant. The generic name comes from the Greek *Ledon,* which was the name used for the Rock Rose in ancient times. Both have a similar aromatic.

6 WESTERN COLTSFOOT *(Petasites palmata)* Sunflower family *(Compositae)*

Height: Perennial herb, 4″-20″ (10-50cm). **Flowers:** In densely crowded corymb, tubular, white, some flower heads with perfect, sterile flowers; fertile heads with mostly pistillate flowers, a few perfect ones in center of head; seeds with long, soft, white bristles when mature. **Leaves:** Scalelike on flower stems; basal leaves large, 5″-16″ (12.5-40cm) long, palmately divided on petioles 4″-16″ (10-40cm) long, opening after flower stems appear; all densely covered with weblike hairs. **In bloom:** March-April. **Habitat-Range:** Deep shade in coniferous forests below 1000′ (300m); Pacific Coast ranges to Alaska, east to New England.

This is one of the earliest spring flowers to appear in moist woods. It is often through blooming when the large-lobed leaf unfolds; the leaf remains most of the summer. Both the generic name, which is Greek for "broad-brimmed hat," and the popular name, referring to a burro's hoof, are based on the shape of the leaf.

7 SPOTTED CORALROOT *(Corallorhiza maculata)* Orchid family *(Orchidaceae)*

Height: Saprophytic herb, 8″-28″ (20-70cm). **Flowers:** Few to many, openly borne in raceme on brown-purple or yellowish stem; 3 sepals, lateral petals alike, crimson-purple to greenish; lower petal white, spotted, veined red, unequally 3-lobed; column of joined stamens, style yellow, curved. **Leaves:** Scalelike. **In bloom:** June-August. **Habitat-Range:** Coniferous forests below 9000′ (2700m); California to British Columbia, east to the Atlantic.

The orchids in this genus live off dead plant material in the soil and do not manufacture their own food. The name refers to the branching root, which is really a stem from which the flower stalks arise. The species name is from the Latin *macula*, meaning spot.

8 FALSE SOLOMON'S SEAL *(Smilacina racemosa)* Lily family *(Liliaceae)*

Height: Perennial herb, 1′-3′ (.3-1m) from stout horizontal rootstalk. **Flowers:** Many, small, in branched panicle at end of leafy stem; perianth of 6 equal segments, white, minute; stamens on filaments longer, broader than segments; fruit, bright red berry. **Leaves:** In two rows, oblong to lance-shaped, 3″-5 1/2″ (7-15cm), pointed at apex, clasping stem with broad base, many-nerved. **In bloom:** March-May. **Habitat-Range:** Shaded woods below 6000′ (1800m) throughout California Coast Ranges, Sierra Nevada to Canada, east to Rocky Mountains.

The various species of *Smilacina* have confusing common names. Star Flower rather clearly defines *S. stellata*, with larger white flowers on a less dense panicle. Two varieties are called Slim Solomon and Fat Solomon, respectively. All are similar in range and habitat and are a familiar part of the western coniferous woodland.

9 SOLOMON'S SEAL *(Smilacina stellata)* Lily family *(Liliaceae)*

Height: Perennial herb, 12″-24″ (30-60cm). **Flowers:** 3-15 in raceme; perianth of 6 equal segments about 1/4″ (6mm) long; white; stamens 6, shorter than perianth segments. **Leaves:** 2″-6″ (5-15cm) long, 3/4″-1 1/4″ (2-3cm) wide, ascending, clasping stem. **In bloom:** April-June. **Habitat-Range:** Wet places, coniferous forests; Sierra Nevada, west coast north to British Columbia.

The common name applies to many New and Old World species, but its meaning is obscure. Another name is Star Flower, as the species name indicates. The flowers are a delicate white addition to the dark green of the forest. Seeds are borne in small red-purple berries that become black when ripe.

10 REIN ORCHID *(Habenaria dilatata)* Orchid family *(Orchidaceae)*

Height: Perennial herb, 16″-30″ (40-75cm). **Flowers:** In terminal spike 4″-8″ (10-20cm) long; green bracts no longer than flowers; flowers about 1/2″ (1cm) long, white; lateral sepals extended outward on back; lateral petals lance-shaped with lower lip broader at base; spur extruding backward about 1/2″ (1cm). **Leaves:** Alternate, sessile, lance-shaped, 3″-9″ (8-24cm) long, becoming shorter near top of stem. **In bloom:** June-September. **Habitat-Range:** Wet meadows and bogs, often under trees in partly shaded situations. Mountains of California to British Columbia, east to the Rocky Mountains, below 11,000′ (3300m).

About 500 species of *Habenaria* grow in temperate and warmer parts of the world. They are called Rein Orchids after the generic name, which is derived from the Latin *habena*, meaning the rein of a horse, because of the reinlike shape of the spur in some species.

YERBA BUENA *(Satureja douglasii)*   Mint family *(Labiatae)*

Height: Trailing perennial herb. **Flower:** Small, solitary in axil of leaf; calyx tubular with marked striations or nerves, 5 lobes; corolla 2-lipped, hairy exterior, 1/4″ (6mm) long, white; stamens 4 with lower 2 longer. **Leaves:** Ovate, 1/2″-1″ (1-2.5cm) long, glandular, especially on underside; stem square. **In bloom:** April-September. **Habitat-Range:** Shaded places, principally in coniferous forests; from southern California to British Columbia.

Yerba Buena, meaning "good herb" in Spanish, is a common aromatic plant along the Pacific coast. Its dried leaves make a pleasant tea and are reputed to give relief from digestive disorders. It is known in many books as *Micromeria chamissonis*.

11 ALKALI GRASS *(Zigadenus elegans)*   Lily family *(Liliaceae)*

Height: Perennial herb, 1′-2′ (.3-.6m). **Flowers:** Many on unbranched raceme; 6 segments in perianth, 1/4″ (6mm) long, yellowish white; stamens 6, equal in length, free from segments. **Leaves:** Basal, linear, smooth, up to 1/2″ (1cm) wide. **In bloom:** July-August. **Habitat-Range:** Coniferous forests; northern Rocky Mountains south to New Mexico.

Some call the Zigadene lilies Death Camas because of the poison that the bulbs contain. The true Camas *(Camassia quamash)* was eaten by the Indians, but even they tell of fatal mistakes in collecting the wrong bulb.

CORN LILY *(Veratrum californicum)*   Lily family *(Liliaceae)*

Height: Perennial herb, 3′-6′ (1-2m). **Flowers:** White, terminal branching spike 1′ (.3m) or more long; corolla in parts of 6; sepals, petals alike, 1/2″ (1cm) long, Y-shaped green gland near base; stamens 6, opposite, free from flower segments, short, curved. **Leaves:** 6″-12″ (15-30cm) long, sheathing stout stalk, broad, strongly veined, plaited. **In bloom:** July-August. **Habitat-Range:** Wet meadows and banks 4500′-8500′ (1400-2600m); Sierra Nevada, north Coast Ranges to Washington, Rocky Mountains to Lower California.

This species and *V. viride*, which grows more to the north, are noted for the chemical qualities of the black roots. As early as the seventeenth century it was written that the roots made a dangerous medicine for skin disorders. The Spaniards fermented the juice to use on arrowheads to make their game more tender for eating. Indians used the root raw in various ways, crushing it for snakebite, putting it in a tea for venereal disease, and chewing it for sore throat. Some stock animals are poisoned by eating the young shoots.

12 GROUND IRIS *(Iris macrosiphon)*   Iris family *(Iridaceae)*

Height: Perennial herb, 6″-8″ (15-20cm). **Flowers:** 1-2 on pedicels about 1/2″ (1cm) long; slender tube 2″-3″ (5-7.5cm) long; sepals 3, narrow to broadly oval, 2″ (5cm) long; petals 3, slightly shorter than sepals, usually veined, erect; color mostly creamy white, also yellow, blue, lavender. **Leaves:** Linear, to 12″ (30cm) long, 1/4″ (6mm) wide. **In bloom:** April-May. **Habitat-Range:** Coniferous slopes below 3000′ (900m); Coast Ranges of California north to Oregon.

This iris shows much variety in color and habitat due to the natural hybrid forms. Its distinctive characteristic is the short flower stem tucked close to the ground and surrounded by longer leaves.

13 MOUNTAIN MISERY *(Chamaebatia foliolosa)* Rose family *(Rosaceae)*

Height: Evergreen shrub, 8″-24″ (20-60cm). **Flowers:** In loose terminal cymes; sepals 5, persisting on calyx; petals 5, ovate, about 1/4″ (6mm) long, white; stamens 50-60 in several rows; pistil single; ovule single, enclosed in calyx. **Leaves:** Thrice pinnate, fernlike, heavily scented, pubescent, 1″-4″ (2-10cm) long. **In bloom:** May-July. **Habitat-Range:** Open coniferous forests to 7000′ (2200m); Sierra Nevada.

This low mountain shrub associated with Yellow Pine forests has a pungent odor that clings to shoes and clothing after one has walked through a pine forest, hence the name Mountain Misery. Other common names are Bear Mat and Tarweed.

SERVICEBERRY *(Amelanchier pallida)* Rose family *(Rosaceae)*

Height: Perennial shrub, 3′-15′ (1-5m). **Flowers:** In racemes; calyx campanulate, with 5 narrow lobes; petals 5, oblong, 1/2″ (1cm) long, white; stamens 15-20; styles 3-4; fruit one-seeded, berrylike, purplish black, about 1/4″ (6mm) in diameter. **Leaves:** Simple, deciduous, 3/4″-1 1/2″ (2-4cm) long, oval, sharply serrate at apex; petioles 1/2″ (1cm) long. **In bloom:** April-June. **Habitat-Range:** Rocky slopes, high coniferous forests to 11,000′ (3300m); California to Alaska, east to Rocky Mountains.

The delicate white flowers mixed with the early leaves makes this a much admired mountain shrub. In late summer the dark fruit, which resembles a small apple, is conspicuous and is pleasing to the taste. Indians gathered and dried it to make large, flat cakes that they added to soups or vegetables during the winter. Dried Serviceberries were combined with buffalo meat to make pemmican, the staple food for travel. Western settlers also found the fruit delicious and useful for jelly, pie, and wine.

14 LEICHTLIN'S MARIPOSA *(Calochortus leichtlinii)* Lily family *(Liliaceae)*

Height: Perennial herb, 2″-24″ (5-40cm). **Flowers:** Open, bell-shaped, erect, 1″-1 1/4″ (2.5-3cm) long; sepals 3, narrow, half as long as petals, bluish on outside; petals 3, spade-shaped, white with slight purplish tinge, yellowish on gland near inner base, with purplish black spot just above. **Leaves:** Single, narrowly linear, approximately length of stem. **In bloom:** June-July. **Habitat-Range:** Common on open dry ground 4000′-11,000′ (1200-3350m) in coniferous areas, Sierra Nevada, western Nevada.

This is one of the open, Mariposa Lily type of *Calochortus* seen commonly in the Sierra Nevada in early and midsummer months. It is named after Max Leichtlin (1831-1910), founder of the famous botanical garden at Baden-Baden, Germany.

SMARTWEED *(Polygonum bistortoides)* Buckwheat family *(Polygonaceae)*

Height: Perennial herb, 1′-2′ (.3-.6m). **Flowers:** In dense, spikelike raceme, 3/4″-1 1/2″

(2-4cm) long, on stems 1′-2′ (.3-.6m) high; petals absent; sepals usually 5, about 1/8″ (3mm) long, white or greenish white; stamens attached to calyx. **Leaves:** Mostly basal, erect, oblong, 4″-10″ (10-25cm) long on petioles half as long. **In bloom:** June-August. **Habitat-Range:** High mountain meadows, wet places in coniferous forests in Sierra Nevada, Coast Ranges of California to Alaska, east to Atlantic coast.

This slender plant often covers mountain meadows. The white flower spikes are delicate and beautiful, giving no hint of the thick roots lying just under the ground. The swollen, starchy rootstock was used as food by the Indians, and the young leaves can be boiled and eaten.

15 GRASS OF PARNASSUS *(Parnassia fimbriata)*   Saxifrage family *(Saxifragaceae)*

Height: Perennial herb, 9″-16″ (23-40cm). **Flowers:** Saucer-shaped, solitary, terminal; calyx deeply 5-lobed, lobes elliptic, 1/2″ (1cm) long; petals 5, ovate, conspicuously veined, fringed basally; 1/2″-3/4″ (1-2cm) long; white to cream; sterile, gland-tipped filaments at base; stamens 5. **Leaves:** Entire, cordate; 3/4″-1 3/4″ (2-4.5cm) broad; mostly basal on petioles 2″-6″ (5-15cm) long; stem leaves sessile, if present. **In bloom:** July-September. **Habitat-Range:** Boggy areas at middle to high elevations in coniferous forests from California to Alaska; Rocky Mountains.

The generic and common names refer to the mountain in Greece where, in mythology, the Muses of song and poetry lived. A closely related species, *P. palustris*, is widespread in wet meadows at lower elevations in California and Oregon and is distinguished from *P. fimbriata* by its elliptic leaves and by petals that lack fringes on the basal edges.

ALUM ROOT *(Heuchera rubescens)*   Saxifrage family *(Saxifragaceae)*

Height: Perennial herb, 4″-12″ (10-30cm). **Flowers:** Small, in spikelike racemes; calyx 5-lobed, urn-shaped, 1/4″ (6mm) long, reddish; petals 5, very small, linear to lance-shaped, white; stamens 5, as long as or longer than petals. **Leaves:** Round-cordate, shallowly lobed, 1/2″-1 1/2″ (1-4cm) across; herbage somewhat bristly, glandular. **In bloom:** May-July. **Habitat-Range:** Dry rocky places, 6000′-12,000′ (1800-3600m), Sierra Nevada east to mountains of Nevada.

Alum Root has astringent qualities and was important to the Indians as an antiseptic. They pounded the root, used it wet as a poultice on sores, and made a concoction for an eyewash. It was also taken internally for digestive upsets. In seventeenth-century England it was reportedly used for secret writing: notes written with the juice were said to be invisible until steeped in running water.

MITERWORT *(Mitella breweri)*   Saxifrage family *(Saxifragaceae)*

Height: Perennial herb, 6″-12″ (15-30cm). **Flowers:** Small, disc-shaped, 8-20 in terminal, spikelike raceme; sepals 5, broad, recurved; petals 5-7, threadlike, greenish white; stamens opposite sepals. **Leaves:** Basal; rounded cordate, slightly lobed with curly lobes on petioles; 1″-2 1/2″ (2.5-6.5cm) broad. **In bloom:** June-August. **Habitat-Range:** Coniferous forests, 6000′-11,500′ (1800-3450m); from California to British Columbia.

Miterwort (from miter, the tall cap worn by bishops) is also known as Bishop's Cap because of the disclike shape of the flower. One of the smaller saxifrages in the higher mountains of the Pacific coast, it frequents melting snowbanks, especially in Red Fir and Mountain Hemlock forests. In subalpine regions it may not bloom until late August

SAXIFRAGE *(Saxifraga punctata)* Saxifrage family *(Saxifragaceae)*

Height: Perennial herb, 8″-16″ (20-40cm). **Flowers:** Saucer-shaped in small clusters in panicle on glandular, pubescent stem; sepals 5, oblong-pointed, reflexed, shorter than petals, purplish; petals 5, rounded, 1/4″ (6mm) long; white with 2 yellow dots at base. **Leaves:** Basal; round to kidney-shaped; toothed; 3/4″-3″ (2-7.5cm) wide on long petioles. **In bloom:** July-August. **Habitat-Range:** Stream banks in coniferous forests from 6500′ to 11,200′ (1950-3360m); California to Washington and Rocky Mountains.

This is a common western North American example of the approximately 250 species of saxifrages found in the cool North Temperate zone. The name means rock-breaker in Latin and is applied to these plants because many grow in rock crevices, and the roots cause the rocks to crack.

16 MARIPOSA LILY *(Calochortus elegans)* Lily family *(Liliaceae)*

Height: Perennial herb, 2″-6″ (5-15cm). **Flowers:** 1-3, open campanulate, somewhat umbellate; sepals 1/2″-3/4″ (1-2cm), lance-shaped; petals wider with claw, greenish white with purple crescent above gland and on sepals; stamens 6, attached to base of flower segments; stigmas 3. **Leaves:** Linear, basal, 4″-8″ (10-20cm) long, under 1/2″ (1cm) wide. **In bloom:** May-July. **Habitat-Range:** Coniferous forests 5000′-7000′ (1500-2150m); northwestern California to Oregon.

The name Mariposa (from the Spanish for butterfly) applies to many of the numerous species of *Calochortus*. The flowers are conspicuous as they appear from among the slender grasslike leaves. The bulbs were dug by the Indians and early settlers, roasted, and eaten as a delicacy. Today every effort is made to discourage people from digging these bulbs because of their declining numbers.

17 INSIDE-OUT FLOWER Barberry family *(Berberidaceae)*
(Vancouveria hexandra)

Height: Perennial herb, 4″-20″ (10-50cm). **Flowers:** Small, nodding, in loose panicle of 5-30 flowers; outer row of sepals small, soon lost, inner sepals 6, 1/4″ (6mm) long, petal-like, reflexed white; petals 6, reflexed, tipped with nectar-bearing appendage; stamens 6, erect around pistil. **Leaves:** Fernlike, from creeping rootstock; divided twice into narrow to ovate leaflets 1″-2″ (2-5cm) long. **In bloom:** May-July. **Habitat-Range:** Deep shaded woods, below 4500′ (1350m), from central California to Washington.

The three species of Vancouveria, or Inside-out Flowers, are limited to the Pacific states. In *V. hexandra* the leaves are lost in the autumn, but in the other two, whose stems are glandular instead of smooth, they persist throughout the winter. *V. planipetala* has white flowers while those of *V. chrysantha* are yellow. Their common name is derived from the reflexed position of the petals.

18 AVALANCHE LILY *(Erythronium montanum)* Lily family *(Liliaceae)*

Height: Perennial herb, 4″-16″ (10-40cm). **Flowers:** One to several on erect stem;

nodding; perianth segments lance-shaped, separate, somewhat recurved; 1″-2″ (2.5 5cm) long; white with yellow near inner base. **Leaves:** Two; basal; elliptic oblong, 4″-8″ (10-20cm) long; green. **In bloom:** July-August. **Habitat-Range:** Near melting snowbanks in the coniferous forests of the Cascades in Oregon and Washington and the northern Rocky Mountains.

The Avalanche Lily, sometimes called Fawn Lily or Dogtooth Violet, is a high-mountain species that blooms just after the snow melts. Mountain slopes are sometimes covered with their blooms as the snow recedes. The bulbs, like those of the closely related yellow Glacier Lily (*E. grandiflorum*), were used by the Indians for food.

19 TWEEDY'S LEWISIA *(Lewisia tweedyi)*   Purslane family *(Portulacaceae)*

Height: Perennial herb, 4″-8″ (10-20cm). **Flowers:** Terminal; sepals 2; petals 8-9, ovate-elongate, 1″-1 1/2″ (2.5-4cm) long; salmon or yellowish. **Leaves:** Basal, 4″-8″ (10-20cm) long; ovate to lance-shaped, tapering basally to long stalk. **In bloom:** May-June. **Habitat-Range:** East of Cascades in Wenatchee Mountains of Washington.

This species has a limited distribution, but it has been included because of its fairly widespread use in horticulture in the Pacific Northwest. The generic name honors Captain Meriwether Lewis of the Lewis and Clark Expedition.

20 INDIAN PIPE *(Monotropa uniflora)* †   Heath family *(Ericaceae)*

Height: Perennial herb, 4″-10″ (10-25cm). **Flowers:** Solitary, nodding, tubular; sepals 2-4; petals 5-6, 1″ (2.5cm) long, waxy white; stamens twice as many as petals; anthers pale yellow. **Leaves:** Lacking on waxy, white, scaly stem. **In bloom:** Summer. **Habitat-Range:** Damp coniferous woods of North America and Asia.

This is an unusual species among saprophytic members of the Heath family. It lacks leaves and chlorophyll, the green coloring matter so important in the plants' production of starches and sugar. Instead it lives on rich organic material in the soil. Its single, waxy white flower on a white stem makes it readily identifiable. Sometimes the plant has a pink tinge, and when it dries it turns black.

WHITE PHLOX *(Phlox diffusa)*   Phlox family *(Polemoniaceae)*

Height: Perennial herb, 4″-12″ (10-30cm). **Flowers:** Largely solitary on ends of short branches, close together; calyx 1/2″ (1cm) long, tubular with 5 lobes; corolla tubular with 5 expanded lobes about 1/2″ (1cm) across; white to pale pinkish or lavender; stamens 5, short. **Leaves:** Linear, about 1/2″ (1cm) long, slightly hairy. **In bloom:** May-August. **Habitat-Range:** Dry slopes in coniferous zone from 3300′-11,500′ (1000-3500m); southern California to Oregon.

White Phlox is most characteristic of open granitic slopes where it may form a carpet in spring and summer, depending on the altitude.

GRANITE GILEA *(Leptodactylon pungens)*   Phlox family *(Polemoniaceae)*

Height: Low, branching shrub, 3″-10″ (8-25cm). **Flowers:** Sessile, solitary or in small, congested cluster; showy; calyx with 5 slender, unequal lobes; corolla with long tube, 3/4″-1″ (2-2.5cm), expanding into 5 lobes 1/4″-1/2″ (6-12mm) long, white to pinkish or purplish-pink. **Leaves:** On branches rising from woody trunk, alternate; palmately divided into needle-like segments 1/4″-1/2″ (6-12mm) long. **In bloom:** April-August. **Habitat-Range:** Dry, rocky slopes, often in granite, from 4000′ to 12,000′ (1200-3700m) in mountains of western Northern America.

This diminutive shrub, looking like an herb unless its wooden base and branches are examined, forms a conspicuous mass of bloom on the ground in summer. It is especially typical of granite slopes in the Rocky Mountains and Sierra Nevada-Cascade axis. While most flowers are nearly white, there is considerable variation as indicated. Growth is slow in the unfavorable habitat this Gilia has selected, and individual plants may be many years old although only a few inches high.

21 LADY'S SLIPPER *(Cypripedium montanum)* †   Orchid family *(Orchidaceae)*

Height: Perennial herb, 1′-2′ (.3-.6m). **Flowers:** 1-3 in axils of leafy bracts; sepals 3, lance-shaped, 1 1/2″-2 1/2″ (4-6cm) long, lateral pair more or less united, purplish brown; petals 3, similar to sepals but smaller, narrower with lower lip ovoid, white with purple veins; 2 fertile stamens. **Leaves:** 4-7, elliptic to ovoid, 3″-6″ (8-15cm) long. **In bloom:** May-August. **Habitat-Range:** Evergreen forests below 5000′ (1500m); from central California to British Columbia, east to Wyoming.

This genus contains many orchids prized by horticulturists. Over 100 species occur in forested parts of Oceania, Eurasia, and America. Many are tropical. Unlike most other orchids, they have two fertile stamens instead of one.

22 SOUTHERN LEWISIA *(Lewisia brachycalyx)*   Purslane family *(Portulacaceae)*

Height: Perennial herb, 1″-2 1/2″ (2.5-6cm). **Flowers:** Solitary on short stem, with 2 petal-like bracts; sepals 2, ovate, 1/4″ (6mm) long; petals 5-9, white, often with pinkish tinge; stamens 9-15; styles 5-7. **Leaves:** Crowded as basal rosette on root crown, spatulate, 1″-4″ (2.5-10cm) long; rather succulent. **In bloom:** May-June. **Habitat-Range:** Wet meadows, 4500′-7500′ (1350-2300m) in coniferous forests; southern California east to New Mexico.

It is probable that the roots of this species, like those of other members of this genus, were used as food by the Indians. They are thick and starchy.

23 BRIDE'S BONNET *(Clintonia uniflora)*   Lily family *(Liliaceae)*

Height: Perennial herb from creeping root stalk, 6″-10″ (15-25cm). **Flowers:** Single, borne on short, slender stem; corolla small, white, bell-shaped of 6 similar petal-like segments; stamens 6, attached at base of segments. **Leaves:** Usually 2-3, basal, oblong, 4″-6″ (10-15cm) long. **In bloom:** May-July. **Habitat-Range:** Shaded woods, 3500′-6000′ (1100-1800m); mountains of northern California, Oregon, Washington to southern Alaska, east to Montana.

Queen Cup and Bead Lily are other common names for this tiny white flower of the shaded coniferous forests. The generic name is for De Witt Clinton, early nineteenth-century naturalist and governor of New York.

24 SYRINGA *(Philadelphus lewisii)*   Saxifrage family *(Saxifragaceae)*

Height: Deciduous shrub 3′-9′ (1-3m). **Flowers:** In terminal raceme, 4-20 in cluster;

calyx 4-5 lobed, 1/4″ (6mm) long, woolly along edges; petals 4-5, white, 1/2″-3/4″ (1-2cm) long, elliptic to obovate; stamens 20-40; styles usually 4; ovary almost completely inferior; seed 4-valved capsule. **Leaves:** Opposite, ovate, 1″-3″ (2.5-8cm) long, slightly hairy to hairy, entire or dentate, on petioles about 1/4″ (6mm) long. **In bloom:** May-July. **Habitat-Range:** Lower mountain slopes, British Columbia to Oregon, Cascade Mountains east to Idaho, Montana, south to California.

One of many kinds of *Philadelphus,* this lovely species is the state flower of Idaho. The common name, Syringa, is also the generic name of Lilac. Mock Orange, another common name, expresses the perfume of the masses of white blossoms. Other species occur in Europe and Asia, and the scientific name honors Ptolemy Philadelphus, a king of ancient Egypt.

25/26 BITTER CHERRY *(Prunus emarginata)*   Rose family *(Rosaceae)*

Height: Deciduous shrub, 3′-18′ (1-6m). **Flowers:** Saucer-shaped, up to 3/4″ (2cm) across; in short corymbs; calyx 5-cleft, small; petals 5, spreading, ovate-oblong; white; stamens 15-30; fruit about 1/4″ (6mm) in diameter; bright red with bitter pulp. **Leaves:** Oblong or oval shaped, 3/4″-1 1/2″ (2-4cm) long. **In bloom:** April-July. **Habitat-Range:** Coniferous forest below 9000′ (2700m); from California to British Columbia, east to northern Rocky Mountains.

This is a member of a famous horticultural genus to which the cultivated cherries, plums, apricots, peaches, nectarines, and their relatives belong. Although it lacks the edible qualities of the cultivated species, the fragrance of its blossoms and the bright color of its bitter fruits compensate for this.

27 BEAR GRASS *(Xerophyllum tenax)*   Lily family *(Liliaceae)*

Height: Perennial herb, stout stem 2′-6′ (.6-2m). **Flowers:** Borne in dense raceme 6″-8″ (15-45cm) long on slender white pedicels 1″-2″ (2.5-5cm) long, each with stiff bract; perianth segments 6, linear, 1/4″ (6mm) long, white or cream, several-nerved; stamens 6, somewhat longer than perianth. **Leaves:** Basal, numerous, 1 1/4′-3′ (.4-1m) long, very slender, dry, rough edges. **In bloom:** May-August. **Habitat-Range:** Open, dry ridges and slopes below 6000′ (1800m); northern California Coast Ranges and Sierra Nevada to Oregon, Washington, east to northern Rockies.

The generic name of this lily means dry leaf, and this feature made its fibers useful to the Indians, who fashioned garments and baskets of the tough leaves. The bulbous root stalk, roasted, furnished food. Some animals also eat the tuberous-like roots. Other common names are Squaw Grass, Elk Grass, Turkey Beard, Bear Lily, Pine Lily, and Indian Basket Grass.

28 ANEMONE *(Anemone drummondii)*   Buttercup family *(Ranunculaceae)*

Height: Perennial herb, 4″-15″ (10-40cm). **Flowers:** Single, arising from involucral bract on a stem that branches from thick root crown; petals absent; calyx 5-8 lobed, corolla-like, white, tinged blue, 1″-1 3/4″ (2.5-4cm) broad; stamens numerous; seeds woolly, in rounded heads. **Leaves:** Arising from branching root crown, on petioles; 1″-2″ (2.5-5cm) wide, divided into linear segments; silky, especially when young. **In bloom:** May-August. **Habitat-Range:** Coniferous forests from 5000′ to 10,600′ (1500-3180m); California north to Alaska, east to Idaho.

This attractive anemone with white to bluish-tinged flowers is an inhabitant of rock slides or gravelly areas in the higher coniferous forests of the West. The color, habitat, and finely dissected leaves provide the clues to its identity.

MEADOW RUE *(Thalictrum fendleri)* Buttercup family *(Ranunculaceae)*

Height: Perennial herb, 2′-5′ (.6-1.5m). **Flowers:** Small, in loose panicles; sepals usually 4, occasionally 5-7, greenish white, petal-like; petals lacking; male, female flowers on separate plants; stamens numerous with long anthers. **Leaves:** Compound, divided several times into broad, lobed or incised leaflets 1/2″-3/4″ (1-2cm) long. **In bloom:** May-August. **Habitat-Range:** Moist, shaded situations in coniferous forests; California to Texas, north to Oregon, Wyoming.

There are over 100 species of Meadow Rue in North America, Europe, and Asia. Some, like the species described here, have stamens and pistils on separate plants; in others they occur in the same flower. Meadow Rues are mostly tall, graceful plants found along streams or the edges of wet meadows where there is considerable shade. The lack of petals and the fact that the sepals fall off soon after the flower opens make the long, loose stamens the most conspicuous part of the flower.

29 MOUNTAIN DOGWOOD *(Cornus nuttallii)* Dogwood family *(Cornaceae)*

Height: Arborescent shrub, 10′-45′ (3-15m). **Flowers:** In dense head on convex receptacle surrounded by 4-7 large petal-like bracts, ovate, 1 1/2″-3″ (4-7cm) long, white; calyx 1/8″ (3mm) long; petals 4-5, 1/4″ (6mm) long; drupes red. **Leaves:** Opposite; elliptic, 3″-5″ (7-12cm) long. **In bloom:** April-July. **Habitat-Range:** Woodland below 6000′ (1800m); California to British Columbia, east to Idaho.

Mountain Dogwood frequently grows to treelike proportions. It is one of the most conspicuous flowering plants in many mountainous parts of the West in spring, and its bright red leaves are equally breathtaking in the fall. What appear to be the flower petals are really large, white, petaloid bracts. The flowers themselves are packed into a compact central disc.

30 PUSSY EARS *(Calochortus tolmiei)* Lily family *(Liliaceae)*

Height: Perennial herb 4″-16″ (10-40cm), from bulb. **Flowers:** Showy on simple or branched stem; 3 petals 1/2″-1 1/2″ (1-4cm) long, oval, fringed on edges, bearded on inner surface, white or cream tinged with rose or purple, raised gland at base; sepals 3, lance-shaped, smooth, shorter than petals; stamens 6 on base of segments, white-purple. **Leaves:** Basal leaf 4″-12″ (10-30cm) long, up to 2 1/2″ (6cm) wide; some cauline leaves present, 2 or more bracts, longer than petals. **In bloom:** April-July. **Habitat-Range:** Dry, rocky soil to grassy or wooded hills below 6000′ (1800m); Coast Ranges of California to Oregon and Washington.

This Mariposa gets its common name because of the abundance of soft hairs on the petals. The bulbs of many species were eaten by the Indians.

31 DEER BRUSH *(Ceanothus integerrimus)* Buckthorn family *(Rhamnaceae)*

Height: Deciduous shrub, 3′-12′ (1-4m). **Flowers:** Small, in showy terminal panicle

2″-6″ (5-15cm) long; calyx 5-lobed; petals 5, each hooded or curved at top with slender base; usually white, sometimes blue or pink. **Leaves:** Broadly elliptic or ovate with one main vein arising from the base instead of three as in several other species; entire or slightly toothed near tip; 1″-3″ (2.5-7cm) long; light green; branches flexible. **In bloom:** May-June. **Habitat-Range:** Dry wooded slopes 1000′-7000′ (300-2100m); southern California to Oregon.

Many of the 50 to 60 species of *Ceanothus* in temperate North America have very local distributions. Deer Brush is one of the more widespread types and is conspicuous at low and middle elevations during the blooming season. Its branches are soft and flexible, unlike many of its relatives. It is a good deer food.

CREAM BUSH *(Holodiscus discolor)* Rose family *(Rosaceae)*

Height: Deciduous shrub, 3′-8′ (1-2.5cm). **Flowers:** Tiny, saucer-shaped, in dense clusters 2″-8″ (5-20cm) long; sepals 5, very small, ovate; petals slightly longer than sepals, oval, white, with several hairs at outer base; stamens about 20 with 3 opposite each petal, 1 opposite each sepal. **Leaves:** Alternate, elliptic, toothed, 3/4″-3″ (2-7cm) long; woolly beneath. **In bloom:** May-August. **Habitat-Range:** Woodlands below 4500′ (1350m); California to British Columbia, northern Rocky Mountains.

This is also known as Ocean Spray because of the white plumelike sprays of flowers produced in profusion in spring and summer. A closely related species, *H. boursieri,* is smaller and restricted largely to the Sierra Nevada between 4000′ and 9600′ (1200-2880m).

32 WHITE GLOBE LILY *(Calochortus albus)* Lily family *(Liliaceae)*

Height: Perennial herb, 1′-2′ (.3-.6m). **Flowers:** Several borne on branching stem, globe-shaped, 6 parts, nodding; sepals greenish white, shorter than petals; petals white, purplish at base with long, silky, yellow hairs above inside gland; gland lunar-shaped; stamens 6, anthers oblong, dilated filaments at base. **Leaves:** Single, basal, lance-shaped, 1′-2′ (.3-.6m) long, bracts 3″-5″ (7-13cm) long, leaflike. **In bloom:** April-June. **Habitat-Range:** Open woods, often rocky places, below 5000′ (1500m) along California coast and Sierra Nevada.

One of many Mariposa Lilies in the West, whose many common names describe the shape of the flower: Fairy Lantern, Snowdrops, Indian Bells, Satin Bells. As these all imply, it is most delightful to come upon the plant in the woods.

33 SALAL *(Gaultheria shallon)* Heather family *(Ericaceae)*

Height: Evergreen shrub, 1′-6′ (.3-2m). **Flowers:** In panicles 1 1/2″-6″ (4-15cm) long; each flower nodding, about 1/2″ (1cm) long; calyx 5-cleft, yellowish; corolla urn-shaped, to 1/2″ (1cm) long, white to pinkish, with 5 small recurved teeth or lobes; stamens 8 or 10, not extending beyond corolla. **Leaves:** Oval to roundish; finely toothed; dark glossy green, somewhat leathery; 1 1/2″-4″ (4-10cm) long. **In bloom:** April-July. **Habitat-Range:** California to British Columbia in woodlands below 2500′ (750m), especially along coast.

Salal is a component of the coastal redwood forest of California and Oregon and is abundant in many other wooded areas along the coast, even forming a brushy cover by itself in some places. It is related to the heathers and huckleberries, and its fruit, a black aromatic berry, was an important food item for coastal Indians. The genus *Gaultheria* is named after an 18th-century Canadian physician.

34 VANILLA LEAF *(Achlys triphylla)*   Barberry family *(Berberidaceae)*

Height: Perennial herb, 12″-18″ (30-45cm). **Flowers:** In short, dense spikes, 1″-2″ (2.5-5cm) long; lacking sepals, petals; stamens 6-13, conspicuous with outer ones dilated upward, white. **Leaves:** Trifoliate with leaflets fan-shaped, narrowly lobed; 2″-4″ (5-10cm) long. **In bloom:** April-June. **Habitat-Range:** Woodlands and coniferous forests below 5000′ (1500m); from northwestern California to British Columbia.

Vanilla Leaf is named for the fragrant odor of its leaves, which contain coumarin, a vanilla substitute. The generic name refers to the god of night, Achlus, because of the dark woods in which this plant grows. Another species occurs in Japan.

35 WOODLAND STAR   Saxifrage family *(Saxifragaceae)*
(Lithophragma heterophylla)

Height: Perennial herb, 1′-2′ (.3-.6m). **Flowers:** In simple racemes of 3-9; sepals 5, short, bluntly triangular; petals 5, wedge-shaped, often toothed or lobed, 1/4″ (6mm) long; white. **Leaves:** Basal leaves 1/2″-1 1/2″ (1-4cm) wide, kidney-shaped, shallowly lobed; stem leaves alternate, deeply 3-cleft. **In bloom:** March-June. **Habitat-Range:** Shaded woodlands below 6500′ (1950m); southern California to Oregon.

Woodland Stars have rootstocks with little bulblets attached. About 12 related species are found in western North America. The five petals, usually lobed or toothed, make these tiny woodland flowers look like fragile stars. The generic name is from the Greek *lithos*, stone, and *phragma*, to break.

WOOD ANEMONE *(Anemone cinquefolia)*   Buttercup family *(Ranunculaceae)*

Height: 4″-12″ (10-30cm). **Flowers:** Solitary on slender stem, star-shaped, 3/4″ (2cm) across; petals absent; sepals 5, petal-like, narrowly ovate; stamens 25-40; center of numerous green achenes, each terminating in short white style. **Leaves:** 3-foliate with leaflet margins incised, except at base; leaflets 1/2″-1 1/2″ (1-4cm) long. **In bloom:** February-June. **Habitat-Range:** Shaded woods, 200′-5000′ (60-1500m); central California to Washington.

This small perennial herb rises from a slender rootstock. An inhabitant of moist evergreen Pacific coast forests, it is related to the cultivated anemones and windflowers. *Anemone,* from the Greek *anemos*, meaning wind, refers to the fact that the delicate flowers are easily disturbed by the wind, and *cinquefolia* is Latin for 5 petals. Other members of the genus occur mostly in more northern coniferous forests, but one Windflower (*A. tuberosa*) is found in desert mountain ranges of Utah, Arizona, and southeastern California. It has a flower with 8-10 white to purplish sepals and woolly achenes.

36 WESTERN AZALEA *(Rhododendron occidentale)*   Heath family *(Ericaceae)*

Height: Deciduous shrub, 3′-9′ (1-3m). **Flowers:** In terminal umbel; calyx 5-lobed, small; corolla funnel-shaped, glandular outside, 1 1/2″-2″ (4-5cm) long with 5 clefts;

white or pinkish with yellow spot on upper lobe; 5 long stamens. **Leaves:** Elliptic, 1″-4″ (2.5-10cm) long, thin, light green. **In bloom:** April-August. **Habitat-Range:** Moist situations such as stream banks in wooded areas below 7500′ (2250m); southern California to Oregon.

This is one of the most beautiful and fragrant shrubs in the West, known to nearly everyone familiar with gardens or wild plants. The genus to which it belongs contains about 200 species, most of which are Asiatic, occurring especially in the Himalayas. The Pacific Rhododendron (*R. macrophyllum*) is the largest representative in western North America (see Red-Pink flowers). Many members of the genus are cultivated.

37 JIMSON WEED *(Datura meteloides)*   Nightshade family *(Solanaceae)*

Height: Perennial herb, 2′-4′ (.6-1m). **Flowers:** Solitary, large; calyx tubular, 5-toothed, up to 4″ (10cm) long; corolla funnel-shaped with 5 slender teeth; 6″-8″ (15-20cm) long; white tinged with violet; stamens 5, not extending beyond mouth of tube. **Leaves:** Alternate, ovate, toothed, 1 1/2″-5″ (4-12cm) long, grayish. **In bloom:** April-October. **Habitat-Range:** Sandy or gravelly situations below 4000′ (1200m). Common in sagebrush scrub, and in coastal brush, desert, foothills; California to Texas, south to South America.

The Indian name of this plant is Tolguacha, from the Aztec *toloatzin-toloa,* to bow the head, and *tzin*, respect. It was used by some tribes of California Indians as a ceremonial narcotic and closely resembles other narcotic species of *Datura* from Asia. Thorn Apple, another name for *D. meteloides,* was used because of the prickly globose capsules which contain the seeds.

38 APACHE PLUME *(Fallugia paradoxa)*   Rose family *(Rosaceae)*

Height: Deciduous shrub, 1′-5′ (.3-1.5m). **Flowers:** Solitary or few on long peduncle; calyx 5-lobed with alternate linear bractlets, much shorter than petals; petals 5, white, orbicular, about 3/4″ (2cm) long; stamens many in 3 rows on calyx tube; pistils numerous, developing achenes with threadlike plumose tails 1″ (2.5cm) long. **Leaves:** About 1/2″ (1cm) long, pinnately divided, 3-5 linear segments with rolled edges, rusty colored underneath. **In bloom:** May-June. **Habitat-Range:** Rocky slopes, Pinyon-Juniper woods; deserts of California, Nevada to New Mexico.

The blooms, resembling apple blossoms, appear in the spring on the straggly shrub and later form fluffy balls of seeds; these balls remain on the bush for some time and are as beautiful as the flowers, giving rise to the name Apache Plume. The genus, which contains a single species, is named after V. Falugi, an Italian abbot. The Hopi Indians steep the leaves for a hair tonic.

39 MILKMAIDS *(Dentaria integrifolia)*   Mustard family *(Cruciferae)*

Height: 6″-20″ (15-50cm). **Flowers:** In racemes; petals, much smaller sepals 4 each; petals alike, about 1/4″ (6mm) long; white to rose pink; stamens 6; pods slender, up to 1 1/2″ (4cm) long. **Leaves:** Simple or trifoliate to linear; stem rising from tuberous rootstock. **In bloom:** Late winter to early spring. **Habitat-Range:** Coast, lower mountain ranges of California in moist, grassy places.

One of the first flowers of spring in California, in favorable years they start blooming by mid-January along with early buttercups. The flowers somewhat resemble those of Wild Radish *(Raphanus sativus)* but are more delicate, nearly white, and the seed pods are slender instead of inflated. In one variety the flowers are rose pink and the leaves marked with purple above and entirely purple below.

40 SEGO LILY *(Calochortus nuttallii)*　　　　Lily family *(Liliaceae)*

Height: 3″-17″ (8-42cm). **Flowers:** Cup-shaped, single on stem; petals 1″-1 3/4″ (2.5-4.5cm) long; white, sometimes shaded with lilac. **Leaves:** Basal, slender, usually shorter than stem. **In bloom:** Late spring, early summer. **Habitat-Range:** Arid mountains, high desert valleys, 5000′-9000′ (1500-2700m) between Sierra Nevada–Cascade ranges and Rocky Mountains.

This is the state flower of Utah because the Ute Indians, who called it "sago," showed the early settlers how to use the bulbs for food. A closely related species is *C. macrocarpus,* the Great Plains Lily, which is taller and has purple-lilac petals.

41 **EVENING PRIMROSE**　　　　Evening-primrose family *(Onagraceae)*
(Oenothera caespitosa)

Height: Perennial herb, up to 8″ (20cm). **Flowers:** Borne in tuft on axis of root crown; calyx tube 2″-4″ (5-10cm) long; petals 4, heart-shaped, 1″-1 3/4″ (2.5-4.5cm) long, white, aging pink; stamens 8, nearly equal length. **Leaves:** In basal rosette; lance-shaped, with margin toothed, wavy, to almost pinnatifid, 1″-4″ (2.5-10cm) long on petiole about half as long. **In bloom:** April-September. **Habitat-Range:** Dry pinyon-juniper or sagebrush slopes 3000′-10,000′ (900-3000m) in western North America.

This is a variable species of wide range in dryer parts of the West. Most forms have no visible stem aboveground. The flowers are interspersed in the basal tuft of leaves.

42 SAND CORN *(Zigadenus paniculatus)*　　　　Lily family *(Liliaceae)*

Height: Perennial herb, 8″-24″ (20-60cm). **Flowers:** In broad compound raceme up to 10″ (25cm) long; perianth segments 6, triangular to ovate with tip pointed, about 1/4″ (6mm) long; greenish white; stamens 6, equal to or longer than perianth segments. **Leaves:** Linear, sheathing stem, 12″-20″ (30-50cm) long, usually less than 3/4″ (2cm) wide. **In bloom:** May-June. **Habitat-Range:** Mostly associated with sagebrush from northeastern California north to Washington and east to Montana.

This Zigadene grows in dry situations and bears a superficial resemblance to a small corn stalk, but its bulb is very poisonous. It is often called Poison Sego and belongs to the same genus as the Death Camas. The first known species has a "yoke" of glands at the base of each flower segment. In this species there is but a single gland.

43 **OUR LORD'S CANDLE** *(Yucca whipplei)*　　　　Lily family *(Liliaceae)*

Height: Perennial shrub, flowering stem 8′-14′ (2.5-4m). **Flowers:** Large, 1 1/4″-1 1/2″ (3-4cm) long in terminal panicle 3′-6′ (1-2m) long; perianth segments 6, creamy white; stamen filaments thickened, shorter than segments. **Leaves:** In basal rosette, narrow, 1′-1 3/4′ (.3-.5m) long, stiff, gray green, with terminal spine 1″ (2.5cm) long. **In bloom:** April-June. **Habitat-Range:** Dry, stony slopes 1000′-4000′ (300-1200m) in chaparral area of southern California.

The Yuccas, called Spanish Bayonets, have several common species. Some botanists place them in the Agave family, but in many ways they are lilylike. The Joshua Tree (*Y. brevifolia*) is an amazing treelike plant growing to a height of 40′ (12m) or more. *Y. schidigera* is common in California on dry, rocky slopes and mesas below 7000′ (2100m), extending through the deserts east to Nevada and Arizona. Fibers from the long leaves of *Y. baccata* were used, and the fruits were eaten by the Indians. Each species is dependent on a particular moth to pollinate its flowers. The female moth gathers pollen from a flower at night, rolls it into a little ball, flies to another plant, deposits her eggs in the ovary, then pushes the ball of pollen into the stigma tube. The larvae, when hatched, are nourished on a few of the fertilized seeds.

44 WESTERN MORNING GLORY Morning-glory family *(Convolvulaceae)*
(Convolvulus occidentalis)

Height: Twining herb with stems several feet long. **Flowers:** Broadly funnel-shaped, 1″-1 1/2″ (2.5-4cm) across; corolla white to pinkish; calyx enclosed in pair of bracts 1/2″-3/4″ (1-2cm) long. **Leaves:** 3/4″-1 1/2″ (2-4cm) long, arrow-shaped, smooth. **In bloom:** February-April. **Habitat-Range:** Sea coast to lower coastal mountains from central California south to Baja California.

Morning Glories of the genus *Convolvulus* are commonly known as Bindweed except in California, where most North American species occur. They are readily recognizable by their twining stems and funnel-shaped flowers that range from white to pink, yellow, blue, or lavender. The Small Bindweed or Creeping Jenny *(C. arvensis)* is common on the Great Plains and is a pest in cultivated areas. Its flowers lack the large sepal-like bracts so conspicuous in the Western Morning Glory. Most members of the family are tropical or subtropical. They include the Morning Glory Tree, Sweet Potato, the parasitic Dodders, and *Dichondra*, often used as a ground cover in place of a lawn.

45 NOLINA *(Nolina parryi)* Lily family *(Liliaceae)*

Height: Perennial herb with stout stem, 3′-6′ (1-2m). **Flowers:** Very small, congested in compound panicle; perianth white, 6 distinct lancelike lobes; stamens 6, very short filaments; flowers white, remaining on stalk, dry, papery. **Leaves:** Rather thick, 3/4″-1 1/4″ (2-3cm) wide, 2′-3 1/3′ (.6-1m) long, saw-edged. **In bloom:** April-June. **Habitat-Range:** Dry mountain slopes below 6000′ (1800m); southern California to Arizona.

This plant is conspicuous in bloom. It is similar to the Yucca but with much smaller flowers. The other desert species of *Nolina*, *N. bigelovii*, differs mainly in having leaves with smooth edges.

46 PARRY MANZANITA *(Arctostaphylos manzanita)* Heath family *(Ericaceae)*

Height: Shrub, 6′-12′ (2-4m). **Flowers:** In terminal nodding clusters; corolla urn-shaped, 1/4″ (6mm) long. **Leaves:** Oblong, 1″-1 1/2″ (2.5-4cm) long; pale green, thick, smooth. **In bloom:** February-April. **Habitat-Range:** Dry canyon slopes, 300′-400′ (90-120m) in Coast Ranges, Sierra Nevada of California.

Manzanitas are typically western and reach their peak in California, where about 25 are recognized. Several low-growing kinds known as Bear Berry or Bear Mat manzanitas are extremely widespread. One species, *A. uva-ursi*, is found throughout the Northern Hemisphere. It forms a ground carpet about 6″ (15cm) high. Most manzanitas are medium to large evergreen shrubs that may form a solid brush cover on unforested slopes or a scattered undercover in coniferous or even broad-leafed forests. Their tough, crooked branches with smooth, polished, dark red bark make generic identification simple, but the many species are difficult to distinguish. The berrylike fruit with slightly acid pulp is harvested by numerous animals and can be made into an interesting jelly.

47 MATILIJA POPPY *(Romneya trichocalyx)*   Poppy family *(Papaveraceae)*

Height: Perennial herb, 3′-8′ (1-2.5m). **Flowers:** Terminal, large, 3″-5″ (8-13cm) broad; calyx smooth, 3-lobed; petals 6, white, frilled, lasting a few days; stamens yellow, numerous; style none; stigmas 7-12, partly joined; fruit an oblong capsule. **Leaves:** Alternate, pinnatifid, 1″-4″ (2.5-10cm) long; stems from creeping underground rootstocks, with colorless bitter juice. **In bloom:** May-July. **Habitat-Range:** Dry Canyons, chaparral-covered slopes; coastal southern California to Baja California.

This beautiful poppy is seen in several forms in the wild and is cultivated in the dry warm areas of California. It was named for the Indian rancheria Matilija near the Mission San Buenaventura, where it grew in profusion.

48 PITCHER SAGE *(Lepechinia calycina)*   Mint family *(Labiatae)*

Height: Perennial shrub, 3′-5′ (1-2m). **Flowers:** Solitary, conspicuous in axils; calyx bell-shaped, veined on outer surface, with 5 pointed lobes; corolla showy, 1″ (2.5cm) long with 4 spreading lobes, a lower fifth lobe longer, erect; white or slightly tinted pink. **Leaves:** Ovate, toothed, veined, hairy, 2″-4″ (5-10cm) long. **In bloom:** April-June. **Habitat-Range:** Chaparral-covered slopes of central, southern California.

This species is not to be confused with another common member of the Mint family, *Salvia spathacea*, also known as Pitcher Sage but with conspicuous purplish-red flowers. *Lepechinia calycina* is a handsome shrub with coarse woolly leaves and large whitish flowers with the lower lobe shaped somewhat like an exaggerated spout of a pitcher.

49 DESERT EVENING PRIMROSE   Evening-primrose family *(Onagraceae)*
(Oenothera deltoides)

Height: Annual herb 2″-12″ (5-30cm). **Flowers:** Solitary, nodding in bud, blooming in evening; sepals 4, 3/4″-1 1/2″ (2-3cm) long with straight, spreading hairs; petals 4, white, becoming pink with age, 3/4″-1 3/4″ (2-4cm) long; stamens 8, shorter than petals; stigma 4-lobed. **Leaves:** Basal, in loose rosette; blades obovate, somewhat toothed, 3/4″-3″ (2-8cm) long with petioles of equal length; some stem leaves smaller. **In bloom:** March-May. **Habitat-Range:** Sandy deserts below 3500′ (1050m); Utah, northern Arizona to southern California, Baja California.

The petals become pinkish when the flower ages and the characteristic long seed pod develops. The pod sometimes reaches a length of 4 1/2″ (11.5cm). This is the common Desert Evening Primrose, with several varieties in different parts of the range.

50 SAND BLAZING STAR *(Mentzelia involucrata)*   Loasa family *(Loasaceae)*

Height: Annual, up to 16″ (40cm). **Flowers:** Solitary, terminal; basal bracts whitish with green-toothed margins; 5 pale gray calyx lobes about 1″ (2.5cm) long, pointed; 5 petals up to 2 1/2″ (6cm) long, abruptly tapering, satiny white with pinkish stripes from middle to base; stamens numerous, short. **Leaves:** Cordate-elongate, spiny; 2″-6 1/2″ (5-16cm) long; gray-green; stems branching, pale flesh color. **In bloom:** March-May. **Habitat-Range:** Gravelly washes, rocky canyon bottoms, Mojave, Colorado deserts, east to Arizona, south to Baja California.

It is a member of a family almost entirely native to the Americas. The foliage is rough and adhesive due to minute barbed hairs.

SAND MAT *(Euphorbia polycarpa)*   Spurge family *(Euphorbiaceae)*

Height: Perennial herb with prostrate stems 2″-10″ (5-25cm) long. **Flowers:** Solitary in axils; campanulate; both pistillate and staminate flowers without sepals or petals; involucre, 1-1.5mm wide, with white appendages, purple glands. **Leaves:** Almost round to oblong, 1/4″ (6mm) long, with fine hairs. **In bloom:** Most of year. **Habitat-Range:** Dry mesas, rocky slopes, Arizona to southern California, Mexico.

This interesting plant forms a mat on the desert floor. On close inspection the tiny blooms appear jewel-like, set in the spreading branches with tiny, stiff leaves. Inside, what appears to be the flower are the numerous simple, naked stamens and the pistil. The dry fruit develops on an extended stalk surrounded by the staminate flowers.

51 DESERT STAR *(Monoptilon bellioides)*   Sunflower family *(Compositae)*

Height: Annual herb, 1″-2″ (2.5-5cm) high, 10″ (25cm) across. **Flowers:** Heads on tips of branches, 1/2″-3/4″ (1-2cm) broad; rays about 1/2″ (1cm) long, white or pinkish; disc, corollas yellow; pappus bristles about half as long as corolla. **Leaves:** Alternate, linear, entire, up to 1″ (2.5cm) long. **In bloom:** February-May; September. **Habitat-Range:** Desert flats, mesas up to 3000′ (900m); Arizona to southern California, northwestern Mexico.

This tiny desert plant is abundant after the infrequent desert rains.

52 CHICALOTE *(Argemone platyceras)*   Poppy family *(Papaveraceae)*

Height: Annual herb, 12″-30″ (30-75cm). **Flowers:** In panicle; each 2″-4″ (5-10cm) in diameter; sepals half as many as petals, prickly, usually lost on opening; petals 6, occasionally 4, spreading, white, slightly crinkled; stamens numerous, yellow; single pistil with thick style, brownish stigma. **Leaves:** Pale gray, pinnatifid, very spiny, 2″-9″ (5-23cm) long; stem spiny, gray-green with acrid orange juice. **In bloom:** April-September. **Habitat-Range:** Open country and roadsides, 1500′-1800′ (450-550m); Nebraska south to Texas and west to eastern California.

This showy, white-flowered, drought-resistant poppy of western North America attracts the attention of motorists because of its large size. The plant is often an indication of overgrazing. It is shunned by livestock because of its spines and acrid juice, but the juice has been used to treat certain skin diseases.

CANBYA *(Canbya candida)*   Poppy family *(Papaveraceae)*

Height: Annual herb 1″ (2-3cm) high. **Flowers:** Borne singly on threadlike stems;

sepals 3, which fall soon after opening; petals 6, white, 1/8″ (3mm) long, remaining attached to seed pod; stamens 6-9, stigmas 3. **Leaves:** Alternate, linear, fleshy, 1/4″ (6mm) long. **In bloom:** April-May. **Habitat-Range:** Sandy washes, western Mojave Desert, California, 2000′-3500′ (600-1050m) elevation.

The only other species of this minute poppy is found in Oregon. The tiny plants can be easily overlooked on the desert sands, but after a rain they flower and are beautiful to see. The almost succulent leaves are well adapted to long dry spells in the desert.

53 PINCUSHION CACTUS *(Mammillaria dioica)* Cactus family *(Cactaceae)*

Height: Perennial succulent, 2″-10″ (5-25cm). **Flowers:** Funnel-shaped, 3/4″-1″ (2-2.5cm) long; petals, sepals not distinguishable; pale cream to light yellow, usually with purplish midrib; stamens numerous; fruit scarlet. **Stems:** Globose to ovoid, 1 1/2″-2 1/2″ (4-6cm) in diameter; spines borne on tubercles; one or more of central spines hooked. **In bloom:** February-April. **Habitat-Range:** Among rocks, gravel, coarse sand in semidesert situations below 5000′ (1500m); from southern California south through Baja California.

Although it often grows in clumps, it can easily be overlooked because its grayish spines make it blend with its environment. It belongs to a large genus represented by many species in North and South America. Most of them are highly sought after by collectors of succulents because of their small size and often-colorful flowers that bloom in the daytime.

JOSHUA TREE *(Yucca brevifolia)* Lily family *(Liliaceae)*

Height: Treelike, 16′-30′ (5-10m). **Flowers:** In large terminal panicles 8″-14″ (20-36cm) long; 6 perianth segments of nearly equal length, 1 1/2″-2″ (4-5cm) long; thick, fleshy, greenish white; stamens 6; fruit oblong, 2″-4″ (5-10cm) long. **Leaves:** Narrow, lance-shaped, 6″-9″ (15-22cm) long, terminating in sharp, stiff spine; margin toothed, lacking free fibers. **In bloom:** April-May. **Habitat-Range:** Desert slopes, mesas, 2000′-6000′ (600-1800m); Utah to southern California.

Some botanists have separated the various species of Yucca or Spanish Bayonet from the Lily family along with the Agaves of the Amaryllis family and placed them in a separate family, the Agavaceae. Joshua Trees, the most conspicuous plants of the high desert, are certainly the largest members of the Lily family in North America. The beautiful flowers, which grow in large clusters, are incapable of self-pollination and have an interesting relationship with a desert moth. The female Pronuba moth gathers pollen from the flower of one plant and carries it to the flower of another, where she lays her eggs in the ovary, then goes to the top of the stigma and deposits the pollen, thus effecting cross-fertilization. Although the larvae of the moth feed on the seeds, they leave some untouched, thus ensuring perpetuation of both plant and moth.

SAHUARO *(Cereus giganteus)* Cactus family *(Cactaceae)*

Height: Columnar, leafless, up to 36′ (11m). **Flowers:** Borne near summit of stem; funnel-shaped; 4″-5″ (10-13cm) long, 2″-3 1/2″ (5-9cm) in diameter; perianth segments resembling petals, white; fruit ovoid, 2″-3″ (5-7.5cm) long, reddish. **Leaves:** Absent. **In bloom:** May-June. **Habitat-Range:** Extreme southeastern California near Colorado River east to Arizona, south to Sonora, Mexico.

The Sahuaro, or Giant Cactus, with its tall columnar trunk and occasional branches which curve upward abruptly and parallel the main stem, is almost symbolic of the southwestern deserts of the United States. It is a night-blooming *Cereus*, but the flowers remain open most of the following day. The fruit was gathered by the Arizona Indians for food and beverages. It is quite edible, like most cactus fruits.

WAND SAGE *(Salvia vaseyi)* — Mint family *(Labiatae)*

Height: Perennial shrub, 3′-5′ (1-1.5m). **Flowers:** In whorls; bracts, calyx lobes long, bristly; calyx, corolla 2-lipped; corolla upper lip with 2 short lobes, lower with 3 lobes, middle one much expanded; white, about 1/4″ (6mm) long; stamens extending conspicuously beyond corolla. **Leaves:** Ovate, often squarish at base, with tips pointed, 1″-1 3/4″ (2.5-5cm) long. **In bloom:** April-June. **Habitat-Range:** West side of Colorado Desert, California south to Baja California.

This is another of the beautiful desert sages, but unlike most other species of *Salvia*, the flowers are white.

54 FLEABANE *(Erigeron divergens)* — Sunflower family *(Compositae)*

Height: Annual or biennial herb, 4″-20″ (10-50cm). **Flowers:** Numerous heads on multibranched stems; ray flowers numerous, 75-150 on disc, 1/4″-1/2″ (6-12mm) long, white to pinkish, sometimes light blue; inner pappus very fragile bristles. **Leaves:** Entire or somewhat toothed, 1″-2 1/2″ (2.5-6cm) long, densely hairy. **In bloom:** March-November. **Habitat-Range:** Arid sandy places, open pine woods from Texas to Colorado and Mojave desert, Baja California, north to Montana and Canada.

These plants were at one time considered to be repellent to fleas. The generic name is more imaginative, combining words meaning "early" and "old man," that is, "old man in the spring." The fleabanes are similar to the asters but usually bloom earlier, are smaller, and have more numerous ray flowers.

WHITE TACK-STEM *(Calycoseris wrightii)* — Sunflower family *(Compositae)*

Height: Annual herb, 4″-20″ (10-40cm). **Flowers:** Heads showy, 3/4″-1 1/2″ (2-4cm) broad, on long peduncles; many raylike flowers in involucre, with white rays 3/4″-1″ (2-2.5cm) long; abundant white bristly pappus forming on seeds. **Leaves:** Mostly basal below branching stem, which is sprinkled with tack-shaped glands; leaves 1″-5″ (2.5-12cm) long, pinnately divided in linear segments. **In bloom:** March-June. **Habitat-Range:** West Texas, Utah, Colorado Desert to southern California deserts, Baja California.

The branching character and open divisions of the leaves give a rather delicate appearance to this lovely white composite. The flowers are all ray type, producing a full petal effect with little center.

WHITE TIDY TIPS *(Layia glandulosa)* — Sunflower family *(Compositae)*

Height: Annual herb, 4″-16″ (10-40cm). **Flowers:** Heads borne on leafless stalks; ray flowers 8-10, white, 1/2″ (1cm) long; disc flowers numerous (25-50), 1/4″ (6mm) long; pappus on seeds glistening white, plumose. **Leaves:** With dark glands, white hairs;

lower 1/2″-1 1/4″ (1-3cm) long, pinnately divided or toothed; upper entire. **In bloom:** March-June. **Habitat-Range:** Sandy soil; California north to Washington, east to Idaho, Utah, New Mexico.

Many species of *Layia* bloom in masses after a wet spring. White Tidy Tips as well as *L. platyglossa*, which has yellow petals with white tips, truly give the appearance of neat and tidy flowers.

55 **DESERT LILY** *(Eremocrinum albomarginatum)*   Lily family *(Liliaceae)*

Height: Perennial herb, up to 12″ (30cm). **Flowers:** Borne in dense cluster close to stem; perianth segments 6, whitish, green-veined; stamens 6; style 3-parted. **Leaves:** About as long as stem, narrow, ribbon-like from base of plant. **In bloom:** June. **Habitat-Range:** Dry deserts, northern Arizona, southern Utah.

Eremocrinum has only one species and it has a limited range. The small white starlike flowers with bright yellow stamens make it an attractive bloom on the dry, sandy desert. There may be more than one flower stalk from the base. The generic name comes from two Greek words: *eremos*, desert, and *krinon*, lily. The specific name refers to the white margin of the perianth segments.

56 **DESERT CHICORY** *(Rafinesquia neomexicana)*   Sunflower family *(Compositae)*

Height: Annual herb, 6″-24″ (15-60cm). **Flowers:** Solitary on ends of small branches; 1″-1 1/4″ (2.5-3cm) in diameter; all of ray type with strap-shaped corollas; of unequal length, toothed at tip; white, veined with rose-purple on outside; stamens yellow. **Leaves:** Oblong, 3/4″-4 1/2″ (2-11cm) long, pinnately lobed to merely toothed. **In bloom:** February-May. **Habitat-Range:** Southwest deserts from Texas to California.

A common spring bloom of the desert, its white flowers, often tinged with rose, grow on a straggly, branching plant with leaves of pale bluish green. The only other species in the genus is *R. californica*, whose white flowers are smaller and lack rose-purple veins; it occurs over much of California and east to Utah. The generic name honors the eccentric nineteenth-century botanist and friend of Audubon, Constantine Rafinesque.

57 **MILKWEED** *(Asclepias engelmanniana)*   Milkweed family *(Asclepiadaceae)*

Height: Perennial herb, 8″-32″ (20-80cm). **Flowers:** Numerous in axillary umbels; calyx with 5 reflexed lobes 1/8″ (3mm) long; corolla 5-lobed, greenish, sometimes tinged with dull purple, 1/4″ (6mm), reflexed. **Leaves:** Narrowly linear, 2″-6″ (5-15cm) long, alternate or sometimes whorled. **In bloom:** May-July. **Habitat-Range:** Grasslands and prairies, Arizona east to Colorado, Nebraska, Texas.

This is a species of the high prairies, where it often grows on rocky ground.

DESERT TOBACCO   Nightshade family *(Solanaceae)*
(Nicotiana trigonophylla)

Height: Perennial herb, 1′-3′ (.3-1m). **Flowers:** In loose racemes; calyx tubular with 5 long lobes; corolla funnel-shaped, nearly 1″ (2.5cm) long, with throat constricted, 5 spreading lobes; white or greenish white. **Leaves:** Oblong; pointed; clasping stem;

2″-5″ (5-12cm) long. **In bloom:** March-June. **Habitat-Range:** Southwestern deserts below 4000′ (1200m); Texas to California.

This heavily scented plant was dried by the Indians and used for smoking. The genus was named after J. Nicot, the French ambassador to Portugal, who introduced tobacco to France about 1560.

58 DESERT LILY *(Hesperocallis undulata)*   Lily family *(Liliaceae)*

Height: Perennial herb from many-coated bulb, 1′-2′ (.3-.6m). **Flowers:** In raceme on stem, 4-18; perianth white, 2 1/4″-2 3/4″ (5-7cm) long, tubular; 6 narrow, petal-like sections with bluish green band on back, spreading open from tube; stamens 6, attached to throat of tube. **Leaves:** Basal, somewhat fleshy, wavy-edged, 1′-2′ (.3-.6m) long, 1/4″-3/4″ (.5-2cm) wide; leaves on stem few, shorter. **In bloom:** March-May. **Habitat-Range:** Dry, sandy flats below 2500′ (800m) in Mojave Desert, Colorado Desert, western Arizona, south into Baja California.

This is an outstanding desert wildflower with the Greek generic name meaning western *(hesperos)* beauty *(kallos)*. The large, fleshy bulbs were used by Indians for food.

SANDPAPER PLANT *(Petalonyx thurberi)*   Loasa family *(Loasaceae)*

Height: Perennial herb, 1′-2′ (.3-.6m). **Flowers:** On short, dense spikes surrounded by greenish, ovate bracts 1/4″ (6mm) long; sepals 4-5, short; petals 4-5, white, 1/4″ (6mm), more or less joined, attached to ovary; stamens 5, projecting beyond petals; style single, ovary inferior. **Leaves:** Alternate, entire, up to 1″ (2.5cm) long, sessile, broad at base. **In bloom:** May-July. **Habitat-Range:** Sandy deserts up to 4000′ (1200m); Mojave, Colorado deserts of southern California to Nevada-Arizona, Baja California.

These plants are woody with spreading, short, barbed hairs. They bloom profusely in sandy places. Their rough texture accounts for the common name, while the generic name is from the Greek *petalon*, petal, and *onyx*, claw. About six species are found in southwest United States and in Mexico.

PINCUSHION FLOWER *(Chaenactis fremontii)*   Sunflower family *(Compositae)*

Height: Annual, 6″-24″ (15-60cm). **Flowers:** Usually several, each on long, slightly glandular stem; heads about 1″ (2.5cm) in diameter; bracts of involucre green, linear, 1/2″-3/4″ (1-2cm) high; marginal flowers large with palmate limbs, white to pinkish, those near center smaller, same color. **Leaves:** 1″-2″ (2.5-5cm) long, pinnatifid to entire, linear, few, scattered along stems; smooth. **In bloom:** March-May. **Habitat-Range:** Sandy deserts, mesas from southern California to Utah, Arizona.

The shape of the tubular florets of this composite suggest a white or pinkish pincushion. In favorable years the species is common among desert flora.

59 WILD ONION *(Allium lacunosum)*   Lily family *(Liliaceae)*

Height: Perennial herb, 3″-6″ (7-15cm). **Flowers:** In umbels of 10-20; small, with 6 perianth segments, ovate, pointed, 1/4"-1/2" (6-12mm) long; varying from white to pink with green or red mid-veins. **Leaves:** Linear, sickle-shaped, 2. **In bloom:** April-May. **Habitat-Range:** Open, dry slopes below 3000' (900m); central and southern California.

There are over 500 species of wild onions in the Northern Hemisphere, most of them difficult to tell apart but easily recognized as onions. Old World species have been cultivated for centuries as food—shallots, leeks, chives, garlic, and various kinds of garden onions. All grow from bulbs and have herbage with a well-known odor. All of the wild onions are edible and can be used as raw or cooked vegetables or for flavoring other foods.

SOAP PLANT *(Chlorogalum pomeridianum)* Lily family *(Liliaceae)*

Height: 2'-10' (.6-3m). **Flowers:** Star-shaped in clusters on a stalk; 6 petals, 3/4" (2cm) long; silvery white with purple veins. **Leaves:** Basal, up to 2' (.6m) long, grasslike with coarse rippled margins. **In bloom:** Late summer. **Habitat-Range:** Dry, open foothills, plains west of Cascade-Sierra Nevada ranges; southwestern deserts.

The bulb is covered with coarse brown fibers that are often seen aboveground. Both Indians and early Spanish settlers had many uses for this plant. The bulb fibers were made into brushes and mattress filling. The bulb itself served as soap because of its lathering quality and was roasted in the ground for food. The juice from cooking bulbs provided a glue used to attach feathers to arrow shafts. Roasted bulbs were made into poultices for sores. The juice from mashed bulbs was put in ponds to stupefy fish. *Pomeridianum* means "in the afternoon," referring to the time that this plant blooms. Another name is Amole.

60 LACE POD *(Thysanocarpus curvipes)* Mustard family *(Cruciferae)*

Height: Annual herb, 1'-1 1/2' (.3-.5m). **Flowers:** Minute, in slender racemes; sepals 4, oval-shaped; petals 4, spade-shaped, whitish; seed pod distinctive, oval, flattened, with entire margin surrounded by membranous perforated wing. **Leaves:** Basal leaves in rosette, entire, oblong with teeth on margin; stem leaves arrow-shaped, clasping stem; hairy. **In bloom:** March-May. **Habitat-Range:** Grasslands below 5000' (1500m); British Columbia to Baja California.

This little member of the Mustard family is known not for its flowers, which are minute, but for its beautiful pods. They are like flattened discs on little curved stems along the stalk, each margined by a transparent membrane containing lines and windows. The generic name *Thysanocarpus* comes from the Greek *thusanos*, meaning fringe, and *karpos*, fruit.

61 CREAM CUPS *(Platystemon californicus)* Poppy family *(Papaveraceae)*

Height: Annual herb, 4"-12" (10-30cm). **Flowers:** Solitary on long stems; sepals 3, ovoid, hairy; petals 6, 1/2" (1cm) long, elliptic; creamy white; stamens numerous. **Leaves:** Opposite, entire, mostly low on plant; linear, 1"-2" (2.5-5cm) long; hairy. **In bloom:** March-May. **Habitat-Range:** Open grassy places below 3000' (900m); California to Utah, Arizona.

This is one of the common spring wildflowers in grasslands of the West. Its open, cream-colored flower and soft hairy foliage make identification easy. It grows in patches much like Baby Blue-eyes, with which it is often associated.

62 MEADOW SIDALCEA *(Sidalcea campestris)*   Mallow family *(Malvaceae)*

Height: Perennial herb, 2'-7' (.6-2m). **Flowers:** In open racemes 4"-14" (10-36cm) long; male, female flowers distinct; sepals 5, often purplish, bristly; petals 5, white to pale rose, 1/2"-1" (1-2.5cm) long, triangular with margin indented. **Leaves:** Deeply cleft with 7-9 toothed lobes, up to 10" (25cm) broad. **In bloom:** May-July. **Habitat-Range:** dry fields, roadsides; Willamette Valley of Oregon.

A closely related species, *S. nelsoniana,* also occurs in central western Oregon, but it has smaller pinkish lavender petals and basal leaves only slightly lobed.

63 BEACH STRAWBERRY *(Fragaria chilensis)*   Rose family *(Rosaceae)*

Height: Perennial herb up to 8" (20cm) high. **Flowers:** Several in cyme on leafless stem; calyx silky with 5 bractlets between sepals, shorter than corolla; petals 5, white, broadly ovate, about 1/2" (1cm) long with short claw; stamens about 20 in 3 series; pistils many, borne on cone-shaped receptacle that enlarges to become fleshy fruit. **Leaves:** From basal tuft, prostrate stems; leaflets 3, 1/2"-1" (1-2.5cm) long, dark green, toothed, smooth above, densely hairy below. **In bloom:** March-August. **Habitat-Range:** Coastal sand dunes and beaches from Alaska to South America.

This strawberry is planted as a ground cover and has edible fruit. The Chilean form was one of the parents of the domestic strawberry.

64 ICE PLANT   Carpetweed family *(Aizoaceae)*
(Mesembryanthemum crystallinum)

Height: Succulent, prostrate, annual herb. **Flowers:** Axillary, terminal; calyx bell-shaped; petals numerous, 1/4" (6mm) long, white to reddish; stamens numerous. **Leaves:** Oval to spade-shaped, 3/4"-4" (2-10cm) long; herbage with numerous crystalline-dewy vesicles. **In bloom:** March-October. **Habitat-Range:** Coastal beaches and bluffs from central California to Baja California.

This is a native of Africa that has become established along parts of the coast of western North America. It is colorful and has beautiful flowers. The leaves and stems appear to be covered with drops of water, which is really contained in vesicles and exudes when the plant is crushed or stepped on.

TREE ANEMONE   Saxifrage family *(Saxifragaceae)*
(Carpenteria californica)

Height: Evergreen shrub, 3'-8' (1-3m). **Flowers:** In terminal cyme, bisexual, 2"-2 1/2" (5-6cm) broad; calyx 5-6 parted, persistent; petals white, 5-7, broad, obovate; stamens numerous, 150-200; style single. **Leaves:** Opposite, oblong, 1 1/2"-4" (4-10cm) long; smooth above, gray, woolly on underside. **In bloom:** May-July. **Habitat-Range:** Foothills of southern Sierra Nevada in California, 1500'-4000' (450-1200m).

This is a species of limited distribution in nature but because of its beautiful, large, anemone-like flowers it is well known as a garden plant. It is the single species of the genus *Carpenteria*, which was named in honor of Professor William Carpenter of Louisiana, a botanist.

65 CANADIAN DOGWOOD *(Cornus canadensis)*   Dogwood family *(Cornaceae)*

Height: Perennial herb, up to 8″ (20cm) tall. **Flowers:** Borne in head surrounded by 4 white ovate bracts about 1/2″ (1cm) long; sepals, petals 4-5, minute; stamens same number as petals; style single; fruit red, 1/4″ (6mm) in diameter. **Leaves:** 4-6, 1″-3″ (2.5-7cm) long in whorl near summit of stem; pair of leaves lower on stem, with scales below. **In bloom:** May-July. **Habitat-Range:** Swampy places below 3500′ (1050m); from Pacific to Atlantic coasts.

Another common name for this tiny plant is Bunchberry. One cannot overlook it when the red berries have formed.

MEADOW FOAM *(Limnanthes douglasii)*   Meadow-foam family *(Limnanthaceae)*

Height: Annual herb 6″-14″ (15-35cm). **Flowers:** From axils on stems 2″-4″ (5-10cm) long; sepals 5, lance-shaped, 1/2″ (1cm) long; petals 5, white, some yellow with white tips, twice as long as sepals, notched at apex, somewhat hairy inside. **Leaves:** Smooth, succulent, pinnately divided, toothed. **In bloom:** March-May. **Habitat-Range:** Moist places below 3000′ (900m); west coast grasslands, low valleys.

This flower seems well named when the white masses of spring bloom cover moist meadows. Some of the plants are 1 foot (.3m) or more in diameter. *Floerkea proserpinacoides*, a member of the same family, has 3-parted flowers with white petals and is found in moist places at higher elevations in coniferous forests.

WESTERN WATER HEMLOCK   Parsley family *(Umbelliferae)*
(Cicuta douglasii)

Height: Perennial herb 3′-4′ (1m) high. **Flowers:** Minute, in loose compound umbels; several narrow bractlets surrounding flower; sepals 5; petals 5, white; fruit with prominent ribs 2-4mm long. **Leaves:** Twice or thrice pinnate; 5″-14″ (12-35cm) long; leaflets lanceolate, 1 1/2″-4″ (4-10cm) long, on petioles sheathing stems; often purplish. **In bloom:** June-September. **Habitat-Range:** Wet places below 8000′ (2400m); California north to Alaska, east to New Mexico.

Cicuta, the Latin name for hemlock, was a plant given as a poison to unwanted citizens in ancient Greece. Our species is poisonous and has been known to be fatal if the leaves are chewed. The true Poison Hemlock (*Conium maculatum*) has been naturalized from Europe. Great care should be taken to avoid both of these plants.

66 MOUSE EAR *(Cerastium arvense)*   Pink family *(Caryophyllaceae)*

Height: Perennial herb, 4″-12″ (10-30cm). **Flowers:** 1-6 in loose cyme; sepals 5, lanceolate, 1/4″-1/2″ (6-12mm) long; petals 5, white, twice length of sepals, deeply notched; stamens 5 or 10; styles 5. **Leaves:** Firm, pubescent, opposite, linear, about 1″ (2.5cm) long. **In bloom:** February-August. **Habitat-Range:** Usually in moist rocky areas on cliffs or banks throughout much of North America and Eurasia.

This pretty little white flower, a chickweed, is seen in abundance in the spring. It grows well where moistened by mist from waterfalls. There are similar species, but the downy hair of *Cerastium* distinguishes it and gives it the name of Mouse Ear Chickweed.

FIVE SPOT *(Nemophila maculata)*   Waterleaf family *(Hydrophyllaceae)*

Height: Annual herb, 4″-12″ (10-30cm) tall. **Flowers:** Solitary, on pedicel; calyx with 5 deeply divided lobes 1/4″-1/2″ (6-12mm) long, with reflexed appendage between each lobe; corolla 5/8″-1 3/4″ (1.5-4.5cm) broad, bell-shaped, 5 white petals, each with large purple blotch; stamens 5, longer than corolla tube; style more or less 2-cleft. **Leaves:** Mostly opposite, oblong, 1/2″-1 1/4″ (1-3cm) long, pinnately divided into 5-9 ovate lobes. **In bloom:** April-August. **Habitat-Range:** Moist places in grasslands, forests up to 7500′ (2250m); western slopes of Sierra Nevada.

Calico Flower and Spotted Nemophila are other names for this plant, which resembles Baby Blue-eyes in form. It is pretty in the unusual marking on its petals and the delicate curve of its stems.

POPCORN FLOWER *(Cryptantha jamesii)*   Borage family *(Boraginaceae)*

Height: Perennial herb, 2″-7″ (5-18cm). **Flowers:** In scorpioid spikes with conspicuous hairy bracts; calyx lobes 5, 1/4″ (6mm) long; corolla white, tube 1/8″ (3mm) long, expanded border about 1/4″ (6mm) broad; stamens 5; pistil attached to superior ovary; nutlets 4. **Leaves:** Pale green, lance-shaped, 1 1/2″-4″ (4-10cm) long, with silky hairs. **In bloom:** May-August. **Habitat-Range:** Dry rocky soil in open woods, widespread 6000′-10,200′ (1800-3060m); southern California, Nevada to mountains of Texas.

This is one of the numerous species of Popcorn Flowers, so called because the white, lobed corolla looks like a small piece of popcorn. Some are difficult to distinguish. Many have very tiny blooms, hence the generic name, meaning "hidden flower." They generally are white, though some are yellow and resemble the Forget-me-nots.

YARROW *(Achillea millefolium)*   Sunflower family *(Compositae)*

Height: Perennial herb, 12″-40″ (30-100cm). **Flowers:** Heads in terminal corymb; ray flowers 4-5, white to rose, round, 1/8″ (3mm) long; disc flowers about 10-75, yellow, fertile. **Leaves:** Aromatic, tripinnately dissected into many small segments; lower leaves 4″-8″ (10-20cm) long. **In bloom:** March-July. **Habitat-Range:** Open slopes or woodlands 200′-9000′ (60-2700m); throughout western states.

This plant was named after the Greek god Achilles but is commonly called Milfoil and Sneezewort because of its finely dissected leaf which is very aromatic. It was thought to be a witch's herb and was used as a tea for various ailments as far back as ancient Greece.

67 COW PARSNIP *(Heracleum lanatum)*   Parsley family *(Umbelliferae)*

Height: Perennial herb, up to 10′ (3m). **Flowers:** Borne in compound umbels 6″-10″ (15-25cm) broad; involucral bracts numerous, falling away; petals white, oval; petals of marginal flowers larger, often cleft into 2 lobes; fruit round, compressed, ribbed, about 1/2″ (1cm) long. **Leaves:** Large, broad, 6″-12″ (15-30cm) long, 3-part, toothed, with petioles sheathing stem. **In bloom:** April-July. **Habitat-Range:** Moist places below 9000′ (2700m); widespread over much of North America.

The lacy umbel of the flowers shows clean and white in the usually dark places where this plant grows. It is named for Hercules, who was supposed to have used it for medicine. It is reported to be poisonous to cattle.

LACE PARSNIP *(Lomatium dasycarpum)*   Parsley family *(Umbelliferae)*

Height: Perennial herb, 1′-1 1/2′ (.3-.5m). **Flowers:** In compound umbel of 6-15 rays, small, petals 5; white; fruit elliptical with thin wing on each side, white to purplish. **Leaves:** Arising from root crown; divided several times into linear segments; somewhat pubescent. **In bloom:** March-May. **Habitat-Range:** Coastal California on dryer hill slopes.

This is one of many kinds of Hog Fennel that grow in western North America. Most are found in open grassland and bear a close resemblance to the sanicles because of their low growth. Like the majority of the Parsley family, they have compound leaves, small flowers in compound umbels, and a strong, spicy odor.

Yellow · Orange

Simplified Key

	HABITAT	HERB	SHRUB
Regular	**ALPINE**	70 Subalpine Buttercup	
Composite		69 Alpine Gold	
		68 Alpine Sunflower	
		Goldenrod	
Regular	**CONIFEROUS**	74 Glacier Lily	87 Oregon Grape
		73 Alpine Lily	
		76 Ground Iris	
		79 California Pitcher Plant	
		84 St. Johnswort	
		71 Evening Primrose	
		72 Cinquefoil	
Irregular		75 Yellow Lady's Slipper	Twinberry
		78 Golden Columbine	
		Mountain Violet	
		77 Wood Violet	
		86 Golden Pea	
Composite		83 Mountain Dandelion	
		82 Pale Agoseris	
		80 Balsam Root	
		81 Heartleaf Arnica	
		Groundsel	
		85 Mule Ears	
Regular	**WOODLAND**	92 Yellow Mariposa	Golden Current
		88 Stonecrop	
		91 Hooker Evening Primrose	
Irregular		90 False Lupine	
		89 Broom Rape	
Regular	**PINYON-JUNIPER-SAGE**	94 Sulphur Flower	
		95 Sagebrush Buttercup	
		97 Prince's Plume	
Composite		96 Sunflower	93 Rabbit Brush
Regular	**CHAPARRAL**	101 Globe Lily	Rock Rose
		100 Humboldt Lily	Fremontia
Irregular			98 Bush Monkey Flov
			99 Bush Penstemon
Regular	**DESERT**	111 Desert Mariposa	103 Prickly Pear
		108 Desert Trumpet	104 Century Plant
		107 Bladder Pod	102 Engelmann Prickly
		Evening Primrose	116 Desert Senna
		106 Sicklepod Rushweed	113 Creosote Bush
		115 Ground Cherry	

Simplified Key

	HABITAT	HERB	SHRUB
	DESERT		
Irregular		109 Lesser Mohavea	114 Yellow Elder
		105 Ghost Flower	
		110 Devil's Claw	
Composite		112 Panamint Daisy	Golden Bush
		Desert Dandelion	
Regular	**GRASS**		
		Yellow Fritillary	
		Golden-eyed Grass	
		California Buttercup	
		Yellow Mustard	
		119 Wild Gourd	
		120 California Poppy	
		121 Frying Pans	
		123 Butterfly Weed	
		124 Fiddleneck	
		125 Great Mullein	
Irregular		Yellow Owl's Clover	
Composite		Goldfields	
		Tarweed	
		122 Tidy Tips	
		Gumweed	
		117 Coneflower	
		118 Cutleaf Coneflower	
		Ragwort	
		Colorado Greenthread	
	SEA COAST		
Regular		126 Yellow Sand Verbena	
		127 Live Forever	
		Beach Primrose	
Irregular			Yellow Lupine
Composite		128 Salt Marsh Gum Plant	California Encelia
		Dune Tansy	
Regular	**AQUATIC**		
		130 Pond Lily	
		129 Skunk Cabbage	
Regular	**WIDESPREAD**		
		Golden Brodiaea	132 Blazing Star
		135 Western Wallflower	
		137 Sticky Cinquefoil	
Irregular		136 Common Monkey Flower	
Composite		Golden Yarrow	
		131 Common Madia	
		133 Common Dandelion	
		134 Salsify	

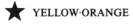

68 ALPINE SUNFLOWER
(*Hymenoxys grandiflora*)[†]   Sunflower family *(Compositae)*

Height: Perennial herb, 4″-12″ (10-30cm). **Flowers:** Large, nodding, solitary; bracts of involucre woolly; ray flowers numerous, notched at tip; disc 1 1/4″ (3cm) in diameter. **Leaves:** Alternate, divided, linear. **In bloom:** July-August. **Habitat-Range:** Alpine tundra of the Rocky Mountains.

Some species of *Hymenoxys* growing at lower elevations are better known. Actinea or Perky Sue *(H. argentea)*, common in the Pinyon-Juniper belt of eastern Arizona and New Mexico, has much smaller flowers and fewer rays. It blooms from April to October. The rubber plant *(H. richardsonii)* of Arizona and New Mexico has even smaller heads and is regarded as poisonous to domestic stock. *Hymenoxys* comes from the Greek *humen*, meaning membrane, and *oxus*, sharp, because of the pointed scales of the seed bristles.

GOLDENROD *(Solidago multiradiata)*   Sunflower family *(Compositae)*

Height: Perennial herb, 2″-16″ (5-40cm). **Flowers:** Heads in terminal cluster; ray flowers 13, yellow, extending beyond the 13-34 yellow disc flowers. **Leaves:** Entire or toothed, 1″-4″ (2.5-10cm) long. **In bloom:** June-September. **Habitat-Range:** High mountains, sunny, grassy, rocky places throughout West to Alaska, Siberia, east to Labrador.

This alpine flower has a wide range in the cold, high mountains, the numerous seeds with fine bristly hairs being easily dispersed by air currents. This group of plants is reputed to have medicinal value. An antiseptic powder can be made from the dried leaves and a lotion of similar properties by boiling the leaves.

69 ALPINE GOLD *(Hulsea algida)*[†]   Composite family *(Compositae)*

Height: Perennial herb, 4″-16″ (10-40cm). **Flowers:** Heads large; rays numerous, small, 1/2″ (1cm) long, linear, yellow; involucres woolly. **Leaves:** Broadly linear with edges often toothed; 1″-4″ (2.5-10cm) long; sticky, pubescent with considerable cottony wool on herbage when young. **In bloom:** July-August. **Habitat-Range:** Alpine fields 10,000′-14,000′ (3050-4300m) from the high Sierra Nevada of California and Cascades of Oregon to the higher peaks of the northern Rocky Mountains.

This rather uncommon flower is found above timberline. A closely related species, *Hulsea nana*, is more common above timberline in the Cascades and Sierra Nevada. It is less succulent, smaller, and lacks the leafy stems, the leaves being in a basal rosette. Both have a strong odor. The generic name is taken from G. W. Hulse, an army surgeon who was the collector.

70 SUBALPINE BUTTERCUP   Buttercup family *(Ranunculaceae)*
(*Ranunculus eschscholtzii*)

Height: Perennial herb, 4″-6″ (10-15cm). **Flowers:** Solitary, terminal; sepals 5; petals 5-9, rounded, about 1/2″ (1cm) long; golden yellow, becoming paler with age; stamens numerous, 20-40. **Leaves:** Rounded, 5/8″-1 1/2″ (1.5-4cm); 3-lobed; smooth. **In bloom:** July-August. **Habitat-Range:** Rocky areas, alpine or subalpine meadows; California east to Rocky Mountains, north to Alaska.

A typical alpine or subalpine species, this plant is small but has relatively large yellow flowers, making it conspicuous. Closely related is the Alpine Buttercup *(R. adoneus)*, found only around or above timberline in the Rocky Mountains and Great Basin. Its three leaf lobes are twice divided into linear segments.

71 EVENING PRIMROSE Evening-primrose family *(Onagraceae)*
(Oenothera xylocarpa)

Height: Perennial stemless herb, 2″-4″ (5-10cm). **Flowers:** Solitary; slender calyx tube arising from root crown, 1″-2″ (2.5-5cm) long; calyx lobes 4, reflexed; petals 4, 1″-1 1/2″ (2.5-4cm) long, yellow, aging salmon; stamens 8. **Leaves:** Pinnatifid, 1″-3″ (2.5-7.5cm), soft pubescent, sometimes spotted red. **In bloom:** July-August. **Habitat-Range:** Sandy flats or benches in coniferous forests; southern Sierra Nevada, California, western Nevada.

This plant has rather limited distribution. Its large and colorful flowers make it conspicuous in the pine forests where it occurs.

72 CINQUEFOIL *(Potentilla gracilis)* Rose family *(Rosaceae)*

Height: Perennial herb, 12″-18″ (30-45cm). **Flowers:** Saucer-shaped, in loose cymes; 3/4″ (2cm) in diameter; sepals 5, pointed, nearly as long as petals; petals 5, heart-shaped with notch at apex, bright yellow; stamens 20-29, inserted on disc. **Leaves:** Palmate with 5 or sometimes 7 toothed leaflets 3/4″-2 1/2″ (2-6cm) long; upper surface dark green, slightly hairy, underside more silvery with many hairs. **In bloom:** May-July. **Habitat-Range:** Moist situations, meadows, streamsides in grassland, woodlands, and coniferous forests from 1500′ to 9000′ (450-2750m); Rocky Mountains to Pacific coast north to Alaska.

This widespread species is known by its yellow flowers and fan-shaped leaf usually divided into five parts, from which the name "Cinquefoil," meaning "five finger," comes. Many other species of this genus of the Northern Hemisphere are difficult to identify.

73 ALPINE LILY *(Lilium parvum)*† Lily family *(Liliaceae)*

Height: Perennial herb, 1 1/2′-7′ (.5-2m). **Flowers:** Bell-shaped; few to many in terminal raceme; perianth segments 6, orange with red spots, 1 1/4″-1 1/2″ (3-4cm) long with lobes turned out; stamens 6, shorter than petals; stigma 3-lobed. **Leaves:** Linear, 2″-5″ (5-12cm) long, in whorls. **In bloom:** July-September. **Habitat-Range:** Wet places along streams or in swamps, 4000′-9000′ (1200-2750m); Sierra Nevada north to Oregon.

This lovely little lily, also called Small Tiger Lily (the species name means "small" in Latin), makes a bright spot in dark coniferous forests. One can watch for it to bloom only to find that deer have nibbled off the bud just before it opened.

74 GLACIER LILY *(Erythronium grandiflorum)* Lily family *(Liliaceae)*

Height: Perennial herb, 3″-16″ (7.5-40cm). **Flowers:** Nodding, showy, 1 to several on erect stem; perianth segments lance-shaped; 1″-1 1/2″ (2.5-4cm) long; recurved; golden yellow, lighter near inside base, green-streaked near outside. **Leaves:** 2, basal, elliptic-oblong, 4″-8″ (10-20cm) long; unmottled green. **In bloom:** June-July. **Habitat-Range:**

High mountains from 6000′ (1800m) to near timberline in moist woods close to melting snow; northern California to British Columbia and east to the Rocky Mountains.

The Glacier Lily, like its close relative the white Avalanche Lily *(E. montanum)*, is often called a Dogtooth Violet, perhaps because of the petal shape. It is a snowline species, usually occurring in large masses in a colorful alpine display. The bulbs were boiled and eaten by the Indians.

75 YELLOW LADY'S SLIPPER   Orchid family *(Orchidaceae)*
(Cypripedium calceolus)

Height: Perennial herb, 1 1/2′-2′ (.5-.6m). **Flowers:** 1-2 from leafy stem; sepals 3, lance-shaped, 2 lower united; purplish brown or greenish yellow; petals 3; lateral twisted, yellow-green; lower saclike, yellow; stamens 2, fertile. **Leaves:** 3-5, broadly ovoid, 3″-6″ (8-15cm) long, deeply veined. **In bloom:** May-August. **Habitat-Range:** Bogs in coniferous forests of North America, also Old World.

This genus includes many striking wild as well as cultivated orchids, especially in the tropics. The generic name is from the Greek *Kypres*, Venus, and *podion*, slipper; *calceolus* means slipper-shaped, describing the petals.

76 GROUND IRIS *(Iris macrosiphon)*   Iris family *(Iridaceae)*

This is a yellow variant of the Ground Iris (see No. 12).

77 WOOD VIOLET *(Viola sempervirens)*   Violet family *(Violaceae)*

Height: Prostrate herb, up to 7″ (18cm). **Flower:** Single on axillary pedicel with irregular corolla consisting of large lower, 2 upper, 2 lateral petals; petals 1/4″ (6mm) long, light yellow with purple veins. **Leaves:** Round or heart-shaped, dark green, smooth; margins notched. **In bloom:** February-April. **Habitat-Range:** Coniferous woods below 3500′ (1050m), especially near coast, from California to British Columbia, east to Idaho.

This little yellow violet often forms a year-round mat on the floor of Pacific coast redwood forests at lower elevations, but its range is far more extensive than that of the conifer. Because of its permanency its specific name is *sempervirens*, meaning "always green." In the higher mountains of California and Oregon the Pine Violet *(V. lobata)*, another common yellow species, has an erect stature and large divided leaves. The leaves of violets may be eaten as greens.

MOUNTAIN VIOLET *(Viola purpurea)*   Violet family *(Violaceae)*

Height: Perennial herb, 2″-6″ (5-15cm). **Flowers:** Lemon yellow, 5 petals, 1/2″ (1cm) long, 2 upper purplish on back, 2 lateral bearded, purplish brown-veined, lower with saclike spur. **Leaves:** On short branches, long petioles; oval to oblong, slightly toothed, somewhat hairy when young. **In bloom:** March-July. **Habitat-Range:** Dry mountain slopes, 1800′-8000′ (550-2400); California to Oregon.

Another species unique to the Pacific coast from California to British Columbia is *V. sempervirens* (meaning "evergreen"), abundant on the floor of Redwood forests. A distinguishing character is the presence of purple veins on the lower three petals.

78 **GOLDEN COLUMBINE**   Buttercup family *(Ranunculaceae)*
(Aquilegia chrysantha)

Height: Perennial herb, 1 1/2′-3′ (.5-1m). **Flowers:** Terminal, showy, mostly erect; sepals 5, yellow; petals 5, with long spur projecting backward 3/4″-1″ (2-2.5cm), yellow; stamens numerous. **Leaves:** Divided into threes with sections trilobed, largely basal. **In bloom:** April-September. **Habitat-Range:** Rich, damp soil in the mountains from southern Colorado to Texas and west to Arizona, 3500′ to 11,000′ (1100-3300m). Primarily found in coniferous regions.

Columbines are plants of moist woods and forests of the North Temperate Zone. The common name is derived from the Latin *columba*, meaning dove, because the spurs project backward like the tails of these birds. The generic name is also thought to come from the Latin *aquila*, meaning eagle, because the spurs also look like an eagle's claw.

79 **CALIFORNIA PITCHER PLANT**   Pitcher-plant family *(Sarraceniaceae)*
(Darlingtonia californica)

Height: Perennial insectivorous herb, 8″-24″ (20-60cm). **Flowers:** Solitary, pendulous; sepals 5, yellowish green; petals 5, 1 1/4″ (3cm) long, dark purple; stamens 12-15. **Leaves:** Enlarged upward into pitcher-shaped hood with opening beneath partly covered by 2-lobed appendage; green with window spots. **In bloom:** April-June. **Habitat-Range:** Bogs or marshes from sea level to 6000′ (1800m); northern California, Oregon.

This strange plant, the only member of the genus, is named after an early American botanist, William Darlington. It can capture insects attracted to nectar secreted at the rim of the pitcher. Some fall into the cavity, which contains a digestive juice, and are unable to climb out because of downward-directed hairs. To further attract insects the hood has window-like spots that permit light to enter.

80 **BALSAM ROOT** *(Balsamorhiza sagittata)*   Sunflower family *(Compositae)*

Height: Perennial herb, 8″-24″ (20-60cm). **Flowers:** One to several large heads on long stems; outer bracts of involucre oblong, woolly, inner linear, less woolly; ray flowers 1″-1 3/4″ (2.5-4.5cm), yellow. **Leaves:** Basal, arrow-shaped, 4″-8″ (10-20cm) long, 2″-4″ (5-10cm) wide at base, silvery haired on long stalk. **In bloom:** May-July. **Habitat-Range:** Open Rocky Mountain forests 4000′-8000′ (1200-2400m); California to Canada, east to Rocky Mountains.

This species resembles Mule Ears *(Wyethia mollis)*, which has larger, ovate leaves. The generic name refers to the healing balsam-like qualities of the plant. The Indians boiled, dried and ground the roots for a medicine. It is reported to be poisonous but possibly, if moderately used, a cure for rheumatism and insect bites.

81 **HEARTLEAF ARNICA** *(Arnica cordifolia)*   Sunflower family *(Compositae)*

Height: Perennial herb, 6″-24″ (15-60cm). **Flowers:** Single heads or few in loose cyme, each on long stem; 7-13 ray flowers, yellow, 3/4″-1″ (2-2.5cm) long; disc deeper yellow, somewhat elevated. **Leaves:** Opposite; basal, lower stem leaves heart-shaped, 1″-3″ (2.5-7.5cm) long on stems 1″-2″ (2.5-5cm) long; herbage somewhat hairy. **In bloom:** May-August. **Habitat-Range:** Moist soil in mountains and valleys between 3500′ and

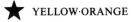

10,000′ (1100-3000m) from the Pacific coast to the Rocky Mountains, north to Alaska.

Most species of *Arnica* in western North America have an aromatic odor. A tincture made from the dried flower heads was popular as a treatment for sprains and bruises.

82 PALE AGOSERIS *(Agoseris glauca)*   Sunflower family *(Compositae)*

Height: Perennial herb 4″-15″ (10-38cm). **Flowers:** Heads single, terminal on long, erect, slightly woolly stem; up to 2″ (5cm) in diameter; bracts of involucre, somewhat woolly, overlapping; ray flowers short; disc, ray flowers yellow. **Leaves:** Generally lance-shaped, either toothed or smooth along edges; 5″-12″ (13-30cm) long. **In bloom:** Midsummer. **Habitat-Range:** Coniferous forests, edges of meadows, sagebrush scrub, 4000′-10,500′ (1200-3200m); Rocky Mountains west to Sierra Nevada and Cascades.

True Dandelions are members of the genus *Taraxacum*, which differs from *Agoseris* in technical details of the seeds and bracts. Both produce seed heads with copious, soft, white bristles attached. The wind carries the individual seeds away with their parachute-like pappus. The name Dandelion comes from the French "dent de lion," meaning tooth of a lion, after the shape of the leaves. Dandelion greens can be cooked as vegetables and are best when young and tender. Older leaves are often bitter.

83 MOUNTAIN DANDELION   Sunflower family *(Compositae)*
(Agoseris aurantiaca)

Height: Perennial herb, 4″-24″ (10-60cm). **Flowers:** Solitary on leafless, erect stem; involucre 3/4″-1″ (2-2.5cm) high; all flowers with petals; burnt orange, darkening with age. **Leaves:** Entire to partly pinnatifid; 2″-10″ (5-25cm) long. **In bloom:** July-August. **Habitat-Range:** Grassy situations in coniferous forests, 6000′-11,500′ (1800-3500m); California to British Columbia, east to Rocky Mountains.

This deeply colored dandelion (*Aurantiaca* means orange in Latin) is one of a large group of composites with many uses for food (such as greens, cooked and uncooked) and beverages made from the flowers, especially Dandelion beer and wine.

GROUNDSEL *(Senecio scorzonella)*   Sunflower family *(Compositae)*

Height: Perennial herb, 1/2′-3′ (.2-1m). **Flowers:** In open cymes of several to many heads; 1/2″-1″ (1-2.5cm) long with 5 or more (sometimes less) bright yellow ray flowers 1/2″-3/4″ (1-2cm) long; disc flowers yellow; bracts of involucre often tipped with purplish black. **Leaves:** Oval to lance-shaped on long petioles near base, 3″-6″ (7.5-15cm) long; stem leaves few, narrow, clasping; herbage woolly. **In bloom:** May-August. **Habitat-Range:** Mountains of western North America, 2500′-10,500′ (750-3200m).

The Groundsels or Ragworts comprise about 1000 species in the genus *Senecio*. They often grow along with larger-flowered composites such as Mule Ears and Balsam Root. The Threadleaf Groundsel (*S. longilobus*), found in Utah and Colorado south to Mexico, has leaves that are linear and matted with woolly hairs. Another species is the Arrowleaf Groundsel (*S. triangularis*), known by its simple, triangular leaves.

84 ST. JOHNSWORT   St. Johnswort family *(Hypericaceae)*
(Hypericum formosum)

Height: Perennial herb, 1′-3′ (.3-1m). **Flowers:** In terminal cymes; saucer-shaped,

1/2″-3/4″ (1-2cm); sepals 5, ovate; petals 5, ovate, yellow with black dots; stamens numerous. **Leaves:** Opposite, entire, ovate, sessile, 1/2″-1 1/4″ (1-3cm) long. **In bloom:** June-August. **Habitat-Range:** Wet meadows up to 7500′ (2300m); from California north to British Columbia, east to Montana.

Ten genera and approximately 300 species of this family are distributed over the temperate and warmer regions of the world. Some are cultivated as an attractive ground cover. The fact that it often blooms about St. John's Day in June is responsible for its common name. A closely related species, Goatweed (*H. perforatum*), has flowers in dense flat cymes and is found over most of the United States and Canada. It has the strange ability to cause sores on white-skinned animals or the white areas of black and white animals, apparently as a reaction to light.

85 **MULE EARS** *(Wyethia mollis)*　　　　　Sunflower family *(Compositae)*

Height: Perennial herb, 1 1/2′-3′ (.5-1m). **Flowers:** Large with one to several heads on long stem; bracts of involucre in several series, 3/4″-1 1/2″ (2-4cm) long; ray flowers showy, 10-17, 1 1/2″-2″ (4-5cm) long, orange-yellow; disc 3/4″-1″ (2-2.5cm) across, orange-yellow. **Leaves:** Elongate-ovate to lance-shaped, 4″-16″ (10-40cm) long, velvety pubescent when young. **In bloom:** May-August. **Habitat-Range:** Dry, wooded slopes, 5000′-10,000′ (1500-3050m); in Oregon, California, and Nevada.

The flower heads of Mule Ears are among the largest native Sunflowers in the West. The showy, bright orange-yellow inflorescences and large gray leaves shaped like a mule's ear are conspicuous even from moving autos. The seeds reportedly were eaten by the Indians. Another common species, the Narrow-leaved Mule Ears (*W. angustifolia*), grows below 5000′ (1500m) in California.

86 **GOLDEN PEA** *(Thermopsis pinetorum)*　　　　　Pea family *(Leguminosae)*

Height: Perennial herb, 1′-2′ (.3-.6m). **Flowers:** In tall racemes; calyx campanulate, 2-lipped; petals yellow; banner about as long as oblong wings, keel almost straight; stamens 10, separate; pistil single, forming flat pod with few seeds. **Leaves:** Palmately 3-foliate; leaflets 1″-2 1/2″ (2.5-6cm) long. **In bloom:** April-July. **Habitat-Range:** Coniferous forests of New Mexico, Arizona to Wyoming, Utah.

These plants resemble Lupines, and the generic name derives from Greek *thermos,* meaning lupine, and *opsis*, likeness. They are common and showy in the forests of the West.

87 **OREGON GRAPE** *(Berberis repens)*　　　　　Barberry family *(Berberidaceae)*

Height: Perennial shrub, 4″-8″ (10-20cm). **Flowers:** In dense raceme, 2″-2 1/2″ (5-6.5cm) long; sepals 6, in 2 circles, petal-like; petals 6, in 2 circles, concave, yellow, 2-cleft to middle; stamens 6; pistil 1, developing blue, berrylike fruit. **Leaves:** 3″-10″ (7-25cm) long, pinnately compound; leaflets ovate, 3-5, many bristlelike teeth on each margin. **In bloom:** April-June. **Habitat-Range:** Open coniferous forests from Sierra Nevada to British Columbia, east to Rocky Mountains; also New Mexico, Texas.

This plant is easily recognized, whether in fruit or in bloom with bright yellow flowers. The leaves are somewhat like the Holly of Europe, and a common name is Mountain Holly. *Repens* means creeping. The state flower of Oregon is *B. aquifolium*. The genus

is often listed as *Mahonia*. The sour berries from these plants are enjoyed by bears; with sugar they make a good juice or jelly. The leaves often turn bright red in the fall and are very decorative. Indians used the yellow stems and roots for a dye.

TWINBERRY *(Lonicera involucrata)*   Honeysuckle family *(Caprifoliaceae)*

Height: Perennial shrub, 2'-3' (.6-1m). **Flowers:** In pairs toward ends of branches; 2 ovate bracts about 1/2" (1cm) long at base of corolla, often turning reddish; calyx missing; petals joined into tube about 1/2" (1cm) long; 5 lobes, unequal, yellow; stamens 5, attached to corolla tube; single pistil becoming black fruit about 3/8" (8mm) in diameter. **Leaves:** Oval, opposite, 1 1/2"-5" (4-12cm) long, hairy underneath. **In bloom:** June-August. **Habitat-Range:** Coniferous forests, 6500'-9500' (2000-2900m); California to British Columbia, east to Rocky Mountains.

This honeysuckle is very attractive with bright red bracts beneath the twin blackberries. Its more trailing relative is *L. ciliosa*, with red berries.

88 STONECROP *(Sedum spathulifolium)*   Stonecrop family *(Crassulaceae)*

Height: Perennial herb, 4"-8" (10-20cm). **Flowers:** Many in branched, flat-topped cluster, yellow; sepals lance-shaped, half as long as petals; petals 4-5, yellow, rarely white, narrow, 1/4" (8mm) long; stamens twice as many as petals. **Leaves:** Thick, flat, in rosettes, rounded apex, 1/2"-1" (1-2.5cm) long, round-toothed edge. **In bloom:** May-July. **Habitat-Range:** Common on rocks in foothills below 7500' (2300m); Coast ranges, Sierra Nevada north to British Columbia.

The plant's generic name comes from the Latin *sedeo*, to sit, referring to its low-growing habit. Stonecrops are rock plants, hence the common name. The succulent leaves are good in salad, especially when young.

89 BROOM RAPE   Broom-rape family *(Orobanchaceae)*
(Orobanche fasciculata)[†]

Height: Perennial herb, 6"-11" (15-28cm). **Flowers:** Solitary on numerous stalks above short, scaly stem; tubes 1"-1 1/2" (2.5-4cm); sepals 5-parted, triangular, usually shorter than flower tube; petals yellow, tinged with purple, 2-lipped, upper with 2 lobes, lower with 3; stamens, 2 pairs, inside floral tube. **Leaves:** Reduced to alternate scales, without chlorophyll. **In bloom:** April-July. **Habitat-Range:** Mountains 2000'-9000' (600-2700m); California to British Columbia, east to Michigan, south to New Mexico.

These fleshy herbs produce no food but live as parasites on roots of plants such as *Eriogonum, Phacelia, Artemisia,* and *Eriodictyon.* The generic name comes from the Greek *orobus*, vetch, and *anchone*, choke, because of the parasitic habit. Cancer Root is a common name for the same reason. The name Broom Rape is based on the habit of some species to parasitize various kinds of Broom. The entire plant can be roasted and eaten, but because the species is rather rare it should not be so used.

90 FALSE LUPINE *(Thermopsis macrophylla)*   Pea family *(Leguminosae)*

Height: Perennial herb, 1'-2' (.3-.6m). **Flowers:** Irregular, in terminal raceme, 3"-6"

(7.5-15cm); calyx campanulate, upper lip notched slightly; corolla yellow, upper petal banner-shaped, roundish, 2 lateral petals oblong, winglike, 2 lower petals joined to form keel; stamens 10, distinct; single pistil. **Leaves:** Palmately 3-foliate, leaflets ovate, 1 1/2″-4″ (4-10cm) long, silky-haired. **In bloom:** April-June. **Habitat-Range:** Open woodlands below 4500′ (1350m); California coastal mountains to southern Oregon.

The False Lupine is more hardy than most lupines in that it can survive cattle grazing and trampling. The stamens, which are not united, and the three leaflets distinguish this group from true Lupines.

GOLDEN CURRANT *(Ribes aureum)*   Saxifrage family *(Saxifragaceae)*

Height: Perennial shrub, 4′-8′ (1-2.5m). **Flowers:** In loose raceme about 1″ (2.5cm) long; calyx tubular, 5 short lobes; petals 5, joined in tube about 1/4″ (6mm) long, yellow; stamens 5, alternate with petals; pistil 1, producing pulpy berry about 1/4″ (6mm) in diameter, either red, yellow, or black. **Leaves:** Nearly smooth, 1/2″-1 1/8″ (1-3cm) broad, 3-5 lobed. **In bloom:** April-May. **Habitat-Range:** Moist woodlands to 7800′ (2400m); California to British Columbia, east to Rocky Mountains, New Mexico.

Ribes, an ancient Arabic name, includes many species with edible berries. Currants and gooseberries, wild and cultivated, are included in the group. *R. aureum* is smooth with golden flowers; *aureum* refers to the gold color. The berries, which ripen in August and September, are good fresh or cooked in jellies. Indians dried them to mix with dried meat and fat for their pemmican, a food they packed in sacks when traveling.

91 HOOKER EVENING PRIMROSE   Evening-primrose family *(Onagraceae)*
(Oenothera hookeri)

Height: Biennial herb, 16″-48″ (40-120cm). **Flowers:** Many on simple or branching stem, 4″-16″ (10-40cm) long; calyx tube 1″-1 1/2″ (2.5-4cm) long, 4-lobed; petals 4, 1″-2″ (2.5-5cm) long, equally broad, yellow; stamens 8; stigma 4-branched, pistil forming woody seed pod. **Leaves:** Ovate, 4″-9″ (10-23cm) long. **In bloom:** June-September. **Habitat-Range:** Moist woodlands to 5000′ (1500m); Coast ranges of California.

As the name implies, these Primroses open in the late afternoon and close by morning. They are very pretty flowers, often blooming in great numbers. Seeds of several species were used as food by the Indians.

92 YELLOW MARIPOSA *(Calochortus luteus)*   Lily family *(Liliaceae)*

Height: Perennial herb, 6″-24″ (15-60cm). **Flowers:** Cup-shaped, erect; single on stem; petals 3/4″-2″ (2-5cm) long, hairy on edge; yellow or orange. **Leaves:** Basal, slender, 2, usually shorter than stem. **In bloom:** May-June. **Habitat-Range:** Hard, packed gravel soil; foothills of Coast Ranges, Sierra Nevada of California.

Mariposa means butterfly in Spanish and refers to the bright, hairy spots on the petals that resemble markings on the wings of some butterflies. This is one of the common species of Yellow Mariposa Lilies. The Yellow Pussy Ears (*C. benthami*) has petals that are thickly covered with yellow hairs. Like many other lilies, some Mariposa bulbs were eaten by the Indians.

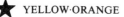

93 RABBIT BRUSH *(Chrysothamnus nauseosus)*   Sunflower family *(Compositae)*

Height: Perennial shrub, 1'-5' (.3-1.5m). **Flowers:** In terminal round clusters; involucre about 1" (2.5cm) high in several series of bracts; corolla lobes 1/2"-1" (1-2.5cm) long, yellow; abundant white bristles attached to seeds. **Leaves:** Linear, 1"-3" (2.5-7.5cm) long, green. **In bloom:** June-September. **Habitat-Range:** Open, dry plains or mountainsides in alkali soil, 3000'-9000' (900-2700m) from the Great Plains west to eastern California.

Many varieties of Rabbit Brush occur over its extensive range, all bearing masses of golden flowers in late summer followed by seed clusters with an abundance of downy white pappus. Latex is obtained from the juice but is of little commercial use; the flowers yield a yellow dye.

94 SULPHUR FLOWER   Buckwheat family *(Polygonaceae)*
(Eriogonum umbellatum)

Height: Perennial herb, 4"-15" (10-37cm). **Flowers:** Borne in clusters on simple umbel, each cluster surrounded by tubular involucre with 8 reflexed lobes; perianth segments 6-parted, all sulphur yellow; calyx gradually narrowing into long stemlike base; stamens 9, attached on base of calyx. **Leaves:** Oval-shaped, basal and at tips of branches; smooth above, white woolly beneath. **In bloom:** June-August. **Habitat-Range:** Sagebrush scrub to coniferous forest, 2500'-10,000' (750-3000m); California, Oregon to Rocky Mountains.

Many species bloom throughout the West, their clear yellow turning reddish in the fall. They are common in Grand Canyon and Mesa Verde national parks.

95 SAGEBRUSH BUTTERCUP   Buttercup family *(Ranunculaceae)*
(Ranunculus glaberrimus)

Height: Perennial herb, 2"-7" (5-18cm). **Flowers:** 1-3 on stems 1/2"-4" (1-10cm) long; sepals 5, spreading, tinged lavender; petals 5, obovate, 1/4"-1/2" (6-12mm) long, almost as wide, yellow; stamens 40-60; pistils forming 75-150 fruits in large rounded head. **Leaves:** Basal roundish, entire or slightly 3-lobed, 1/2"-1 1/4" (1-3cm) long; leaves on stem few, 3-lobed. **In bloom:** April-May. **Habitat-Range:** Sagebrush flats, moist mountain meadows; California to British Columbia, throughout Rocky Mountains.

In many places this is the first buttercup to bloom in the spring. *Ranunculus,* which has about 300 species, is Latin for little frog, a good name for the many species that like moist situations. *Glaberrimus* means baldest, referring to the complete absence of hair on the leaves. Most Buttercups contain ingredients that are irritating to the skin and poisonous if eaten; however, boiling or drying makes them harmless.

96 SUNFLOWER *(Helianthus nuttallii)*   Sunflower family *(Compositae)*

Height: Perennial herb, up to 12' (4m). **Flowers:** Heads in loose, flat-topped raceme; ray flowers, about 17, up to 1 1/2" (4cm) long; disc yellow, near 1" (2.5cm) in diameter. **Leaves:** Mostly alternate; entire; elongate lance-shaped; 2 1/2"-6" (6-15cm) long; herbage pubescent, glandular-dotted. **In bloom:** July-September. **Habitat-Range:** Moist meadows in pinyon-juniper areas, 4000'-8000' (1200-2400m); eastern California to Canada and New Mexico.

These are among the largest composites in North America. The Common Sunflower (*H. annuus*), the state flower of Kansas, is the familiar cultivated variety. Sunflower seeds, especially when roasted, are a popular grocery item; early Spanish settlers used them for meal or gruel. The Indians made an oil from the flower heads, and sunflower oil is still fed to domestic stock and poultry. Purple and black dye is obtained from the seeds and yellow dye from the flowers. The stalks yield a useful fiber.

97 PRINCE'S PLUME *(Stanleya pinnata)* — Mustard family *(Cruciferae)*

Height: Perennial herb, 2'-4' (.6-1m). **Flowers:** In elongate, showy spike-like racemes; sepals 4, spreading, reflexed, greenish-yellow; petals 4, bright yellow, 1/4" (6mm) long; stamens, pistil extend beyond petals; pods slender, drooping, up to 2" (5cm). **Leaves:** Entire to deeply pinnatifid, up to 6" (15cm); pale gray, smooth. **In bloom:** May-June. **Habitat-Range:** Dry plains and foothills in desert and semidesert areas.

The showy yellow plumes may be seen for quite a distance in late spring and early summer, especially when silhouetted on a ridge. It is used by Indians as a potherb.

98 BUSH MONKEY FLOWER — Figwort family *(Scrophulariaceae)*
(Mimulus aurantiacus)

Height: Perennial shrub, 2'-5' (.6-1.5m). **Flowers:** Funnel-shaped with upper, lower lips, solitary in axils, up to 3" (7cm) long, yellow to salmon red. **Leaves:** Opposite, 1"-3" (2.5-7cm) long, dark green, sticky-glandular. **In bloom:** Spring-Fall. **Habitat-Range:** Open rocky, well-drained slopes of California, western Oregon.

This is one of several sticky-leafed, bushy Monkey Flowers (see also Common Monkey Flower) found in dry, brush-covered areas of the Pacific coastal region. Because of their abundance and long blooming season, the brightly colored, velvety flowers are an important source of nectar to certain hummingbirds. *M. aurantiacus* hybridizes with *M. longiflorus* of southern California and northern Mexico. The Scarlet Monkey Flower (*M. cardinalis*) is also a large, sticky-leafed species but with red flowers; it favors streamsides.

99 BUSH PENSTEMON — Figwort family *(Scrophulariaceae)*
(Penstemon antirrhinoides)

Height: Perennial, evergreen shrub, 1'-8' (.3-2.5m). **Flowers:** Crowded in broad, leafy clusters, tubular; sepals 5, much shorter than flower tube, rounded, coming to sharp point; petals yellow, in broad tube, 1" (2.5cm) long, upper lip erect, arched, lower lip 3-lobed, open widely; stamens showing on lips, sterile stamen densely hairy. **Leaves:** Linear or oblong, less than 1/2" (1cm) long, with tiny hairs. **In bloom:** April-May. **Habitat-Range:** In chaparral on dry, rocky slopes below 4500' (1400m) in California.

Many species have forms with slight variations and extended range. In this Penstemon a form called *microphyllus* has yellowish gray-green leaves and is found in a more desert-like area along with Creosote Bush, Pinyon, and Juniper on dry, rocky slopes and mesas below 5000' (1500m) in the Colorado and Mojave deserts to Arizona.

ROCK ROSE *(Helianthemum scoparium)* — Rock rose family *(Cistaceae)*

Height: Somewhat shrubby perennial, 8"-12" (20-30cm). **Flowers:** In terminal panicle:

sepals 5, outer 2 linear, short, inner 3 ovate, 1/8″ (4mm) long; petals 5, expanded, 1/4″ (6mm) long, yellow; stamens numerous. **Leaves:** Alternate, narrowly linear, up to 1″ (2.5cm) long, sometimes slightly hairy. **In bloom:** March-May. **Habitat-Range:** Dry chaparral slopes up to 4000′ (1200m); central California south to Baja California.

The Rock Roses derive their name from the Greek *helios,* sun, and *anthemon,* flower, not because they turn toward the sun as do the *Helianthus,* Sunflowers, but because they open only in sunlight. There are many species in the Mediterranean region as well as in North and South America, and they are grown as ornamentals.

100 HUMBOLDT LILY *(Lilium humboldtii)* Lily family *(Liliaceae)*

Height: Perennial herb, 3′-5′ (1-1.5m). **Flowers:** Few to many in terminal raceme; large, 2 1/2″-4″ (6-10cm) long, nodding; corolla 6 equal segments, strongly recurving, orange-yellow with maroon or purple spots; stamens 6, conspicuous, about 2″ (5cm) long; style as long as stamens, 3-branched. **Leaves:** Lanceolate, 3 1/2″-4 3/4″ (9-12cm) long, bright green or purplish, in 4-6 whorls of 10-20. **In bloom:** June-July. **Habitat-Range:** Chaparral, yellow pine forests below 4500′ (1350m); Sierra Nevada.

This is one of our most beautiful wild lilies, named for Alexander von Humboldt, the famous German naturalist and explorer.

FREMONTIA Cacao family *(Sterculiaceae)*
(Fremontodendron californicum)

Height: Shrub, up to 15′ (4.5m). **Flowers:** 1 1/2″-2″ (4-5cm) in diameter, showy, composed of open corolla-like calyx with 5 deep clefts, rich yellow; 5 stamens united to middle. **Leaves:** Up to 1″ (2.5cm) long, usually trilobed or palmately lobed, green, shiny above, densely hairy beneath. **In bloom:** February-June. **Habitat-Range:** Dry foothills, interior mountain slopes; California, parts of Arizona.

Fremontia, often called Flannel Bush, was named for its discoverer, General John C. Frémont, explorer of the Far West and first Senator from California. Fremontia has been cultivated as an ornamental plant. It belongs to the same family as the Central American Cocoa Tree, the source of cocoa and chocolate.

101 GLOBE LILY *(Calochortus amabilis)* Lily family *(Liliaceae)*

Height: Perennial herb, 6″-20″ (15-50cm). **Flowers:** Terminal or in loose umbel, nodding; globose, 1″-1 1/2″ (2.5-4cm) long; sepals lance-shaped, greenish yellow; petals eye-shaped, uncurved, golden yellow with margins toothed. **Leaves:** Single; basal; narrow, about as long as stem; linear bracts present on stem. **In bloom:** April-June. **Habitat-Range:** Dry loamy or rocky soil, usually near chaparral on slopes up to 3000′ (900m) in north Coast ranges of California.

This species is yellow, like the Yellow Mariposa, but the flowers are globe-shaped rather than open, and are nodding. This is another of the nearly 60 species of *Calochortus,* a name meaning beautiful grass, found in western North America from British Columbia to Guatemala. They are commonly divided into three groups, the Mariposas, the Star Tulips, and the Globe Lilies, based upon the shape of the flower.

102 **ENGELMANN PRICKLY PEAR**   Cactus family *(Cactaceae)*
(Opuntia phaeacantha)

Height: Succulent perennial shrub, main stems horizontal. **Flowers:** Solitary, sessile, perianth segments with sepals grading into petals, usually folded longitudinally in middle to form angle, 1 1/4″-2 1/2″ (3-6cm) long, yellow. **Leaves:** Absent; stems flattened, jointed, spiny; fruit red or purple. **In bloom:** March-June. **Habitat-Range:** Deserts, grasslands below 5000′ (1500m); Southwest from California to New Mexico.

This species is often listed as *Opuntia mojavensis.* The name *phaeacantha* means brown spines, although the spines are not always brown. It is a sprawling plant, often forming low clumps many yards across, and is one of the best-known cacti of its type in the southwestern deserts. Like other Prickly Pears, the fruit and pods have long been used for food in the Southwest. A delicious syrup is made from boiling and straining the peeled fruit. It can also be made into jelly, candy, or a paste called *queso de tuna.*

103 **PRICKLY PEAR** *(Opuntia occidentalis)*   Cactus family *(Cactaceae)*

Height: Succulent perennial shrub, 3′-4 1/2′ (1-1.5m). **Flowers:** Solitary, sessile (stemless); perianth segments with sepals grading into petals, 1 1/2″-2″ (4-5cm) long, yellow; stamens numerous; fruit purple-red, 2″-3″ (5-7cm) long. **Leaves:** Absent; stems flattened pads, jointed, spiny. **In bloom:** May-June. **Habitat-Range:** Sandy or gravelly mesas, washes up to 7000′ (2150m); principally in western desert areas, also into coastal scrub, pinyon-juniper region.

This species appears to be a hybrid; however, it is so well known that its description here seems justified. The Prickly Pear has been an important food for man in the Southwest for centuries. The Indians used the fruit and seeds. The Mexicans to this day use not only the fruit, which they call tuna, but the young pads or *nopalitos* for salad or cooked green vegetable. The plants are raised commercially and *nopalitos* sold in some markets in the United States.

104 **CENTURY PLANT** *(Agave shawii)*   Amaryllis family *(Amaryllidaceae)*

Height: Perennial shrub, 8′-12′ (2.5-4m). **Flowers:** In dense panicle at end of long stem arising from basal rosette of leaves; perianth (sepals, petals) funnel-shaped with 6 segments; 2 1/2″-4″ (6-10cm) long; yellowish green. **Leaves:** Mostly in basal rosette, thick, fleshy, broadly lance-shaped with horny margined teeth, 8″-20″ (20-50cm) long; gray-green. **In bloom:** September-May. **Habitat-Range:** Coastal bluffs, slopes of southern California (formerly), Baja California.

Several hundred species of Agaves, commonly called Century Plants, occur in the warm, dry parts of the Western Hemisphere. Those in the southwestern desert areas of the United States are easily recognized by their basal rosette of large, thick, pointed leaves. The many uses of Agaves include sisal fibers and strong fermented drinks such as pulque, from the juice, and tequila, made by distilling a fermented mash from the woody base. *A. shawii,* one of the most beautiful species, unfortunately has disappeared from southern California because of human encroachment.

105 **GHOST FLOWER** *(Mohavea confertiflora)*   Figwort family *(Scrophulariaceae)*

Height: Annual herb, 4″-16″ (10-40cm). **Flowers:** In dense, leafy spikes; calyx up to

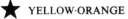

1/2" (1cm) long with 5 narrow lobes; corolla closed at throat, about 1" (2.5cm) long, pale yellow with palate of throat purple-dotted. **Leaves:** Linear to broadly lance-shaped, 1/2"-2 1/2" (1-6cm) long; sticky. **In bloom:** March-April. **Habitat-Range:** Gravelly slopes and sandy washes below 3000' (1000m) in the deserts of southern California, Nevada, Arizona, and northern Baja California.

The Ghost Flower is larger and has paler flowers than its only close relative, the Lesser Mohavea, which occurs in similar desert habitats. The pale yellow, almost transparent petals account for its name.

106 SICKLEPOD RUSHWEED
Pea family *(Leguminosae)*
(Hoffmannseggia drepanocarpa)

Height: Perennial herb, up to 8" (20cm). **Flowers:** Few, small, in racemes; calyx in 5 nearly equal parts; petals 5, yellow, oval, nearly equal; stamens 10, separate; single pistil forming large, curved, flat pod. **Leaves:** Twice pinnately compound with many pairs of lightly hairy leaflets. **In bloom:** May-September. **Habitat-Range:** Dry deserts, 4000'-5500' (1200-1650m), Arizona east to Colorado, Texas.

The species name describes the large flat pod. In Latin *drepano* means sickle and *carpa*, fruit. The genus is named for the Count of Hoffmannsegg, co-author of a study of the flora of Portugal.

107 BLADDER POD *(Lesquerella ludoviciana)*
Mustard family *(Cruciferae)*

Height: Perennial herb, 6"-18" (15-40cm). **Flowers:** Small, in racemes; sepals 4, shorter than petals; petals 4, entire, yellow. **Leaves:** Linear, entire or slightly toothed, 1"-4" (2.5-10cm) long, hairy; seed pods pendulous. **In bloom:** May-August. **Habitat-Range:** Grassy areas, rocky slopes, 3500'-7500' (1050-2300m); Arizona north to Montana, east to Illinois.

This genus is confined largely to western North America, where about 50 species are found. The common name derives from the shape of the seed capsule, which is inflated and often "pops" when stepped on. Most species are spreading, but *L. ludoviciana* is erect, and the herbage is quite woolly. The roots of *L. intermedia* were used by the Hopi Indians as an antidote for rattlesnake bites.

EVENING PRIMROSE
Evening-primrose family *(Onagraceae)*
(Oenothera brevipes)

Height: Herbs, 4"-22" (10-55cm). **Flowers:** In racemes, with tips sometimes nodding, cup-shaped, 3/4" (2cm) in diameter; calyx tube short, lobes 1/4" (6mm) long, pointed, reflexed; petals 4, 1/4"-1/2" (8-12mm) long, bright yellow; stamens 8, yellow, slightly unequal in length; seed capsule slender, up to 2 3/4" (7cm) long, on short pedicel. **Leaves:** Coarse, mostly basal, ovate, 1"-3" (2.5-7.5cm) long, varying from entire to pinnatifid. **In bloom:** March-May. **Habitat-Range:** Dry desert slopes, washes below 5000' (1500m); Utah, Nevada, Arizona, southern California.

Members of the genus *Oenothera* are called Evening Primroses because many of them open in the late afternoon or evening and remain open until the next day. *O. brevipes* is an abundant plant after good spring rains on the desert. The flower heads are large and colorful. The long seed capsule with its short stem helps in field identification.

108 DESERT TRUMPET
Buckwheat family *(Polygonaceae)*
(Eriogonum inflatum)

Height: Perennial herb, 8″-32″ (20-80cm). **Flowers:** Involucre borne singly on stalks from axils or ends of branches, 5-lobed, turbinate, surrounding several minute flowers; calyx hairy, petal-like, yellow, in 3 segments about 1/8″ (2mm) long; petals 3, same as calyx. **Leaves:** Mostly basal, heart-shaped, 1/2″-1″ (1-2.5cm) long on stalks twice as long. **In bloom:** September-October. **Habitat-Range:** Along washes, mesas below 6000′ (1800m); deserts of California east to Utah, Arizona, and south to Lower California.

The peculiar, swollen stems are responsible for the species name *inflatum. Eriogonum* is a large genus of wild buckwheat with some 150 species. As the name implies —*erion* is Greek for wool and *gonu* means knee or joint—some are hairy at the stem joints. The inflated stems of Desert Trumpet have been dried and used by the Indians as tobacco pipes. It is said that some were also used for whistles or trumpets.

109 LESSER MOHAVEA
Figwort family *(Scrophulariaceae)*
(Mohavea breviflora)

Height: Annual herb, 2″-8″ (5-20cm). **Flowers:** In leafy spikes; calyx 5-parted; corolla with short tube; upper and lower lips lobed, lower with hairy palate but not conspicuously dotted; 1/2″ (1cm) long; lemon yellow. **Leaves:** Broadly lance-shaped, 1/2″-1 1/2″ (1-4cm) long; foliage very sticky. **In bloom:** March-April. **Habitat-Range:** Sandy washes and gravelly slopes below 3000′ (900m) in Death Valley, western Nevada, and northwestern Arizona.

This genus was named for the Mohave River where it was discovered by Captain John Frémont. The only other Mohavea is *M. confertiflora,* the Ghost Flower, which is larger and has pale lemon, almost transparent petals, responsible for the common name. They occur in similar desert habitat.

110 DEVIL'S CLAW *(Proboscidea altheaefolia)*
Devil's-claw family *(Martyniaceae)*

Height: Perennial herb, 6″-10″ (15-25cm). **Flowers:** 3-7 in racemes; calyx 5-lobed; corolla 5-lobed, 1″-1 1/2″ (2.5-3.5cm) long, campanulate, slightly 2-lipped, yellow or brownish; stamens 4, long pair sterile, short pair with anthers; pistil single, developing into fruit 3″-4″ (7.5-10cm) long with 2 long, curved claws twice as long. **Leaves:** Mostly opposite, broader than long, 1 1/4″-2″ (3-5cm) wide, with shallow lobes. **In bloom:** June-September. **Habitat-Range:** Dry sandy desert below 5000′ (1500m); southern California to Arizona, Mexico.

The generic name, from the Greek *proboscis,* meaning "beak," refers to the long, curved, beak-shaped seed pods that cling to anything they come in contact with and often get attached to the nostrils of cattle. When softened, the pods furnish black fibers for Indian baskets.

111 DESERT MARIPOSA *(Calochortus kennedyi)*
Lily family *(Liliaceae)*

Height: Perennial herb, 4″-8″ (10-20cm). **Flowers:** 2-4 in umbels; sepals 3, ovate, 1/2″-1″ (1.5-2.5cm) long; petals 3, 1″-2″ (2.5-5cm) long, nearly as broad, orange or vermilion with brown spots near base of each segment. **Leaves:** 2 basal, linear. **In bloom:**

April-June. **Habitat-Range:** Dry rocky slopes, deserts, 2000'-6500' (600-2000m); southern California to Arizona, south to Mexico.

The many species of Mariposa Lilies exhibit a wide range of colors. This desert Mariposa is yellow in Arizona but usually vermilion in California.

112 PANAMINT DAISY   Sunflower family *(Compositae)*
(Enceliopsis argophylla)

Height: Perennial herb, 1'-2' (.3-.6m). **Flowers:** Heads large, single, on naked stem; bracts of involucre, lance-shaped; 24-26 yellow rays, 1"-2" (2.5-5cm) long; disc flat, yellow. **Leaves:** Mainly basal; broad, often pointed, 2"-3" (5-7.5cm) long on short petiole; silvery, velveted. **In bloom:** April-June. **Habitat-Range:** Desert scrub from 1200'-4000' (370-1200m) in Utah, Arizona, Nevada, and southeastern California.

The three species of *Enceliopsis* in southwestern United States are very much alike. Their large, sunflowerlike flowers resemble members of the Brittle Bush genus *Encelia*. The Panamint Daisy is named after the Panamint Mountains that border Death Valley, which are named for some Shoshonean Indians who formerly inhabited the area.

DESERT DANDELION *(Malacothrix glabrata)*   Sunflower family *(Compositae)*

Height: Annual herb, 3"-16" (7-40cm). **Flowers:** Heads solitary, 1"-1 3/4" (2.5-4.5cm) across; bracts linear in about 3 rows, greenish to white, often with short, woolly stripe up middle; limbs of ray flowers pale yellow; disc flowers deeper yellow, often with small red "button" in center. **Leaves:** Mostly basal with some on stems; 2 1/2"-5" (6-13cm) long; pinnatifid into very narrow lobes. **In bloom:** March-June. **Habitat-Range:** Dry, sandy desert from southern California east to Arizona, north to southern Idaho.

In years of heavy rain the Desert Dandelion becomes one of the most conspicuous plants. The pale yellow head, often with a tiny red center, can be seen in colorful masses for miles, and when the air is still they may fill it with their delicate fragrance. Deserts are subject to much wind, but these dandelions can withstand days of such weather.

113 CREOSOTE BUSH *(Larrea divaricata)*   Caltrop family *(Zygophyllaceae)*

Height: Perennial shrub, 3'-12' (1-4m). **Flowers:** Terminal, solitary on short lateral branches; open saucer-shaped; sepals 5, soon lost; petals 5, narrowed toward base, twisted, yellow. **Leaves:** A pair of divergent, oblong, slightly curved leaflets, 1/2" (1cm) long; dark green; resinous. **In bloom:** February-June. **Habitat-Range:** Sonoran Desert of southwestern United States and Mexico below 5000' (1500m); also found in Chile and Argentina.

These dominant desert plants are regularly spaced since their root systems are extensive and spread out near the surface. The common name is derived from the abundance of strong-smelling resin exuding from the leaflets. The Indians used the juice as an antiseptic and the wood for cooking. Because of the presence of latex in Creosote Bush, an attempt was made to cultivate it for a rubber substitute during World War II. It is also known as Greasewood.

BURRO FAT *(Isomeris arborea)*   Caper family *(Capparidaceae)*

Height: Annual shrub, 2'-4' (.6-1m). **Flowers:** Large in bracted racemes; calyx 4-lobed, 1/4" (6mm) long; petals yellow; stamens 6, extending beyond petals; pistil single, forming large, inflated, 2-parted capsule which hangs down. **Leaves:** Alternate, 1/2"-1 1/2" (1-3.5cm) long, 3-parted on stalks half as long, heavily scented. **In bloom:** February-May. **Habitat-Range:** Alkaline, desert areas; southern California.

This may be called Burro Fat because of its strong odor. Another name is Bladder Pod, referring to the large seed pod. The generic name is from the Greek *isos*, equal, and *meris*, part, describing the equally divided pod.

114 **YELLOW ELDER** *(Tecoma stans)*   Trumpet-vine family *(Bignoniaceae)*

Height: Shrub, 5'-12' (1.5-4m). **Flowers:** In terminal racemes; calyx of 5 sepals, united, about 1/4" (6mm) long; petals 5, united into funnel-like corolla with wavy lobes, 1 1/4"-1 3/4" (3-4.5cm) long, bright yellow; 2 long, 2 short stamens. **Leaves:** 4"-8" (10-20cm) long; opposite; pinnately compound with 7-9 leaflets. **In bloom:** June-September. **Habitat-Range:** Desert areas from southern Arizona to Texas.

Yellow Elder is closely related to the Catalpa *(Catalpa speciosa)*, which is native to east Texas and southern United States. It is a colorful species, sometimes cultivated, blooming with the summer rains. In parts of Mexico the stalks are used to make the walls and ceilings of small houses.

GOLDENBUSH *(Haplopappus linearifolius)*   Sunflower family *(Compositae)*

Height: Perennial shrub, 1.5'-5' (.5-1.5m). **Flowers:** Heads terminal, on ends of many nearly leafless stalks; involucres round, glandular; ray flowers 13-18, yellow, about 1/2" (1cm) long; disc flowers numerous. **Leaves:** Linear, entire, 1/2"-1 1/2" (1-3cm) long, glandular. **In bloom:** March-May. **Habitat-Range:** Arid, rocky, shrubby woods, deserts, below 6000' (1800m); southern California east to Arizona, Utah, south to Baja California.

The genus name is from the Greek *haploos*, single, and *pappos*, referring to the pappus or bristles, which are white and in a single circle around the apex of the mature achenes. *Linearifolius* refers to the narrow foliage of the plant. About 150 species are now grouped in this genus, found chiefly in the western hemisphere.

115 **GROUND CHERRY** *(Physalis crassifolia)*   Nightshade family *(Solanaceae)*

Height: Perennial herb, 1'-2' (.3-.6m). **Flowers:** Campanulate with spreading lobes, pale yellow, on pedicels 2-3 times length of flower; calyx bell-shaped, lobes short, pointed; petals joined, longer than calyx, turned back, 1/2" (1cm) broad, 5 hairy bands at summit opposite each lobe; stamens with hairy filaments. **Leaves:** With minute hairs, 1/2"-1" (1-2.5cm) long, entire or with few teeth, broadly ovate on petiole. **In bloom:** March-May. **Habitat-Range:** Sandy, rocky washes or canyon beds, desert ranges, with Creosote Bush; Colorado Desert, east Mojave Desert to Utah, Texas, and lower California, below 4000' (1200m).

A related species called Strawberry Tomato *(P. fendleri)* is common in mesa and Grand Canyon country along with Pinyon and Juniper trees. The round yellow berry, covered with the thin, papery calyx when ripe, is edible raw or cooked.

116 DESERT SENNA *(Cassia covesii)*   Pea family *(Leguminosae)*

Height: Shrub, 1′-2′ (.3-.6m). **Flowers:** In 1″-2″ (2.5-5cm) long axillary racemes; 5 distinct sepals; corolla saucer-shaped, composed of 5 petals each 1/2″ (1cm) long; yellow; 7 fertile, 3 sterile stamens; pods straight. **Leaves:** Pinnate with 3 pairs of elliptic leaflets 1/2″-1″ (1-2.5cm) long; densely white, pubescent. **In bloom:** April-June. **Habitat-Range:** Dry washes below 2000′ (600m), often with Creosote Bush; Colorado Desert east to Arizona.

A closely related species of Senna in Nevada, Arizona, and southeastern Alaska, *Cassia armata*, has smooth leaves, terminal racemes 3″-7″ (7.5-18cm) long and curved pods. A cathartic drug derived from the dried leaves of an Old World species of *Cassia* is called Senna.

117 CONEFLOWER *(Ratibida columnaris)*   Sunflower family *(Compositae)*

Height: Perennial herb, 1′-4′ (.3-1m). **Flowers:** Borne on cylindrical disc nearly 2″ (5cm) long, one quarter as thick; ray flowers yellow or purplish, 3/4″-1 1/2″ (2-3.5cm) long, often hanging down; disc flowers tubular, purplish brown, covering cone-shaped disc, forming flattened seeds. **Leaves:** Narrow or divided in 5, 7, or 9 narrow segments. **In bloom:** July-September. **Habitat-Range:** Open plains, prairies, foothills from Texas, New Mexico north to Arkansas, Minnesota, Canada.

This Coneflower once was grouped with the *Rudbeckia*, but the fruit structure is different. The name *columnaris* means columnar, referring to the shape of the disc. Indians used the leaves and flower heads for tea and as a yellow-orange dye.

118 CUTLEAF CONEFLOWER   Sunflower family *(Compositae)*
(Rudbeckia laciniata)

Height: Perennial herb, 2′-10′ (.6-3m). **Flowers:** Borne on cone-shaped disc 1″ (2.5cm) in diameter; ray flowers about 8, 1″-2″ (2.5-5cm) long, yellow or orange, turning downward; disc flowers covering dark-colored cone, forming 4-angled seeds. **Leaves:** Smooth, irregularly divided in 3, 5, or 7 lobes. **In bloom:** July-September. **Habitat-Range:** Wet fields, roadsides; Arizona, Texas, north through Rocky Mountains to Canada.

The leaves of *laciniata* are more divided than those of other Coneflower species, as the name indicates. The generic name honors father and son Olaf Rudbeck, professors of botany at Uppsala, Sweden, who lived just before Linnaeus. A garden plant, Golden Glow, is a variety of this Cutleaf Coneflower.

TARWEED   Sunflower family *(Compositae)*
(Hemizonia multicaulis, ssp. vernalis)

Height: Annual herb, 4″-12″ (10-30cm). **Flowers:** In flat raceme; heads up to 1″ (2.5cm) across; involucre bracts oblong-pointed; sticky; ray, disc flowers bright lemon yellow; ray flowers deeply 3-lobed. **Leaves:** On erect sticky, pubescent stems; slender, grasslike; 2″-6″ (5-15cm) long. **In bloom:** April-June. **Habitat-Range:** Open brushland, grassy woods; central California.

This is one of the few spring-blooming tarweeds, a group associated principally with late summer and fall. Like most members of the genus, it has sticky aromatic herbage; hence its common name. All of the approximately 30 species in the genus are in California and Baja California, where the dry summer climate seems to favor their growth.

119 WILD GOURD *(Cucurbita foetidissima)*   Gourd family *(Cucurbitaceae)*

Height: Perennial herb, trailing stems 5′-15′ (1.5-4.5m). **Flowers:** Large, bell-shaped, solitary in axils of stem; calyx 5-lobed, narrow; corolla tubular, 5-lobed, yellow; male flowers 4″-5″ (10-12cm) long, rough-haired, ribbed, with broad lobes; female flowers shorter, hairy; stamens 5 with 2 pairs united; pistil 3-celled, into smooth, globular fruit, light green with white stripes, round, 3″-3 1/2″ (8-9cm). **Leaves:** Triangular, somewhat rounded at base, 4″-10″ (10-25cm) long, erect from trailing stem. **In bloom:** May-August. **Habitat-Range:** Sandy, shrubby, grassy areas below 2000′ (600m); southern California, Mexico, east to Texas, north to Nebraska.

The gourds, melons, and pumpkins have the generic name *Cucurbita* from the Latin, meaning gourd. The odor of this wild gourd is very strong, as the specific name indicates. Fruit and seeds can be eaten fresh or dried for future use. A common Spanish name, *Calabazilla*, means little gourd.

YELLOW FRITILLARY *(Fritillaria pudica)*†   Lily family *(Liliaceae)*

Height: Perennial herb, 3″-10″ (7-30cm). **Flowers:** 1-3 on terminal raceme; corolla bell-shaped, nodding, 6 segments, less than 1″ (1.5-2cm) long, yellow or orange, purple-tinged; stamens 6, half length of segments; pistil single. **Leaves:** Alternate, 3-8, lanceolate, 3″-8″ (6-20cm) long. **In bloom:** April-June. **Habitat-Range:** Grassy wooded slopes below 5000′ (1500m); northern California north to British Columbia, east to Montana, Wyoming.

This small Fritillary comes from a bulb surrounded by many bulblets shaped like rice grains, all edible whether raw or boiled. Some species are thought to contain an alkaloid that is poisonous. It seems best to admire the flowers for their beauty and try their edibility only in an emergency. The generic name is from the Latin *fritillus*, meaning dice box, referring to the capsule, and the specific name means modest.

GOLDEN BRODIAEA *(Brodiaea lutea)*   Lily family *(Liliaceae)*

Height: Perennial herb, 4″-18″ (10-46cm). **Flowers:** 6-11 in loose umbel; star-shaped, 3/4″-1″ (2-2.5cm) in diameter; 6 perianth segments (sepal and petals), yellow with purple-black midvein; stamens 6, alternating long, short; anthers purple to yellow on broad, winged filaments. **Leaves:** Narrowly linear, nearly as long as stem. **In bloom:** May-August. **Habitat-Range:** Open to shaded places in sandy or gravelly soil in coniferous forests of California and southern Oregon, from near sea level to 10,000′ (3000m).

Most of the more than 40 species of *Brodiaea* in western North and South America are some shade of blue, purple, or red. The Golden Brodiaea is an exception, as is the White Brodiaea *(B. hyacinthina)*, whose many white-flowered umbels may be found in low, moist places in California.

GOLDEN-EYED GRASS *(Sisyrinchium californicum)*   Iris family *(Iridaceae)*

Height: Perennial herb, 6″-12″ (15-30cm). **Flowers:** In umbels of 3-7; perianth segments 6 (sepals, petals), 1/2″-3/4″ (1-2cm) long, bright yellow, each with 5-7 dark nerves; stamens 3; pistil single, forming capsule about 1/2″ (1cm) long. **Leaves:** Grasslike, basal, thin, half as long as stem, dull green, drying almost black. **In bloom:** May-June. **Habitat-Range:** Moist grassy places, marshes; California coast north to Oregon.

At first glance this plant might be thought a grass, but the lovely flower with six parts and the seed pod beneath it place it in the Iris family.

120 CALIFORNIA POPPY   Poppy family *(Papaveraceae)*
(Eschscholtzia californica)

Height: Annual or perennial herb, 8″-24″ (20-60cm). **Flowers:** Terminal, showy; open funnel-shaped; sepals 2, joined to form cap which is cast off as petals expand; petals 4; rounded triangular; 1″-2 1/2″ (2.5-6cm) long; deep orange to yellow; receptacle on which flower is borne with conspicuous rim. **Leaves:** Alternate; divided several times into linear segments 1″-2 1/2″ (2.5-6cm) long on long stems; grayish green. **In bloom:** February-September. **Habitat-Range:** Widely distributed over much of the open grasslands of California up to 6500′ (2000m).

This showy poppy (the state flower of California) has been cultivated in many parts of the world. The genus was named after Dr. J. F. Eschscholtz, surgeon and naturalist with the Russian expeditions to the Pacific coast of North America in 1816 and 1824. Several other species occur in western North America, but only the California Poppy has a rim on the receptacle that bears the flower. All flowers of the genus close at night.

121 FRYING PANS *(Eschscholtzia lobbii)*   Poppy family *(Papaveraceae)*

Height: Annual herb, 4″-12″ (10-30cm). **Flowers:** Erect; open funnel-shaped; terminal on stem; sepals 2, united into cap that is lost when petals expand; petals 4, rounded triangular; 1/2″-1 1/2″ (1-4cm) long, yellow; prominent rim lacking beneath petals. **Leaves:** Largely basal; 1/2″-1 1/2″ (1-4cm) long on stems; finely divided; herbage smooth, greenish. **Habitat-Range:** Open grassy slopes of Sierra Nevada foothills and inner north coast ranges of California below 2000′ (600m).

This species differs from California's state flower *(E. californica)* in its smaller size (generally), greener foliage, and the lack of a prominent rim below the petals. Its range is much more restricted.

122 TIDY TIPS *(Layia platyglossa)*   Sunflower family *(Compositae)*

Height: Annual herb, 4″-16″ (10-40cm). **Flowers:** Heads terminal, showy, 1″-1 1/2″ (2.5-4cm) in diameter; ray flowers 13, notched at tip, about 1/2″ (1cm) long, yellow with creamy or white tips; disc yellowish, not elevated. **Leaves:** Entire or lower one pinnatifid, linear, alternate, with short bristles, glandular. **In bloom:** March-May. **Habitat-Range:** Open grassland in western California.

Tidy Tips are related to the Tarweeds but are early spring bloomers with showy flowers. They often occur with Goldfields *(Baeria chrysostoma)* and Baby Blue-eyes *(Nemophila menziesii)*. Another closely related species is *Layia chrysanthemoides*, which occurs in the same area but has nonglandular herbage.

RAGWORT *(Senecio plattensis)*   Sunflower family *(Compositae)*

Height: Perennial herb, 8″-20″ (20-50cm). **Flowers:** Heads borne in corymbs; involucre cup-shaped, bracts equal in length, soft-hairy, about 1/4″ (6mm) high; ray flowers yellow-orange; fruit an achene with short bristles. **Leaves:** Alternate, ovate to linear, pinnatifid or toothed, 1″-2″ (2.5-5cm) long, woolly. **In bloom:** May-August. **Habitat-Range:** Mountain grasslands; New Mexico, Arizona, Texas, Utah north to South Dakota.

This genus, one of the largest, covers much of the world and ranges from tiny herbs to the giant tree senecio of Africa. *Senex* means old man in Latin and describes the white hairlike bristles on the seeds.

COLORADO GREENTHREAD   Sunflower family *(Compositae)*
(Thelesperma megapotamicum)

Height: Annual herb, 1′-3′ (.3-1m). **Flowers:** Borne in heads on ends of long slender stalks; involucre with outer row of bracts, short, spreading, inner bracts 4 times as long; disc flowers numerous, yellow; ray flowers lacking. **Leaves:** Mostly basal, narrow, threadlike. **In bloom:** May-October. **Habitat-Range:** Plains, mesas, 3500′-6500′ (1050-2000m), Arizona, Texas, north to Colorado, Wyoming, Nebraska.

The cultivated Coreopsis is closely related to the Greenthreads. The seeds of *Thelesperma* are rough with small projections, accounting for the Greek name *thele*, nipple, and *sperma*, seed. A similar species, *T. longipes*, is more common in the Southwest. The Indians call it *cota* and use it as a tea and for a reddish dye.

GOLDFIELDS *(Baeria chrysostoma)*   Sunflower family *(Compositae)*

Height: Annual herb, 5″-10″ (13-25cm). **Flowers:** Heads on slender stems, 1/2″-1″ (1-2.5cm) in diameter; 5-15 ray flowers, usually notched at end; disc yellow. **Leaves:** Linear, entire, 1/2″-1 1/2″ (1-4cm) long; herbage slightly pubescent. **In bloom:** January-May. **Habitat-Range:** Sandy or clay soil in open grassland, up to 3000′ (1000m), California to Oregon.

This colorful and widespread species may occur in such abundance that it produces a carpet of gold visible many miles away. The generic name *Baeria* honors the early Russian zoologist K. E. Baer.

123 BUTTERFLY WEED *(Asclepias tuberosa)*   Milkweed family *(Asclepiadaceae)*

Height: Perennial herb, 12″-32″ (30-80cm). **Flowers:** In umbels, mostly terminal; sepals small, reflexed; corolla lobes 5, about 1/4″ (6mm) long, reflexed, with 5 cups rising at top of corolla tube, ranging from bright orange to orange-red. **Leaves:** Alternate, sessile, linear to oblong, roughly hairy. **In bloom:** June-September. **Habitat-Range:** Dry, open grasslands from New England to Arizona.

This is one of the many colorful species of Milkweeds but unlike most, the juice is not milky. The root has been used as a cure for pleurisy.

124 FIDDLENECK *(Amsinckia intermedia)*   Borage family *(Boraginaceae)*

Height: Annual herb, 1′-3′ (.3-1m). **Flowers:** In scorpioid (coiled) spikes; 5 calyx lobes, sometimes partly united, hairy on outside; corolla about 1/2″ (1cm) long, somewhat funnel-shaped, with 5 lobes; yellow to orange. **Leaves:** Oblong to lance-shaped, 4″-8″ (10-20cm) long; herbage coarse, bristly. **In bloom:** March-June. **Habitat-Range:** Open grassland of western North America from desert to mountains below 5000′ (1500m).

The common name "Fiddleneck" refers to the curved or scorpioid shape of the flower spike. It is also known in Arizona as "Saccato Gordo," meaning fat grass, because of its abundance and value as a grazing plant for stock. In certain areas of the West in spring, Fiddleneck is the dominant plant and yellow-to-orange fields of it are visible several miles away.

CALIFORNIA BUTTERCUP
Buttercup family *(Ranunculaceae)*
(Ranunculus californicus)

Height: Up to 18″ (45cm). **Flowers:** With distinct sepals, petals; petals 9-16, up to 1/2″ (1cm) long, yellow, with nectar pit at base covered by scales; sepals 5, reflexed, yellowish green; stamens numerous. **Leaves:** Palmately lobed, usually somewhat hairy, 1″-3″ (2.5-8cm) long, divided. **In bloom:** Early spring. **Habitat-Range:** Throughout lowlands of California in moist situations on grassy hillsides, valleys.

Of the many kinds of buttercups, this is a common species in the West. It is among the first and most conspicuous flowers of spring in most areas. Generally buttercups are easily recognizable by the numerous glossy yellow petals, but in some species the blooms are white or even pink. Roots and foliage are cooked and eaten by many, and Indians have used the seeds parched and ground in making bread. Thorough cooking removes the poisonous volatile oil protoanemonin, which is present in all buttercups.

125 GREAT MULLEIN
Figwort family *(Scrophulariaceae)*
(Verbascum thapsus)

Height: Perennial herb, 3′-6′ (1-2m). **Flowers:** In crowded spikes 1′-3′ (.3-1m) long, 1 1/4″ (8.5cm) thick; calyx 5-lobed; corolla yellow, spreading, in nearly equal segments; stamens 5, all with anthers; stigma single, capsule with 2 parts. **Leaves:** Hairy, oval; basal in rosettes, 4″-16″ (10-40cm) long, on shorter petiole. **In bloom:** June-September. **Habitat-Range:** Grassy or sandy waste places; most of North America up to 8000′ (2450m); introduced from Europe.

Only three of the almost 250 species of *Verbascum* have settled in western America. The generic name is from old Latin *barbascum*, and *thapsus* is from an ancient North African town on the Mediterranean. Leaves of this plant are used to make a skin lotion.

126 YELLOW SAND VERBENA
Four-o'clock family *(Nyctaginaceae)*
(Abronia latifolia)

Height: Perennial herb, up to 4″ (10cm) tall on prostrate stem, 1′-3′ (.3-1m) long. **Flowers:** Many in terminal heads; involucre of 5 ovate bracts; calyx tubular with spreading tips; corolla tubular, 4-5 lobed, yellow; stamens 5, unequal in length within tube; pistil single; fruit top-shaped with 5 winged lobes attached. **Leaves:** Round, thick, succulent, 1/2″-1 1/2″ (1-4cm) long, glandular. **In bloom:** May-October. **Habitat-Range:** Sea coast, southern California to British Columbia.

The fragrant Sand Verbenas are common and showy on the sands of the Pacific coast and in deserts of the West, varying in color from white to yellow and from rose to lavender. They are not related to the true verbenas. The Greek *abros*, meaning graceful, gives the Yellow Sand Verbena its generic name.

127 LIVE FOREVER *(Dudleya farinosa)*   Stonecrop family *(Crassulaceae)*

Height: Perennial herb, 5″-12″ (13-30cm). **Flowers:** In cymelike clusters on stem with many scalelike leaves arising from basal rosette; calyx with 5 deeply cleft, erect lobes; corolla cylindrical, composed of 5 erect petals joined near base, lemon yellow, about 1″ (2.5cm) long. **Leaves:** Principally in basal rosette; smooth, gray, with red to purple tinges; thick; oblong; 1″-2″ (2.5-5cm) long, 1/2″-1″ (1-2.5cm) wide. **In bloom:** May-September. **Habitat-Range:** Sea bluffs and coastal scrub from southern California to Oregon.

Live Forever, referring to the ability of these plants to survive for many years, is also known as Hen and Chickens or Sea Lettuce. Most of the species are rock inhabitants. The genus was named in honor of an early Stanford University botanist, Professor W. R. Dudley.

GUMWEED *(Madia gracilis)*   Sunflower family *(Compositae)*

Height: Annual herb of varying height, 4″-40″ (10-100cm). **Flowers:** In loose racemes; involucre ovoid to globose with bracts deeply grooved; very glandular, aromatic, pointed; heads 1/2″-1″ (1-2.5cm) in diameter; ray, disc flowers lemon yellow; ray flowers 8-12, 3-lobed. **Leaves:** Mostly linear, coarse, up to 4″ (10cm) long; stem glandular, hairy. **In bloom:** April-August. **Habitat-Range:** Wooded hillsides, open situations from sea level to 7800′ (2400m); British Columbia, Montana south to Chile.

The flowers of this plant open in the evening and close about noon each day. The strongly scented, glandular, sticky herbage places it with the tarweeds. The genus *Madia*, restricted to North and South America, consists of 18 species.

128 SALT MARSH GUM PLANT   Sunflower family *(Compositae)*
(Grindelia stricta)

Height: Perennial herb, 12″-16″ (30-40cm). **Flowers:** Heads large, solitary, 1 1/2″-2″ (4-5cm) across; gummy bracts composing broad involucre; ray flowers bright yellow. **Leaves:** Alternate, spade-shaped, 1″-2″ (2.5-5cm) long, thick, resinous. **In bloom:** June-September. **Habitat-Range:** Coastal salt marshes and seaside bluffs from central California to Oregon.

Some species of *Grindelia* are restricted to salt marshes, others are found about freshwater or semialkaline marshes, and still others occur in dry brushland. One of the widest ranging is *G. squarrosa*, found from New Mexico and Texas to the northern Mississippi Valley. All are coarse, summer-blooming composites with sticky flowerheads. Gum Plants have been used for many medicinal purposes. The Indians boiled the roots for various ailments and the buds for the treatment of smallpox. Spanish Americans drank the juice of boiled buds and flowers for kidney ailments. They are now used for asthma and bronchitis, as an antispasmodic and in a common cough remedy, Pertussin.

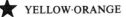

DUNE TANSY *(Tanacetum camphoratum)*   Sunflower family *(Compositae)*

Height: Perennial herb, 1'-2 1/2' (.3-.8m). **Flowers:** Borne in clusters in small flat heads; involucre with many overlapping scalelike bracts; ray flowers missing; disc flowers tubular, yellow, 5-toothed, on disc 1/2"-3/4" (1-2cm) broad. **Leaves:** Alternate, bipinnately dissected, with fine hairs; aroma of camphor. **In bloom:** June-September. **Habitat-Range:** Coastal sand dunes; northern California.

Perhaps the origin of the common name, from the Greek *athanasia*, meaning "to ward off death," accounts for the fact that the Tansies, all strong-scented herbs, are credited with many cures. They have been used for skin irritations, bruises, sprains, rheumatism, and as a douche. But when taken internally, they have proved fatal.

CALIFORNIA ENCELIA   Sunflower family *(Compositae)*
(Encelia californica)

Height: Shrub, 2'-4' (.6-1m). **Flowers:** In solitary heads 2"-4" (5-10cm) across; disc maroon to brown, ray flowers 14-25, bright yellow. **Leaves:** Elongate, 1"-3" (2.5-7cm) long, essentially smooth, green, on long, naked stalk rising from wooden base. **In bloom:** February-May. **Habitat-Range:** Dry foothills, coastal bluffs of southern California.

This is a conspicuous early spring composite seen everywhere along roads in coastal southern California. It is found from sand dunes just back of beaches to dry barrancas inland, with several related species on the southwestern deserts. Most common in gravelly washes and mesas is *E. virginensis*, which has a yellow disc, smaller ray flowers, and downy foliage.

129 **SKUNK CABBAGE** *(Lysichitum americanum)*   Arum family *(Araceae)*

Height: Perennial herb, without stem, from thick rootstalk. **Flowers:** Foul smelling, clustered on fleshy spike 2"-6" (5-15cm) long, sheathed by yellow bract; corolla 4-lobed, bractlike; stamens 4. **Leaves:** Basal, oblong, becoming huge (to 3', 1m) after flower appears. **In bloom:** April-June. **Habitat-Range:** Open swamps, wet woods, often as snow melts; California north coast to Alaska, east to northern Rocky Mountains.

The bright yellow, hood-shaped covering of the flower stalk is conspicuous as it develops along wet places. By the end of summer the tall leaves are all that remains. When crushed, the leaves produce a strong skunklike odor—hence the name. The fleshy roots are eaten by bears and elk. Indians baked the roots to supplement winter food.

130 **POND LILY** *(Nuphar luteum)*   Water-lily family *(Nymphaeaceae)*

Height: Aquatic perennial herb. **Flowers:** Large, cup-shaped, 2"-3" (5-7.5cm) diameter; sepals 5-7, rounded, concave, yellow; petals, stamens similar, numerous, yellow. **Leaves:** Oval to heart-shaped; 4"-16" (10-40cm) long, floating on water surface. **In bloom:** April-September. **Habitat-Range:** Ponds and slow streams, sea level to 7500' (2300m), over much of the West. Not restricted to any special plant community.

Pond lilies are characteristic of quiet waters where other water plants usually occur. Their large, yellow, globelike flowers are conspicuous. In California the Klamath Indians used the ripened seeds to make flour, and some of the seeds were roasted like popcorn.

131 COMMON MADIA *(Madia elegans)*   Sunflower family *(Compositae)*

Height: Annual herb, 3/4'-2 1/2' (.2-.8m). **Flowers:** Heads few to many on long stems, showy, 1"-1 1/2" (2.5-4cm) in diameter; rays 8-20, 3-lobed at tip; yellow (sometimes with red spot at base); disc flat. **Leaves:** Alternate, linear, 3"-5" (7-12cm) long near base of stem; coarse, hairy, sticky. **In bloom:** April-November, varying with locality, habitat. **Habitat-Range:** Dry grassy or wooded slopes below 10,000' (3000m); California, Oregon.

The several subspecies of Common Madia vary in size, form of flower, and habitat, some occurring in coniferous forests at high elevations, others in lowland woods or meadows. The Woodland Madia (*M. madioides*) has fewer and less showy flower heads only 1/2"-3/4" (1-2cm) in diameter.

GOLDEN YARROW *(Eriophyllum lanatum)*   Sunflower family *(Compositae)*

Height: Perennial herb, 4"-36" (10-80cm). **Flowers:** Showy in loose corymbs; involucres bell-shaped to round, 1/4"-3/4" (6-20mm) broad; ray flowers 8-13, yellow; disc flowers yellow, 5-lobed on glandular tube. **Leaves:** Woolly, usually toothed or divided, 1/2"-3" (1-8cm) long. **In bloom:** June-July. **Habitat-Range:** Many plant communities; up to 10,000' (3,000m); southern California north to British Columbia, east to Great Basin, Rocky Mountains.

There are many varieties of this species within the widespread habitat. The white woolly stems and leaves account for both the genus name, from the Greek *erion*, wool, and *phyllon*, leaf, and for the species name, from the Latin *lanatum*, meaning woolly. The woolly hairs help prevent evaporation of water and allow these plants to grow in dry locations.

132 BLAZING STAR *(Mentzelia laevicaulis)*   Loasa family *(Loasaceae)*

Height: Biennial shrub, 2'-4' (.6-1m). **Flowers:** In terminal clusters of 1-3, star-shaped; calyx 5-lobed with lobes lance-shaped, 1"-1 1/4" (2.5-3cm) long; petals 5, pointed, 1 3/4"-2 1/2" (4.5-6cm) long, light yellow; stamens numerous, long. **Leaves:** Lance-shaped or narrowly oblong, toothed, 3"-7" (7.5-18cm) long; stems white; herbage with barbed hairs. **In bloom:** June-October. **Habitat-Range:** Dry, gravelly streambeds from desert to mountains below 8500' (2600m) from California north to Washington and east to Montana and Utah.

The many species of *Mentzelia* in the West are often called Stickleaf because of the minute barbed hairs on leaves and stem. The flowers are closed during much of the day, opening only in late afternoon. Seeds of the Yellow Mentzelia and related kinds of the Southwest were parched and used by the Indians for meal.

133 COMMON DANDELION   Sunflower family *(Compositae)*
(Taraxacum officinale)

Height: Perennial herb, 3"-10" (7.5-25cm). **Flowers:** In single heads, 3/4"-2" (2-5cm) broad, on long stems; involucre with 2 circles of bracts, outer smaller than inner; all flowers strap-shaped, yellow; seeds with numerous thin white hairs. **Leaves:** Basal, pinnately lobed or toothed. **In bloom:** Throughout the year. **Habitat-Range:** Widespread in moist places in western United States.

This true Dandelion, a native of the Old World, has become known as a bothersome weed in many places where it crowds out other plants. It is useful as a food for many birds and forest mammals. The leaves and roots are used in salads, the flowers for making wine. The root also contains a drug used for centuries as a mild laxative and diuretic. The species name means that the plant is recognized as an official drug.

134 SALSIFY *(Tragopogon dubius)*   Sunflower family *(Compositae)*

Height: Perennial herb, 24"-48" (60-120cm). **Flowers:** Heads solitary; bracts about 13, long, narrow, exceeding corollas; flowers all rays with corolla pale lemon yellow. **Leaves:** Grasslike, clasping, 4"-12" (10-30cm) long. **In bloom:** May-July. **Habitat-Range:** Widespread, 3500'-7000' (1000-2100m); Idaho south to Arizona, New Mexico.

This species, naturalized from Europe, is also known as Goatsbeard and Goat Dandelion, probably because of the long, slender bracts that extend beyond the corollas of the head. In some respects it resembles a very large dandelion. It is closely related to the Oyster Plant (*T. porrifolius*), which has purple instead of yellow flowers.

135 WESTERN WALLFLOWER   Mustard family *(Cruciferae)*
(Erysimum asperum)

Height: 1'-2 1/2' (.3-.8m). **Flowers:** In raceme, each 3/4" (2cm) in diameter with 4 petals, 4 sepals; orange; pods 4 sided, 3"-4" (7-10cm) long. **Leaves:** Entire, very narrow, 3"-6" (7-15cm) long; numerous. **In bloom:** February-June. **Habitat-Range:** Sierra Nevada to subalpine situations.

Many kinds of Wallflowers grow throughout the Northern Hemisphere. Their large, fragrant flower heads range from cream to brilliant orange or orange-red with long, slender pods and narrow leaves. Their name derives from their preference for growing in old walls or against rocks. Cultivated varieties are common in old-fashioned gardens. A coastal species, *E. capitatum,* ranges from California to Washington and has cream or yellowish flowers. Another yellow species that occasionally has a lavender form and is alpine is *E. nivale* of the Rocky Mountains.

YELLOW MUSTARD *(Brassica campestris)*   Mustard family *(Cruciferae)*

Height: Annual herb, 1'-6' (.3-2m). **Flowers:** In elongated racemes; sepals 4, oblong, 1/4" (6mm) long, yellowish; petals 4, yellow, spreading, slightly longer than sepals; stamens 6, 2 shorter than others; pistil single, forming pod 1 1/4"-1 1/2" (3-4cm) long. **Leaves:** Smooth, succulent, entire or lobed, 4"-8" (10-20cm) long. **In bloom:** January-May. **Habitat-Range:** Open grassy fields throughout West.

Brassica is Latin for cabbage and includes the cultivated cauliflower, turnip, broccoli, and other vegetables. The leaves of Mustard are used as a green vegetable; but the seeds are potent and can be toxic to animals and humans. The flowers bloom early in spring in a solid mass of yellow in orchards and fields.

136 COMMON MONKEY FLOWER   Figwort family *(Scrophulariaceae)*
(Mimulus guttatus)

Height: 1'-2' (.3-.6m). **Flowers:** Tubular with 2 lips, strongly angled calyx; solitary in axils; 3/4″-1 1/2″ (2-4cm) long; yellow, often with reddish spot in throat. **Leaves:** Opposite; broad, toothed on edges; smooth or slightly hairy. **In bloom:** March-August. **Habitat-Range:** Rich, moist soil in suitable situations below 10,000′ (3050m) throughout western North America.

It is widespread, with many related species throughout its range. The name Monkey Flower is applied to the group because dots of color on the lobes of several species suggest a face. The smallest forms are found in alpine and desert regions.

YELLOW OWL'S CLOVER   Figwort family *(Scrophulariaceae)*
(Orthocarpus hispidus)

Height: Annual herb, 4″-12″ (10-30cm). **Flowers:** In terminal spikes with conspicuous bracts; calyx with 4 narrow divisions about 1/2″ (1cm) long; corolla 1/2″-3/4″ (1-2cm) long, yellow; 2-lipped, upper narrow, straight, lower with 3 sacs, longer than deep; stamens 4, attached near top of corolla tube; pistil single. **Leaves:** 1/2″-1 1/2″ (1-4cm) long, finely hairy, entire or few narrow divisions. **In bloom:** May-August. **Habitat-Range:** Grassy meadows, 3000′-7000′ (900-2150m) elevation; southern California north to Alaska, east to Nevada, Idaho.

Owl's Clover, so named for the eyelike spots on the petals, has many widespread species. In the genus name, *orthos* is Greek for straight, and *karpos,* fruit, refers to the straight seed pod. *Hispidus* refers to the hairy stems and foliage of this small yellow species.

BEACH PRIMROSE   Evening-primrose family *(Onagraceae)*
(Oenothera cheiranthifolia)

Height: Prostrate perennial. **Flowers:** Solitary in axils of leaves along stem; calyx lobes 4, up to 1/4″ (6mm) long, reflexed; petals 4, bright yellow, up to 1/2″ (1cm) long; stamens 8, of unequal length. **Leaves:** In basal rosette and along the stem; basal leaves up to 3″ (7cm) long, those on stem 3/4″-1 1/2″ (2-4cm) long; thick, white, pubescent. **In bloom:** February-August. **Habitat-Range:** Sandy beaches, coastal dunes from Oregon to Baja California.

Evening Primroses are members of the same family as the cultivated Fuchsia. Found over much of the world, they reach a peak of abundance in western North America, and the genus *Oenothera* is one of the largest. Despite the name "Evening Primrose," only a few species bloom at twilight. This beautiful species is often seen on the beach in spring and on dunes with the colorful pink Sand Verbena. The bright yellow flowers, reclining stems, and grayish white foliage identify it.

137 STICKY CINQUEFOIL *(Potentilla glandulosa)*   Rose family *(Rosaceae)*

Height: Perennial herb, 1′-4′ (.3-1m). **Flowers:** Saucer-shaped in loose cyme, 1/2″ (1cm) in diameter; sepals 5, pointed, slightly longer than petals; petals 5, rounded at apex, pale yellow; stamens 25, in groups of 5, variable in length, with flat anthers, inserted on marginal disc. **Leaves:** Pinnate, 2″-8″ (5-20cm) long; leaflets 5-7; herbage hairy, stems glandular. **In bloom:** May-July. **Habitat-Range:** Dry to moist situations from 500′ to 11,000′ (150-3300m); western North America.

This wide-ranging species is found in many kinds of plant communities from the

Pacific coast to subalpine regions. Its pale yellow flowers, pinnate leaf with 5 to 7 leaflets, and slightly glandular stems distinguish it from *P. gracilis* with which it is often associated. A number of subspecies show a difference in height of plant and size of flower. The species is sometimes placed in a separate genus, *Drymocallis*.

YELLOW LUPINE *(Lupinus arboreus)*   Pea family *(Leguminosae)*

Height: Perennial shrub, 3 1/2'-8' (1-2.5m). **Flowers:** In racemes 4"-12" (10-30cm) long; calyx 2-lipped; petals broad, round, bright yellow, irregular, pea-flowerlike; stamens 10, united into single ring; pistil single, forming 2-celled dark brown pod 2"-3" (5-8cm) long. **Leaves:** Palmately compound, 5-12 leaflets, 3/4"-2 1/4" (2-6cm) long, silky-haired. **In bloom:** March-June. **Habitat-Range:** Sandy coastal area in California.

This coastal Lupine forms masses of lovely yellow flowers, but the species, whose name means treelike, can also have blue or violet blooms. The generic name is from the Latin *lupus*, wolf, because the plants were thought to rob the soil of nutrient, but it is now known that members of the Pea family, by means of bacteria in the root nodules, return nitrogen from the air to the soil.

Red·Pink

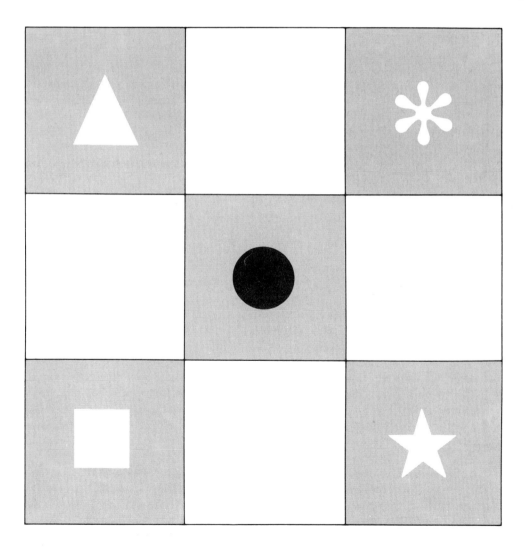

Simplified Key

	HABITAT	HERB	SHRUB
Regular	ALPINE	138 Rose Epilobium 139 Parry's Primrose	140 Red Mountain Heather

Regular	CONIFEROUS	141 Mariposa Lily
		    Red Clintonia
		167 Coast Trillium
		169 Common Trillium
		165 Pussy Paws
		163 Lewisia
		162 Bitterroot
		164 Indian Pink
		148 Western Peony
		157 Fringe Cups
		159 Fireweed
		149 Old Man's Whiskers
		    Red Potentilla
		142 Redwood Sorrel
		160 Sugar Stick
		158 Pinesap
		156 Wintergreen
		161 Snow Plant
		151 Shooting Star
		170 Star Flower
		171 Dogbane
		155 Skyrocket Gilia
		144 Gilia
			Pacific Rhododendron

Irregular		150 Red Columbine
		146 Western Corydalis
		153 Bleeding Heart
		152 Grassleaf Peavine
		143 Hedge Nettle
		173/174 Scarlet Paint Brush
		168 Pink Monkey Flower
		147 Indian Warrior
		154 Barbey Penstemon
		    Scarlet Penstemon
		145 Mountain Pride
		166 Rock Penstemon
		    Figwort	

Composite		172 Thistle	
Regular	WOODLAND	Western Wood Lily 177 Lewisia	175 Fuchsia-flowered Gooseberry 178 Sweetbrier
Irregular		176 Red Larkspur 179 Lupine	

Simplified Key

HABITAT	HERB	SHRUB
PINYON-JUNIPER-SAGE		
Regular	182 Rocky Mountain Bee Plant	181 Fairy Duster
	184 Strawberry Cactus	
	180 Pink Phlox	
Irregular	183 Scarlet Locoweed	
	185 Desert Monkey Flower	
CHAPARRAL		
Regular	186 Catchfly	
	192 Coast Morning Glory	
Irregular	189 Crimson Sage	193 Dutchman's Pipe
	Scarlet Bugler	190 Western Redbud
	188 Cardinal Flower	187 Chaparral Pea
		191 Snapdragon
DESERT		
Regular	194 Hedgehog Cactus	199 Ocotillo
	195 Fishhook Cactus	197 Barrel Cactus
	198 Fivespot Mallow	196 Beavertail Cactus
	200 Purple Mat	202 Bouvardia
Irregular		204 Hummingbird Flower
		201 Desert Willow
		203 Chuparosa
GRASS		
Regular	208 Wild Poinsettia	
	215 Firecracker Flower	
	209 Giant Four O'clock	
	206 Red Maids	
	217 Sugarbowl	
	211 Summer's Darling	
	213 Farewell-to-Spring	
	207 Wine Cups	
	210 Checkerbloom	
	205 Scarlet Globe Mallow	
	Shooting Star	
Irregular	212 Horse Mint	
	214 Shrubby Red Sage	
SEA COAST		
Regular	220 Pink Sand Verbena	
WIDESPREAD		
Regular	216 Windmill Pink	
Irregular	219 Stream Orchid	
	218 Foxglove	

138 ROSE EPILOBIUM
(*Epilobium obcordatum*)

Evening-primrose family *(Onagraceae)*

Height: Perennial herb on creeping stems 2″-6″ (5-15cm) long. **Flowers:** One to few in axils of upper leaves; calyx 4-lobed; petals 4, rose-purple, heart-shaped, 1/2″-1″ (1-2.5cm) long; stamens 8, yellow on purplish stalks; pistil purplish, forming capsule 1″-1 1/2″ (2.5-3.5cm) long. **Leaves:** Opposite, small, ovate, smooth. **In bloom:** July-September. **Habitat-Range:** Dry ridges, alpine slopes, 8000′-13,000′ (2450-3950m); California north to Oregon, east to Nevada, Idaho.

This genus includes many large, conspicuous plants. The Fireweed (*E. angustifolium*) is one of the better known. Seed pods of the entire group are easily identified, being long and narrow below the calyx lobes. The generic name comes from the Greek *epi,* "upon," and *lobon,* "capsule," referring to this characteristic.

139 PARRY'S PRIMROSE
(*Primula parryi*)

Primrose family *(Primulaceae)*

Height: Perennial herb, 2′ (.6m). **Flowers:** In umbels of 3-12 blooms; calyx bell-shaped, 5-toothed; funnel-shaped with 5 lobes, 1″ (2.5cm) across, magenta pink; stamens 5, opposite petals; pistil single. **Leaves:** In basal rosette, smooth, narrow, 4″-12″ (10-31cm) long. **In bloom:** June-August. **Habitat-Range:** Wet, rocky alpine areas, 8000′-12,000′ (2450-3650m); Nevada east to New Mexico and north to Idaho, Wyoming.

This tall, brilliantly red flower, a favorite of mountain hikers, may be found at the edge of melting snow banks and along streams, where most wildflowers are tiny and matted. The genus name, meaning first, refers to its early blooming. Of the 150 or so species, most are found in the Orient and Old World. Our garden varieties come from these foreign lands. This Rocky Mountain species is named for Charles C. Parry, a botanist with the Mexican Boundary Survey in the late nineteenth century.

140 RED MOUNTAIN HEATHER
(*Phyllodoce empetriformis*)

Heath family *(Ericaceae)*

Height: Perennial shrub, 4″-12″ (10-30cm). **Flowers:** In crowded racemes; calyx with 5 lance-shaped lobes; petals rose-purple, joined into bell-shaped tube about 3/8″ (9mm) long; stamens 7-10 inside tube; seed capsule 5-celled. **Leaves:** Evergreen, linear, 1/4″-5/8″ (6-15mm) long. **In bloom:** July-August. **Habitat-Range:** Rocky alpine slopes, 5000′-9000′ (1500-2750m); northern California north to Alaska, east to the Rocky Mountains.

These tiny alpine shrubs are a beautiful sight when they bloom on rugged mountain slopes and in dark forests. They remind one of the true heathers of the Old World. *P. breweri* is a similar species but with a more open, cup-shaped flower. The genus is named for a Greek nymph.

141 MARIPOSA LILY (*Calochortus gunnisoni*)†

Lily family *(Liliaceae)*

Height: Perennial herb, 8″-20″ (20-50cm). **Flowers:** Borne singly or few on erect stem; sepals 3, lance-shaped, colored; petals 3, broad, reddish purple, white, or pale yellow, densely hairy at base around gland; stamens 6 on base of floral segments; styles 3, pistil forming 3-sided seed pod. **Leaves:** Narrow, basal, few. **In bloom:** June-August.

Habitat-Range: Coniferous forests, mountains of New Mexico, Arizona, north to South Dakota.

The generic name is from the Greek *kalos*, "beautiful," and *chortos*, "grass"—the beautiful flowers with grasslike leaves. Mariposa is Spanish for butterfly. These lilies grow from a bulb that is eaten by Indian people and was considered a delicacy by the early pioneers. The flowers are too scarce now to encourage their use as food..

142 REDWOOD SORREL *(Oxalis oregana)* Wood-sorrel family *(Oxalidaceae)*

Height: Low perennial herb from creeping rootstock. **Flowers:** Complete, regular, single on stem; 5 small sepals; 5 petals up to 1″ (2.5cm) long, oblong, white to rose, often purple-veined. **Leaves:** Trifoliolate, closing at night. **In bloom:** March-September. **Habitat-Range:** Coastal area from central California to southern Oregon, in redwoods.

The Yellow Sorrel (*O. corniculata*) is a common European weed that most gardeners try to eliminate, but the pink-flowered Redwood Sorrel is a conspicuous part of the Pacific coast redwood forest, forming a carpet of green with delicate pink flowers early in the spring. The name Sour Grass is often used for members of the family because of their extremely tart juice. An introduced species now becoming common in gardens and orchards is Bermuda Buttercup (*O. pes-caprae*). It has showy yellow flowers about 1″ (2.5cm) in diameter. One may use the leaves and stems of *Oxalis* in salads or the juice as a flavoring, but care must be taken not to consume a large quantity since these plants contain oxalic acid, which may have a toxic effect.

143 HEDGE NETTLE *(Stachys cooleyae)* Mint family *(Labiatae)*

Height: Perennial herb, 2′-5′ (.6-1.5m). **Flowers:** In interrupted spikes with whorls arising from axil of bracts; corolla tubular, with ring of hairs near inner base, about 1″ (2.5cm) long, 2-lipped, lower bent down, about 1″ (2.5cm) long; deep red-purple; stamens 4. **Leaves:** Opposite, lanceolate or ovate, with small scalloped edges, hairy, 2″-4″ (5-10cm) long; stem square. **In bloom:** June-August. **Habitat-Range:** Moist or swampy areas in coniferous forests; Cascades of Oregon, Washington, and coastal British Columbia.

Hedge Nettles derive their name from the habit that some species have of growing near hedges. They are not true nettles but members of the Mint family, as their aromatic odor and square stems indicate. The species is named in honor of Grace E. Cooley, who collected the type specimen at Nanaimo, British Columbia in 1891.

144 GILIA spp. Gilia family *(Polemoniaceae)*

This is one of the Gilias whose flowers are in dense heads rather than open panicles. For comparison see Skyrocket Gilia *(G. aggregata)*, No. 155.

145 MOUNTAIN PRIDE Figwort family *(Scrophulariaceae)*
(Penstemon newberryi)

Height: Perennial herb, 8″-20″ (20-50cm). **Flowers:** Borne on short racemes; calyx 3/8″-1/2″ (8-12mm) high, lobes lance-shaped; corolla crimson, 1″-1 1/8″ (2.5-3cm) long, throat of tube widened, upper lip erect, lower hairy; fertile stamens 4, sterile, woolly, 5th with beard at tip; style single. **Leaves:** Rounded, 3/4″-1 1/4″ (2-3cm) long, serrate edges. **In bloom:** June-August. **Habitat-Range:** Rocky coniferous forests, 5000'-11,000' (1500-3350m); Sierra Nevada, western Nevada to Washington.

This Penstemon, often creeping and matlike, is one of the beautiful wildflowers of the high mountains. The sterile, bearded stamen gives rise to the common name Beard-tongue, which is also applied to other members of the genus.

146 WESTERN CORYDALIS   Bleeding-heart family *(Fumariaceae)*
(Corydalis scouleri)

Height: Perennial herb, 2'-4' (.6-1m). **Flowers:** In racemes, both terminal, axillary; sepals 2, scalelike; petals 4, in 2 pairs, about 1" (2.5cm) long; outer upper petal spurred for 2/3 length; pink. **Leaves:** Pinnately divided several times with segments about 5/8" (15mm) long. **In bloom:** June-July. **Habitat-Range:** Coniferous woodlands, western slopes of Cascades, northern Oregon north to British Columbia.

Members of this genus are closely related to Bleeding Heart or Dutchman's Breeches, *Dicenta*, but the latter has a 2-spurred, not single-spurred corolla.

147 INDIAN WARRIOR   Figwort family *(Scrophulariaceae)*
(Pedicularis densiflora)

Height: Perennial herb, 8"-24" (20-60cm). **Flowers:** Each about 1" (2.5cm) long, in dense, elongate, spikelike head with bracts; corolla strongly 2-lipped with upper forming sharp, elongate, downcurved beak; lower formed of 3 small rounded lobes; corolla crimson, bracts greenish red. **Leaves:** Pinnately divided, alternating on stem. **In bloom:** February-March. **Habitat-Range:** Coastal California on wooded slopes.

This is one of the very early spring wildflowers in California, flowering before winter ends. The crimson spikes often occur in dense clusters, probably inspiring the name Indian Warrior. Members of the genus are known as Louseworts because of an old belief among farmers that sheep feeding upon the plants would become infested with lice. This also accounts for the generic name *Pedicularis*, derived from the name of the parasitic human body louse *Pediculus*.

148 WESTERN PEONY *(Paeonia brownii)*†   Buttercup family *(Ranunculaceae)*

Height: Perennial herb, 8"-14" (20-35cm). **Flowers:** Solitary, terminal, nodding, 3/4"-1 1/2" (2-4cm) broad; sepals 5-6, round, concave, green inside, purplish outside; petals 5-8, round, about 1/2" (1cm) long, brown-red in center, yellow toward tips; stamens numerous, yellow; pistils 2-5, becoming large fleshy follicles with several large seeds. **Leaves:** Large, chiefly basal, fleshy, smooth, grayish, 4"-8" (10-20cm) long, twice or three times divided. **In bloom:** April-June. **Habitat-Range:** Dry slopes, forests, 3000'-7500' (900-2300m); California, Nevada north to Canada, east to Wyoming.

This wild Peony is often overlooked in the forest because the large, beautiful flowers have their heads hanging down under rather dense foliage. The flower can be called either dark red or yellow. The seed pods become large and heavy, bending over to touch the ground. There are many uses for the Peony as charms and medicine. It is named after Paion, physician of the Greek gods. The Paiute and Washoe Indians made tea from the roots for lung trouble. The roots of *P. albiflora* have been used by the Tartars for food for centuries.

149 OLD MAN'S WHISKERS *(Geum triflorum)*   Rose family *(Rosaceae)*

Height: Perennial herb, 6″-20″ (15-50cm). **Flowers:** Broad, few, pendant on long stalks; calyx with 5 lance-shaped lobes, 3/8″-3/4″ (1-2cm) long, with longer bracts, purplish red; petals 5, reddish, about as long as calyx; stamens, pistils numerous, crowded on receptacle, developing achenes with long feathery plumes. **Leaves:** Mostly basal, 1 1/2″-7″ (3-18cm) long, hairy, pinnately divided, fernlike. **In bloom:** May-July. **Habitat-Range:** Coniferous forests, 4000′-8000′ (1200-2450m); northern California north to Canada, east to the Atlantic.

The common name is descriptive of the flower in fruit, with the heads of the feathery styles, which are easily carried by the wind, accounting for the wide distribution of this pretty plant. The generic name is an old Latin one for herb bennet, the Eurasian *G. urbanum*; another common name is Avens. Many species have thick roots that can be boiled for a refreshing chocolate-like drink to which sugar should be added. In early England the roots were soaked in wine for flavor and eaten to relieve heart trouble.

RED POTENTILLA *(Potentilla thurberi)*   Rose family *(Rosaceae)*

Height: Perennial herb, 12″-15″ (30-38cm). **Flowers:** Borne singly or in small clusters, 1/2″-3/4″ (1-2cm) across; sepals 5 with 5 bracts alternating below; petals 5, oval, bright red; stamens, pistils numerous, red. **Leaves:** Basal leaves with 5 or 7 segments, finely toothed, smooth above, hairy below. **In bloom:** July-October. **Habitat-Range:** Coniferous forests from Arizona to New Mexico.

This is an unusual and beautiful species of *Potentilla* because of its red rather than yellow or white flowers. Another red-flowered species, *P. palustris*, occurs in the Rocky Mountains. *Potentilla*, "the little potent one," refers to the medicinal qualities of Silverweed *(P. anserina)*, a yellow-flowered species widespread in North America, Europe, and Asia. It grows in moist situations along lakes and streams, and its roots, when cooked, taste like sweet potatoes or parsnips.

150 RED COLUMBINE *(Aquilegia formosa)*   Buttercup family *(Ranunculaceae)*

Height: Perennial herb, 1 1/2′-3 1/2′ (.5-1m). **Flowers:** Terminal, nodding, showy; sepals spreading, slightly turned back, broadly lance-shaped, up to 1″ (2.5cm) long, red; petals rounded in front, yellow with long red spurs extending backward 1/2″-3/4″ (1-2cm); stamens numerous. **Leaves:** Largely basal, trilobed with each lobe again trilobed. **In bloom:** June-August. **Habitat-Range:** Moist situations in coniferous forests up to 10,500′ (3200m); California north to Alaska, east to Utah.

Columbines come in red, yellow, blue, and white, depending on the species. This is the common species of the mountains. In the Southwest the Yellow Columbine *(A. chrysantha)* is the commonest form. The state flower of Colorado is the Blue Columbine *(A. caerulea)*, a common subalpine species. Columbines have had many uses. The Indians used the boiled roots as a cure for diarrhea, and old herbals recommend the leaves in a lotion for sore mouths and throats and the seeds in wine for jaundice. The leaves can be eaten as a salad green or as a cooked vegetable.

151 SHOOTING STAR *(Dodecatheon jeffreyi)*   Primrose family *(Primulaceae)*
Height: Perennial herb, 12″-21″ (30-53cm). **Flowers:** 3-18, nodding, in umbel on long

stalk; calyx tube with 4-5 lobes; petals 4-5, 1/2″-1″ (1-2.5cm) long, magenta, lavender, or white, turned back tightly on tube; stamens 5, often united, extending beyond corolla tube, resembling bill; pistil single, long with many-seeded capsule. **Leaves:** Basal, entire, oblanceolate, 4″-20″ (10-50cm) long. **In bloom:** June-August. **Habitat-Range:** Coniferous forests, wet places, 2300′-10,000′ (700-3050m); California north to Alaska, east to Montana.

The genus is well represented in North America and Asia. The Greek *dodeca*, twelve, and *theos*, god, suggest that the flower is under the care of twelve deities, or that the cluster of flowers might resemble a group of gods. It is a lovely plant, blooming gracefully, often in masses. Another common species, *D. hendersonii*, has ricelike grains on the rootstocks. Roots and leaves are edible when roasted but should be used only in dire emergencies.

152 GRASSLEAF PEAVINE *(Lathyrus graminifolius)*   Pea family *(Leguminosae)*

Height: Perennial herb, 6″-14″ (15-35cm). **Flowers:** Few in raceme; calyx teeth 5, irregular lengths; corolla pink, purple-tinged, or white, pea-shaped; stamens 10; style single, forming pod. **Leaves:** Branched into linear leaflets 1″-3″ (2.5-7.5cm) long, ending in long tendrils. **In bloom:** May-August. **Habitat-Range:** Open coniferous forests, 4400′-6600′ (1300-2050m); California south to Mexico, east to Arizona, Texas.

Lathyrus is the old Greek name for pea, and our cultivated Sweet Pea was developed from a Mediterranean species, *L. odoratus*. The Peas resemble the Vetches *(Vicia)* in many characteristics such as the segmented leaves and tendrils. Seeds from pea plants have been a favorite food of people all over the world. The bean from Europe, *Vicia faba*, is one of the most ancient cultivated plants.

153 BLEEDING HEART   Bleeding-heart family *(Fumariaceae)*
(Dicentra formosa)

Height: Perennial herb, 8″-18″ (20-45cm). **Flowers:** Borne in cluster on leafless stalk; calyx with 2 small oval parts; petals 4, outer 2 enlarged, flattened, heart-shaped base about 3/4″ (2cm) long, inner 2 narrow; stamens 6; style single. **Leaves:** Basal on long stems, lacy, pinnately divided. **In bloom:** March-July. **Habitat-Range:** Shady coniferous woods to 7000′ (2150m); California to British Columbia.

There are about 15 species of *Dicentra* in North America and east Asia. The name comes from the Greek *dis*, "twice," and *kentron*, "spur," describing the shape of the flower. The common name is more romantic, suggesting that the red flower, which hangs down, looks like a heart with a crack in it. Some species contain an alkaloid poisonous to man and cattle.

154 BARBEY PENSTEMON   Figwort family *(Scrophulariaceae)*
(Penstemon barbatus)

Height: Perennial herb, 12″-28″ (30-70cm). **Flowers:** Many on long, slender panicle; calyx with 5 ovate sepals; corolla tubular, crimson, up to 1 1/2″ (4cm) long, upper lip erect, lower divided; stamens 4 fertile, fifth a sterile filament; style single. **Leaves:** Mostly basal, narrowly linear, smooth, 2″-4 1/2″ (5-11cm) long. **In bloom:** June-August.

Habitat-Range: Dry rocky slopes, coniferous forests, 5000'-10,000' (1500-3050m); southern California, Mexico east to Arizona, New Mexico, Utah, Colorado.

The Penstemons belong to the largest genus in the Figwort family, with many interesting variations. The name, derived from Greek *pente*, "five," and *stemon*, "stamen," refers to a distinguishing characteristic. Four stamens are fertile, with the fifth often having hairs and no pollen. This gives rise to a common name for the group, Beardtongue. This red species is listed by some botanists as *P. labrosus*.

155 SKYROCKET GILIA *(Gilia aggregata)*   Phlox family *(Polemoniaceae)*

Height: Perennial herb, 12"-30" (30-76cm). **Flowers:** In elongate panicle, somewhat nodding; calyx up to 1/2" (1cm) long with sepals united for half length; corolla 1"-1 1/2" (2.5-4cm) long, tubular with 5 lobes, lance-shaped, extending outward to form star-shaped pattern; bright red, or pink to salmon in some areas; stamens 5, extending beyond corolla. **Leaves:** 1 1/2"-2 1/2" (4-6cm) long, alternate, finely divided into linear segments on erect stem; herbage glandular, aromatic. **In bloom:** June-September. **Habitat-Range:** Open, rocky or sandy slopes, 3500'-10,500' (1050-3200m); western United States.

Where this species has red flowers it is often confused with the Scarlet Bugler, which is a Penstemon, not a Phlox. The strong scent of the glandular foliage as well as of the flower itself accounts for the name Skunk Flower often applied to it.

156 WINTERGREEN *(Pyrola asarifolia)*   Heath family *(Ericaceae)*

Height: Perennial herb, 9"-18" (22-45cm). **Flowers:** In terminal raceme, open cup-shaped; calyx 5-parted, reddish; petals 5, concave, ovate, 3/8" (9mm) long, dull red to rose-purple, sometimes whitish later. **Leaves:** Basal, evergreen, oval to elliptic, finely toothed, green, 1 1/4"-3 1/2" (3-8cm). **In bloom:** June-July. **Habitat-Range:** Moist coniferous forests, northern California to British Columbia, east to Rocky Mountains.

Most of the dozen or so species of *Pyrola* in the Northern Hemisphere resemble each other. *Pyrola* comes from the Latin *pyrus*, meaning pear, referring to the shape of the leaf. The true Wintergreen used in flavoring belongs to another genus of the Heath family; the same common name is used for members of the genus *Pyrola* because of their evergreen leaves, which are conspicuous in fall and winter. Another common species is *P. picta*, whose leaves are white-veined.

PACIFIC RHODODENDRON   Heath family *(Ericaceae)*
(Rhododendron macrophyllum)

Height: Evergreen shrub, 4'-12' (1-4m). **Flowers:** Showy in terminal umbels; calyx very small, 5-lobed; corolla broadly bell-shaped, rose-purple, 1 1/2"-1 3/4" (3-4cm) long; stamens 10, short; style covered with red, silky hairs. **Leaves:** Leathery, oblong, entire, 2 1/2"-8" (6-20cm) long. **In bloom:** April-July. **Habitat-Range:** Shaded coniferous forests below 4000' (1200m); northern California coast to British Columbia.

The wild Rhododendrons have been developed into popular cultivated plants with much variety in size and color. Many species come from Asia. The Western Azalea (*R. occidentale*), deciduous with cream to light pink flowers, is especially lovely. The generic name is Greek—from *rhodos*, "rose," and *dendron*, "tree."

157 FRINGE CUPS *(Tellima grandiflora)*   Saxifrage family *(Saxifragaceae)*

Height: Perennial herb, 1 1/2′-3 1/2′ (.5-1m). **Flowers:** In terminal raceme on simple stem; calyx bell-shaped with 5 sepals, 10-nerved; petals 5, about 1/4″ (6mm) long, each narrowly divided, pinnate, reflexed, whitish at first, soon becoming red. **Leaves:** Mainly basal, rounded or heart-shaped, shallowly lobed, 2″-4″ (5-10cm) across. **In bloom:** April-July. **Habitat-Range:** Evergreen forests of Pacific coast below 5000′ (1500m) from California to Alaska.

This is the only species in this genus, which incidentally is an anagram of *Mitella*, a closely related genus that includes the Miterwort or Bishop's Cap.

158 PINESAP *(Monotropa hypopithys)*†   Heath family *(Ericaceae)*

Height: Saprophytic herb, 4″-12″ (10-30cm). **Flowers:** Solitary, nodding; sepals 2-5, slender, bractlike, 5/8″ (15mm) long; petals 5 or 6, oblong, somewhat saclike at base, longer than sepals, waxy, pinkish to white. **Leaves:** Bractlike along waxy, reddish to whitish stem. **In bloom:** June-July. **Habitat-Range:** Shaded, moist coniferous forests below 2000′ (600m); northern California north to British Columbia, east to Atlantic coast.

Pinesap is widespread over northern North America and northern Asia but is of relatively rare occurrence. Its translucent quality gives it a somewhat ghostlike appearance, especially when it is more whitish than pink. It is also commonly known as Indian Pipe because of the shape of the stem and flower. *Monotropa* means "one turn," referring to the top of the stem, which is turned down on one side before it terminates in the flower.

159 FIREWEED   Evening-primrose family *(Onagraceae)*
(Epilobium angustifolium)

Height: Perennial herb, 2′-6′ (.6-2m). **Flowers:** Large in long racemes; calyx with 4 linear lobes; petals 4, rose, purple, or white, 1/2″-3/4″ (1-2cm) long; stamens 8, often unequal, shorter than petals; pistil single, longer than stamens, forming seed capsule. **Leaves:** Numerous, lance-shaped, 4″-8″ (10-20cm) long. **In bloom:** July-September. **Habitat-Range:** Coniferous forests, especially burned areas, Mexico to Alaska, from west to east coast.

This plant is common especially in places where the soil has been disturbed by fire or clearing. It forms a bright coloration in devastated areas, in Europe as well as this country. There are many ways to use Fireweed for food: boiling young shoots like asparagus, mixing with other greens as salad, in dried form as tea, and for soups. The generic name is from the Greek *epi*, "upon," and *lobon*, "capsule," referring to the calyx attached to the upper end of the seed pod.

160 SUGAR STICK *(Allotropa virgata)*†   Heath family *(Ericaceae)*

Height: Saprophytic herb, 4″-20″ (10-50cm). **Flowers:** In dense, spikelike raceme; perianth segments 5, regarded by some as sepals, by others as petals, reddish to whitish, up to 1/4″ (6mm) long, thin; stamens 10, purplish black; ovary red, style white. **Leaves:** Scalelike on bright red stem striped with white. **In bloom:** June-August. **Habitat-Range:** Coniferous forests, 2000′-10,000′ (600-3050m); California north to British Columbia.

Most of the saprophytic members of the Heath family that lack the usual green coloring matter or chlorophyll of flowering plants are striking in appearance, but none more than Sugar Sticks. This species looks like a miniature barber pole or Christmas candy cane. It is the only member of the genus.

161 **SNOW PLANT** *(Sarcodes sanguinea)*†   Heath family *(Ericaceae)*

Height: Saprophytic herb, 6″-20″ (15-50cm). **Flowers:** In raceme, fleshy, campanulate (bell-shaped); sepals 5, ovate, about 1/2″ (1cm) long, red; corolla with 5 spreading lobes, slightly longer than calyx, red. **Leaves:** Lance-shaped, scalelike, red, on thick, fleshy red stem. **In bloom:** May-July. **Habitat-Range:** Coniferous forests, 4000′-8000′ (1200-2450m); California, Oregon, Nevada, Baja California.

One of the best known and most protected plants of the mountains, it is like an enormous, brilliantly red asparagus stalk. At first it seems difficult to accept it as a member of a family that contains the heathers, huckleberries, and blueberries, but a close examination of the flower shows that it has the same bell-shaped flowers with 5 corolla lobes and 5 sepals. The main difference, as with the other saprophytic heaths, is the lack of chlorophyll. It does not manufacture its own food but secures it from decaying organic matter in the soil.

162 **BITTERROOT** *(Lewisia rediviva)*†   Purslane family *(Portulacaceae)*

Height: Perennial herb, 1″-2″ (2.5-5cm). **Flowers:** Terminal on stems 1″-3″ (2.5-7.5cm) long, 1″-2″ (2.5-5cm) broad; sepals 6-8, petal-like, rose to whitish; petals 12-18, oblong, pink or bright rose to whitish. **Leaves:** Linear, thick, up to 2″ (5cm) long; often lost before flowers appear. **In bloom:** March-June. **Habitat-Range:** Rocky or gravelly situations, 2500′-6000′ (750-1800m), coniferous forests from California north to British Columbia, east to Rocky Mountains.

Its generic name honors Captain Meriwether Lewis of the Lewis and Clark Expedition, who collected this species in the Bitterroot Valley of Montana. The species name, *rediviva*, means "brought to life."

163 **LEWISIA** *(Lewisia cotyledon)*†   Purslane family *(Portulacaceae)*

Height: Perennial herb, 4″-12″ (10-30cm). **Flowers:** In panicles on long stem with paired bracts; sepals 2, round, with gland-tipped teeth; petals 8-10, oblong to spatulate, 1/2″-3/4″ (1-2cm) long, whitish with red tinge, reddish stripe. **Leaves:** In basal rosette, succulent, spatulate, 1 1/2″-3″ (4-7.5cm). **In bloom:** June-July. **Habitat-Range:** Rocky areas, 4000′-7500′ (1200-2300m) in coniferous forests of northern California.

The flowers of many of the beautiful species of *Lewisia* arise, like the leaves, from short stems on the root crown. *L. cotyledon,* however, has lovely pink flowers borne on a number of relatively long stems on which are one or two short, paired bracts. The root, like that of other members of the genus, is starchy and probably edible, but the plant is rare and should be protected.

164 **INDIAN PINK** *(Silene californica)*†   Pink family *(Caryophyllaceae)*

Height: Perennial herb, 6″-12″ (15-30cm). **Flowers:** In cymes; calyx tubular, 5-toothed;

petals 5, 1″ (2.5cm) across, 4-lobed, crimson. **Leaves:** Elliptic to ovate, opposite, up to 3 1/2″ (9cm) long, somewhat glandular. **In bloom:** March-August. **Habitat-Range:** Coniferous forests or woods below 5000′ (1500m), California north to Oregon.

With its large scarlet-red flowers, this is one of the West's most beautiful wildflowers. It is not abundant and is always a thrill to find. The generic name *Silene* supposedly refers to Silenus (foster father of Bacchus), who was covered with foam. The plant is high in saponin, which served as a primitive form of detergent.

165 PUSSY PAWS *(Calyptridium umbellatum)*   Purslane family *(Portulacaceae)*

Height: Perennial herb, 3″-15″ (7.5-37cm). **Flowers:** Small, crowded in coiled spikes in terminal umbels; calyx of 2 pink scalelike sepals; petals 4, pink or white, ovate, less than 1/4″ (6mm) long; stamens 3, each enclosed by folding petal; pistil single, enclosed by petal. **Leaves:** In basal rosette 3/4″-3″ (2-7cm) long, rounded, wider at end than base. **In bloom:** May-August. **Habitat-Range:** Gravelly places, coniferous forests, 2500′-11,000′ (750-3350m); California, Nevada, north to British Columbia, east to Rocky Mountains.

The name Pussy Paws best describes this flower. The clusters are soft to look at and touch on the forest floor. The generic name derives from the Greek *kaluptra*, a cap or covering, so called because as the seed matures it is covered by the caplike petals.

166 ROCK PENSTEMON *(Penstemon rupicola)*   Figwort family *(Scrophulariaceae)*

Height: Perennial herb, less than 4″ (10cm). **Flowers:** Few in raceme; calyx with 5 oblong lobes; corolla deep rose, 1″-1 1/2″ (2.5-3.5cm) long, throat of tube widened; stamens 5 with 4 fertile, slightly longer than tube, one sterile with beard at tip. **Leaves:** 3/8″-3/4″ (9-20mm) long, roundish, serrate edges, from low, matted stems. **In bloom:** June-August. **Habitat-Range:** Rocky, red fir forest; northern California to Washington.

There is so much variation in this genus that species are numerous and often hard to distinguish. Thus this low-growing, brightly colored Penstemon is considered by some to be the species *newberryi*.

167 COAST TRILLIUM *(Trillium ovatum)*[†]   Lily family *(Liliaceae)*

Height: Perennial herb, up to 10″ (25cm). **Flowers:** Single on stem; 3 slender herbaceous sepals; 3 petals 1″-1 1/2″ (2.5-4cm) long; white, changing to rose with age. **Leaves:** In whorl of 3 at summit of stem; usually ovate, pointed with netted veins; green, smooth. **In bloom:** February-April. **Habitat-Range:** Coast of central California north to British Columbia, east to Idaho.

Trilliums or Wake Robins symbolize early spring in the moist, shaded woods and deep humus of temperate North America. The Common Trillium (*T. sessile*) with its deep red to lilac flowers is much more widespread than the Coast Trillium but grows from the center of the leaf whorl without any stem.

168 PINK MONKEY FLOWER   Figwort family *(Scruphulariaceae)*
(Mimulus lewisii)

Height: Perennial herb, 1′-2 1/2′ (.3-.7m). **Flowers:** Funnel-shaped, 2-lipped with lobes spreading; up to 2″ (5cm) long; rose to pink with 2 hairy yellow ridges on lower lip and throat. **Leaves:** Opposite, lanceolate, only slightly toothed; bright green, sticky, hairy. **In bloom:** Spring-summer. **Habitat-Range:** Stream banks in higher mountains throughout western North America.

This is one of the more beautiful plants of the western mountains. Unlike *M. lewisii*, some smaller pink and red species of *Mimulus* are annuals rather than perennials, for example, *M. rubellus,* the Little Red Mimulus, found in moist, sandy places east to Colorado. It too is montane but rarely reaches a height of more than 8 inches (20cm).

SCARLET PENSTEMON Figwort family *(Scrophulariaceae)*
(Penstemon bridgesii)

Height: Perennial herb, 1′-3′ (.3-1m). **Flowers:** Arranged irregularly along stem; calyx 5-parted, lobes lance-shaped; corolla tubular, glandular, scarlet to vermilion, 2-lipped, 1″ (2.5cm) or more in length. **Leaves:** Largely basal on branched, woody stems; linear to spatulate; 1″-2 1/2″ (2.5-6cm) long. **In bloom:** Midsummer, time varying with elevation. **Habitat-Range:** 5000′-11000′ (1500-3350m), in mountains from California to Colorado.

The Scarlet Bugler (*P. eatonii*), which occurs in Arizona and Utah in the spring, is similar in color but has a funnel- or bugle-shaped corolla that essentially lacks lips.

FIGWORT *(Scrophularia californica)* Figwort family *(Scrophulariaceae)*

Height: Perennial herb, up to 6′ (2m). **Flowers:** In panicles on branchlets along tall stalk; usually about 1/4″ (6mm) long, urn-shaped with upper lip 2-lobed; reddish. **Leaves:** Opposite, distributed along square stem from base to inflorescence; ovate; toothed; 1″-4″ (3-10cm) long. **In bloom:** February-July. **Habitat-Range:** Often found in roadside thickets or along streams in open, moist situations from California to British Columbia.

This plant is an important source of nectar for honey bees; hence its other name— Bee Plant.

169 **COMMON TRILLIUM** *(Trillium sessile)*† Lily family *(Liliaceae)*

Height: Perennial herb, 1′-1 3/4′ (.3-.5m). **Flowers:** Sessile on round base at attachment of leaves; calyx 3 lance-shaped, leafy sepals; petals ovate, 1 1/2″-3″ (4-7.5cm) long, deep red to dull white; styles 3, pistil forming 3-celled reddish berry. **Leaves:** 3, ovate, 2 1/2″-5″ (6-12.5cm) long in whorl on naked stem. **In bloom:** February-May. **Habitat-Range:** Coniferous woods below 3500′ (1050m); California to Washington.

The generic name, from the Latin *triplum,* refers to the obvious three leaves and flower parts. A common name, Wake Robin, indicates the early spring arrival of the flower and bird. An obscure common name for some of the species is Birthroot, so called because Indian women are reported to have used the thick roots to ease childbirth.

RED CLINTONIA *(Clintonia andrewsiana)*† Lily family *(Liliaceae)*

Height: Perennial herb, up to 20″ (50cm). **Flowers:** In terminal cluster on long naked stem; each about 3/4″ (2cm) long on short pedicel (lateral stem); deep rose-pink to crimson; perianth (petals and sepals) alike. **Leaves:** 5-6; elliptic; up to 12″ (30cm) long, 6″ (15cm) wide; bright glossy green. **In bloom:** May-July. **Habitat-Range:** Shaded redwood forests from central coastal California to southern Oregon.

Clintonias are limited to about 6 species found in North America and Asia. The Red Clintonia is one of the more beautiful components of the redwood forests of the Pacific coast. Another western species, the White Clintonia (*C. uniflora*), occurs from the northern Rocky Mountains of Montana north to British Columbia and south to the Sierra Nevada of California. Its flowers are white and more than an inch across although there are only 1 or 2 to a stalk. The generic name honors De Witt Clinton, Governor of New York in the early nineteenth century.

170 STAR FLOWER *(Trientalis europea)*   Primrose family *(Primulaceae)*

Height: Perennial herb, 4″-8″ (10-20cm). **Flowers:** Single on stalk above whorl of leaves at top of stem; calyx with 5-7 narrow lobes; corolla red-pink with 5-7 spreading petals, somewhat joined, about 1/2″ (1cm) across, sharply pointed; stamens opposite lobes of corolla; pistil single. **Leaves:** Lower few, scalelike, upper 4-6, ovate, 1 3/4″- 3 3/4″ (4-8cm) long, in whorl. **In bloom:** April-July. **Habitat-Range:** Coniferous woods below 4500′ (1350m); coastal California north to British Columbia.

These dainty plants often bloom in the dense shade, bright as little stars. The circle of leaves at the base of the flower stalks is easily recognized. The generic name is Latin for one-third of a foot, a reference to the height of these small plants.

171 DOGBANE *(Apocynum androsaemifolium)*   Dogbane family *(Apocynaceae)*

Height: Perennial herb, 5″-18″ (12-45cm). **Flowers:** In short clusters at ends of much-branched stems; calyx small, 5-toothed; corolla 5-lobed, bell-shaped, about 1/4″ (6mm) long, pink with white, pink-veined lobes; stamens, style minute, inside base of floral tube; seed pods 2″-7″ (5-18cm) long, seeds plumed. **Leaves:** Ovate, 3/4″-3 1/2″ (2-8cm) long. **In bloom:** June-August. **Habitat-Range:** Dry places in coniferous forests, 5000′-9500′ (1500-2900m); California, Arizona, north to British Columbia, east to Atlantic coast.

The flowers are fragrant little bells. The peculiar meaning of the name, given to the ancient Dogbane of the Old World, is from the Greek *apo*, "from," and *kuon*, "dog" —literally, harmful to dogs. One would hardly expect such long, useful seed pods from this tiny flower. Fibers from the stem were used for making string and nets and weaving rough cloth. Early settlers on the Delaware River bought such ropes from the Indians, 14 yards of it for a piece of bread.

172 THISTLE *(Cirsium wheeleri)*   Sunflower family *(Compositae)*

Height: Perennial herb, 15″-30″ (37-75cm). **Flowers:** Heads borne at tips of branches; involucre bracts ovate, inner with twisted tips; ray, disc flowers alike, rose-purple, tubular with linear lobes; pappus on achenes feathery, bristles on receptacle stiff. **Leaves:** Alternate, prickly, toothed, mostly at base of plant. **In bloom:** June-October. **Habitat-Range:** Open pine forests, southern New Mexico, Arizona.

The name of this large genus of Thistles comes from the Greek *kirsion,* "thistle." Some species are considered weeds and their bristles can make walking among them difficult, but the flower heads are bright and beautiful. The roots can be eaten raw or prepared by boiling or roasting; in addition, the stems can be peeled and cooked. The Artichoke, *Cynara scolymus*, is a European Thistle of a closely related genus.

173/174 SCARLET PAINT BRUSH *(Castilleja miniata)*

Figwort family *(Scrophulariaceae)*

Height: Perennial herb, 1'-2' (.3-.6m). **Flowers:** In spikelike racemes with upper leaves becoming scarlet-tipped, hairy bracts with incised tips; calyx tubular, 2 lobes on each side, scarlet with green base, about 1" (2.5cm) long, deeply cleft in middle; corolla tubular, 1"-1 1/2" (2.5-4cm) long, compressed, 2-lipped with upper extended into long beak, margined with red. **Leaves:** Broadly lance-shaped, pointed, 1"-2" (2.5-5cm) long; alternate. **In bloom:** May-September. **Habitat-Range:** Moist meadows and streamsides below 11,000' (3300m); coniferous forests of western North America.

This is probably the commonest montane species of *Castilleja* encountered in the western mountains. It belongs to a large group of about 200 species, all but one occurring in the New World. A beautiful species common on ridges, mesas, and high meadows in the Rocky Mountains is the Orange Paint Brush (*C. integra*), which has brilliant red-orange bracts and velvety stems.

175 FUCHSIA-FLOWERED GOOSEBERRY *(Ribes speciosum)*

Saxifrage family *(Saxifragaceae)*

Height: Evergreen shrub, 4'-10' (1-3m). **Flowers:** 1-4 on drooping stalk; calyx with 4 red erect sepals; petals red in short campanulate tube with 4 lobes about as long as sepals; stamens 4, extending beyond tube; style single; berry dry, bristly, about 1/2" (1cm) long. **Leaves:** Rounded, somewhat 3-lobed, shiny dark green above, 1/2"-1 1/2" (1-3.5cm) broad; spines at nodes in branches heavy. **In bloom:** January-May. **Habitat-Range:** Shaded coastal woods below 1500' (450m); central California to Baja California.

The name *Ribes* is from the ancient Arabic *ribas*, meaning a plant with a sour juice. This species is truly spectacular, as the species name implies, because of its bright red flowers pendant among the delicate foliage. Many of the Gooseberries furnish food for man and animal. In the late summer and fall some bushes produce lovely juicy fruits, but they are covered with bristly spines. The berries can be eaten fresh, dried, or cooked as jams or in pies.

WESTERN WOOD LILY *(Lilium umbellatum)*†

Lily family *(Liliaceae)*

Height: Perennial herb, 1'-4' (.3-1m). **Flowers:** One or several at top of stem, erect, goblet-shaped; sepals 3, petals 3, alike, 2"-4" (5-10cm) long, red with dark spots; stamens 6, showy; style single, as long as stamens. **Leaves:** Narrow, lanceolate, borne singly except for whorl at top. **In bloom:** June-August. **Habitat-Range:** Moist wooded places, northern Rocky Mountains, south to Arizona, New Mexico.

This species and *L. columbianum* are the only true lilies found in the Rocky Mountains. They are bright and lovely to look at but are in danger of extinction from being picked. *Lilium* is from the classic Greek *lirion*, for lily. *Umbellatum* refers to the umbel arrangement of the blooms.

176 RED LARKSPUR *(Delphinium nudicaule)*   Buttercup family *(Ranunculaceae)*

Height: Perennial herb, 1′-2′ (.3-.6m). **Flowers:** 2-12 in loose raceme; calyx red, with 5 lobes, 1 developed into spur 5/8″-3/4″ (1.5-2cm) long; petals 4, in unequal pairs, yellow with red tips; stamens many; pistils 3, becoming many-seeded pods. **Leaves:** Mostly basal, 3-5 parted into broadly lobed divisions; smooth, somewhat succulent. **In bloom:** March-June. **Habitat-Range:** Dry slopes in woods below 8000′ (2450m); central, northern California.

The generic name derives from the Greek *delphinus*, "dolphin," because some flower shapes suggest this animal. Cattle on range land may die of an alkaloid poisoning if they eat a large amount of any of several common species of these plants in spring. Sheep are not affected.

177 LEWISIA *(Lewisia cotyledon howelii)*   Purslane family *(Portulacaceae)*

A curled-leaf variety of *L. cotyledon* (see No. 163) occurring in oak woodland below 1000′ (300m) in northwestern California and Oregon.

178 SWEETBRIER *(Rosa rubiginosa)*   Rose family *(Rosaceae)*

Height: Deciduous shrub, to 10′ (3m). **Flowers:** 1-4 on short glandular stalks; calyx 5-cleft, lobes lance-shaped; petals 5, pink-whitish, 1″-2″ (3-5cm) broad; stamens numerous, attached to disc at edge of receptacle; pistils many within and free of recepacle, forming many seeds surrounded by the fleshy fruit (rose hip). **Leaves:** Pinnately compound, 7-9 leaflets, serrate, glandular, 1/2″-1″ (1-3cm) long with curved prickles at base, on stem. **In bloom:** May-July. **Habitat-Range:** Naturalized from Europe in woods and pastures; western United States.

The Rose is one of the oldest-known and best-loved flowers. This European species has become widely established in thickets, where the brilliant red fruits appear in quantity in late summer. The Rose hips, like small apples, have many uses as food; they may be eaten raw, stewed, candied, or juiced for jams and jellies. Rose petals are sometimes candied or used fresh in salads. The Sweetbrier is also known as *R. eglanteria*.

179 LUPINE *(Lupinus stiversii)*   Pea family *(Leguminosae)*

Height: Annual herb, 4″-18″ (10-45cm). **Flowers:** In racemes about 1″ (2.5cm) long; calyx 2-lipped with upper cleft, lower entire, finely hairy, petals 5, bright yellow, lateral petals or wings slightly longer, rose pink, lower petals or keel hairy near base, whitish. **Leaves:** Palmately compound, with 6-8 segments 1/2″-1 1/2″ (1-4cm), finely haired. **In bloom:** April-July. **Habitat-Range:** Sandy or gravelly soil, 1600′-4600′ (480-1380m).

There are more than 100 kinds of lupines in western North America. Because of their palmate leaves and pealike flowers borne in racemes, the genus is easily identified, but the species often troubles even the most experienced botanists. *L. stiversii* is one of the exceptions because of its distinctive yellow banner and rose-colored wings. Like other legumes, it enriches the soil because of nitrogen-fixing bacteria in the roots.

180 PINK PHLOX *(Phlox austromontana)*   Gilia family *(Polemoniaceae)*

Height: Perennial herb, matted, 3″-10″ (7.5-25cm) across. **Flowers:** Usually solitary at ends of numerous branches; calyx tubular, 5-cleft, 1/4″-1/2″ (6-12mm) long, corolla about 1/2″ (12mm) across, tubular basally with 5-6 spreading lobes, pink. **Leaves:** Opposite, linear, about 1/2″ (1cm) across, grayish green, pubescent. **In bloom:** May-July. **Habitat-Range:** Dry rocky situations in Pinyon-Juniper or yellow pine woods, 4500′-8000′ (1350-2450m); southern California east to Colorado, New Mexico.

Pink Phlox grows from a woody base, forming colorful mats that hug the ground in mountainous parts of the Southwest. The flowers have a delicate fragrance and although usually pink, may be whitish or lavender.

181 FAIRY DUSTER *(Calliandra eriophylla)*   Pea family *(Leguminosae)*

Height: Deciduous shrub, 8″-14″ (20-35cm). **Flowers:** In dense heads on short stems; calyx 5-toothed, red; petals 5, red, about 1/4″ (6mm) long; stamens many, reddish, extending about 1″ (2.5cm) beyond corolla; pistil narrow, developing pealike pod. **Leaves:** Pinnately divided into small leaflets on densely branched, gray, hairy stems. **In bloom:** February-March. **Habitat-Range:** Gullies, sandy washes in Pinyon-Juniper areas below 1000′ (300m); southern California, Baja California, central Mexico to Texas.

This plant belongs to a part of the Pea family with the acacias and mimosas. The flowers are not irregular with the typical Sweet Pea structure, but regular and fluffy-looking due to the long stamens. Many tropical trees and shrubs are included in this group. The name is from the Greek *kallos*, "beautiful," and *andra*, "stamen." The plant forms characteristic pea pods, often large, with edible peas.

182 ROCKY MOUNTAIN BEE PLANT   Caper family *(Capparidaceae)*
(Cleome serrulata)

Height: Annual herb, 1′-3′ (.3-1m). **Flowers:** In dense racemes; calyx lobes 4, short; petals 4, reddish to purplish or white; stamens 6, long; pistil one, developing into linear capsule 1″-2 1/2″ (2.5-6.5cm) long on stalk equally long. **Leaves:** Palmately compound, 3 leaflets 1″-2″ (2.5-5cm) long. **In bloom:** May-August. **Habitat-Range:** Pinyon-Juniper, Sagebrush scrub; California north to eastern Washington, east to Rocky Mountains.

The Caper family gets its name from the generic name for goat, *Capra*, because the plants have a strong odor similar to that of goats. This Bee Plant looks and tastes much like Mustard; the generic name is an ancient one meaning "mustard." The flowers and leaves of these strong-tasting plants can be boiled and eaten. Other common names are descriptive: Spider Flower, Pink Cleone, and Stinkweed.

183 SCARLET LOCOWEED   Pea family *(Leguminosae)*
(Astragalus coccineus)

Height: Perennial herb, 3 1/2″-6″ (8.5-15cm). **Flowers:** Borne in a few flowered spikes; calyx 5-toothed, half as long as corolla, reddish; corolla narrow with 5 petals of equal length, 1 1/4″-1 1/2″ (3-4cm) long, upper petal tending to turn upward, lateral petals or wings more or less parallel to keel, bright scarlet; pods somewhat inflated, densely hairy. **Leaves:** Pinnate, 2″-4″ (5-10cm) long with 7-15 leaflets, densely silky, grayish white. **In bloom:** March-June. **Habitat-Range:** Pinyon-Juniper areas, edges of deserts,

2000'-8000' (600-2450m); southeastern California south to Baja California, east to Arizona.

This is an enormous genus containing approximately 2000 species, about 400 of which occur in North America. Most are impossible for anyone but an expert in this group to identify, but the Scarlet Locoweed is unique within its range because of its coloration. The name Locoweed (from Spanish *loco*, "insane") is applied to many species of *Astragalus* because they absorb selenium from the soil. This chemical is poisonous and when such plants are eaten may cause death or nervous derangement, especially to horses.

184 STRAWBERRY CACTUS   Cactus family *(Cactaceae)*
(Echinocereus mojavensis)

Height: Succulent perennial, 2"-8" (5-20cm). **Flowers:** Solitary; perianth funnel- or bell-shaped, segments broad, rounded, 2"-3" (5-7cm) long, reddish. **Leaves:** Lacking; long spines borne on ribs of thick fleshy stem. **In bloom:** April-June. **Habitat-Range:** Rocky areas of Pinyon-Juniper, certain desert areas, 3000'-7000' (900-2150m); southern California, Nevada, Arizona, northern Baja California.

Members of the genus *Echinocereus* are known as Hedgehog Cactus because of the derivation from Latin *echinos*, "hedgehog," and *cereus*, "spiny." The Strawberry Cactus is also called Mound Cactus because numerous plants form broad moundlike masses. The fruits of all Hedgehog Cacti are edible, and the Indians depended on some, such as the Pitayas, as a seasonal food. They are still prized by the people of northern Mexico.

185 DESERT MONKEY FLOWER   Figwort family *(Scrophulariaceae)*
(Mimulus bigelovii)

Height: Annual herb, 2"-10" (5-25cm). **Flowers:** Near tips of stems on short pedicels; calyx with 5 unequal teeth; corolla funnel-shaped, about 1" (2.5cm) long, 2-lipped with 2 lobes above, 3 below, lobes rounded, red with purplish tinge. **Leaves:** Opposite, entire, ovate to oblong, 1/2"-1" (1-2.5cm) long, densely glandular, hairy. **In bloom:** March-June. **Habitat-Range:** Pinyon-Juniper-Sagebrush, Joshua tree woodlands, edges of deserts, below 10,000' (3050m); southern California east to Nevada, Arizona.

This species of Monkey Flower is small but has large, colorful flowers. Because of its preference for rocks it often grows in the bottom of dry washes. *M. fremontii*, a somewhat similar species below 7000' (2100m) in southern California, has rose-purple flowers and a reddish stem and leaves.

186 CATCHFLY *(Silene laciniata)*   Pink family *(Caryophyllaceae)*

Height: Perennial herb, 2'-5' (.6-1.5m). **Flowers:** Up to 1" (2.5cm) broad at ends of leafless stalks; calyx tubular, 5-toothed; petals 5, showy, scarlet, deeply divided into 4 parts; stamens 10, standing above petals; styles 4; fruit a toothed capsule. **Leaves:** Narrowly lance-shaped, glandular, fine-hairy, 2"-6" (5-15cm) long. **In bloom:** May-July. **Habitat-Range:** Chaparral below 5000' (1500m); coastal southern California east to New Mexico, south to Mexico.

Many species of this genus have a sticky secretion that supposedly captures insects.

This characteristic gave rise to the name, an allusion to the Greek god Silenus, who was covered with foam. Most of the flowers in the Pink family have conspicuous petals, usually divided, and seed pods toothed at the top, opening to discharge the many seeds. Carnations and Sweet Williams are well-known members of the family.

187 CHAPARRAL PEA *(Pickeringia montana)* Pea family *(Leguminosae)*

Height: Evergreen shrub, 3'-8' (1-2.5m). **Flowers:** Solitary in axils, pealike; calyx campanulate with 5 low, wide teeth; corolla 3/4" (2cm) long, banner (upper petal) large with sides expanded, turned back, wings (lateral petals), keel (2 lower petals) smaller, oblong; rose-purple with white or yellow spot at base of banner. **Leaves:** Small, pod 2" (5cm) long divided into 3 leaflets; stems rigid, branched, spiny. **In bloom:** May-August. **Habitat-Range:** Chaparral below 5000' (1500m); California.

This is a colorful but very thorny component of the California chaparral.

188 CARDINAL FLOWER

(Lobelia cardinalis)

Bellflower family *(Campanulaceae)*

Height: Perennial herb, 1 1/2'-3' (4.5-1m). **Flowers:** In terminal racemes; calyx tubular, short, with 5 lobes; corolla 1"-1 1/2" (2.5-4cm) long, bright red, tubular, upper lip 2-lobed with central split to base, lower with 3 lobes; anthers united into tube around style. **Leaves:** Alternate, linear to lanceolate, 3 1/2"-5 1/2" (8-14cm) long. **In bloom:** August-October. **Habitat-Range:** Moist areas in chaparral or scrub below 7000' (2150m); California east to Texas, south to Panama.

Lobelia is a well-known and widely distributed genus but has relatively few representatives in the West. These are easily recognized by the 2-lipped corolla, with a split in the upper lip between the 2 lobes that extends nearly to the base of the tube, and by the tube the stamens form around the protruding style. The Cardinal Flower is seen by many summer visitors to the Grand Canyon and Zion Canyon.

189 CRIMSON SAGE *(Salvia spathacea)* Mint family *(Labiatae)*

Height: Perennial herb, 1'-3' (.3-1m). **Flowers:** In 5 or more whorls, each with purplish, sticky basal bracts; calyx about 5/8" (1cm) long, 2-lipped with upper larger, lower 2-toothed; corolla crimson, 2-lipped with upper straight, lower with 2 spreading lobes, 2 lateral lobes very short; stamens extending beyond corolla. **Leaves:** Triangular, margins bluntly toothed, 4"-8" (10-20cm) long, coarsely hairy, glandular. **In bloom:** March-May. **Habitat-Range:** Chaparral, coastal brush, or woodland below 2000' (600m); west central to southern California.

This species is sometimes referred to as Pitcher Sage, but that name is more properly applied to *Lepechinia (Spacele) calycina*, which often grows in the same region but is larger and has a different, whitish flower. Like all Sages, the stems are squarish and the leaves aromatic. *Salvia* has more than 500 species; many are used for flavoring food or are grown as ornamentals.

190 WESTERN REDBUD *(Cercis occidentalis)* Pea family *(Leguminosae)*

Height: Deciduous shrub, 6'-15' (2-5m). **Flowers:** In lateral fascicles; calyx broadly bell-shaped with 5 lobes; corolla up to 1/2″ (1cm) long, pealike, reddish purple, with upper petal (standard) enclosed by 2 lateral wings, 2 lower petals forming keel not united; pod flat. **Leaves:** Round or cordate, 2 1/2″-3 1/2″ (6-9cm) across. **In bloom:** February-April. **Habitat-Range:** Chaparral of foothills from California east to Texas.

Redbud or Judas Tree is one of the most colorful shrubs of the western foothills. In spring the bushes are covered with showy reddish flowers, and in autumn the leaves turn a beautiful pinkish red before they are shed. The bark of the Redbud was used by Indians to weave into baskets and also, because of its astringent quality, as a remedy for diarrhea. Flowers and pods are both regarded as edible.

191 SNAPDRAGON *(Galvezia speciosa)* Figwort family *(Scrophulariaceae)*

Height: Evergreen shrub, 3′-8′ (1-2.5m). **Flowers:** In terminal raceme; calyx 5-parted; corolla tubular, enlarged at base, 2-lipped, 1″ (2.5cm) long, scarlet. **Leaves:** Mostly in threes, elliptic, smooth, or finely hairy, 1″-1 1/4″ (2.5-3cm) long. **In bloom:** February-May. **Habitat-Range:** Rocky canyons on offshore islands of southern California and Baja California.

This species with its large scarlet flowers was formerly placed with other Snapdragons in the genus *Antirrhinum*. However, its woody character and leaves mostly in whorls of 3 indicate a closer relationship to *Galvezia*. This genus is named after José Galvez, a Spanish administrator in South America in the eighteenth century, and contains about 4 species found between California and Peru.

SCARLET BUGLER Figwort family *(Scrophulariaceae)*
(Penstemon centranthifolius)

Height: Perennial herb, 1′-4′ (.3-1m). **Flowers:** Borne in long, slender panicles; calyx short with 5 rounded lobes; corolla tubular, 1″ (2.5cm) long, scarlet, slightly 2-lipped with 2 upper, 3 lower lobes nearly equal. **Leaves:** Opposite, ovate to lance-shaped, sessile, smooth, entire, thickish, with whitish bloom. **In bloom:** April-July. **Habitat-Range:** Dry chaparral, especially where soil has been disturbed; central California south to Baja California.

This tall slender *Penstemon* has leaves similar in shape to *Centranthus*, the Spur Valerian; hence the species name, *centranthifolius*. *P. eatonii*, also known as the Scarlet Bugler, occurs from southern California east to Utah below 8000′ (2450m). It differs in having green rather than grayish leaves.

192 COAST MORNING GLORY Morning-glory family *(Convolvulaceae)*
(Convolvulus cyclostegius)

Height: Perennial trailing herb, 4′-12′ (1-4m). **Flowers:** 1-3 on stalks 1 1/2″-4″ (4-10cm) long; calyx lobes 5, folded over, twisted in bud, with 2 bracts below; corolla 1/2″-1 1/2″ (1-4cm) long, pinkish or white, bell-shaped, folded, twisted in bud; stamens 5 within corolla tube; pistil single, forming round capsule. **Leaves:** Triangular to lance-shaped, 3/4″-2″ (2-5cm) long, often toothed. **In bloom:** March-August. **Habitat-Range:** Coastal chaparral under 2000′ (600m); southern California.

The generic name, from the Latin *convolvere*, "to entwine," is descriptive of this large group. The lovely name Morning Glory refers to the morning blooming of the flowers. The twining, creeping habit often makes a pest of some species, such as *C. sepium*, introduced from Europe. In England some of the less-flattering common names are Bindweed, Devil's Garter, Devil's Gut, Daddy's White Shirt, and Granny's Nightcap. Our popular Moon Flowers and Morning Glories are descended from a Mexican species of a different genus, *Ipomoea*.

193 DUTCHMAN'S PIPE
Birthwort family *(Aristolocheaceae)*
(Aristolochia californica)

Height: Deciduous, woody vine, up to 12′ (3m). **Flowers:** Pendulous, axillary, irregular; calyx tubular, pipe-shaped, 1″-1 1/2″ (2.5-4cm) long, 5-cleft, 2-lipped, green-veined or tinged with reddish purple, petals lacking. **Leaves:** Cordate to ovate, 1 1/2″-3″ (4-7cm), silky. **In bloom:** January-April. **Habitat-Range:** Principally chaparral, occasionally woodland; northern California.

This climbing vine with strange-looking reddish-green to flesh-colored flowers, bent like the lower part of a pipe, belongs to a genus of tropical plants containing about 180 species. The generic name refers to its supposed usefulness in childbirth and comes from the Greek *aristos*, "best," and *locheia*, "parturition."

194 HEDGEHOG CACTUS *(Echinocereus fendleri)*
Cactus family *(Cactaceae)*

Height: Succulent, spiny, up to 4″ (10cm) high, 2″ (5cm) wide. **Flowers:** Borne near top of plant, funnel-shaped, 2″-3 1/2″ (5-9cm) long; perianth segments reddish purple; fruit ovoid, about 1″ (2.5cm) long, red, spiny. **Leaves:** Absent; spines on 10-12 vertical ribs, up to 1 3/4″ (4cm) long. **In bloom:** April-June. **Habitat-Range:** Dry plains; Arizona, New Mexico north to Utah.

This species of Hedgehog Cactus sometimes grows solitary, but often many plants grow together in a mass. The fruit is edible, but care should be taken to brush off the spines.

195 FISHHOOK CACTUS
Cactus family *(Cactaceae)*
(Mammillaria tetrancistra)

Height: Succulent perennial, 4″-10″ (10-25cm). **Flowers:** Borne in axils of tubercles around upper part of stem; campanulate, about 1″ (2.5cm) long, perianth segments white to pinkish with rose mid-stripe, outer segments fringed; fruit ovoid, about 1/2″ (1cm) long, scarlet. **Leaves:** Absent; spines arranged on tubercles on thick rounded stem, some spines longer, hooked. **In bloom:** April. **Habitat-Range:** Gravelly areas in deserts of southern California, Nevada, Utah, Arizona.

The Mammillarias are small, rounded cacti with delicate flowers and fruits too small to be of significance as food. Some, like this species, have spines with hooks on the end that others lack. Most are inconspicuous and difficult to locate but are sought after by collectors of succulents.

196 BEAVERTAIL CACTUS *(Opuntia basilaris)*
Cactus family *(Cactaceae)*

Height: Succulent perennial, 4″-12″ (10-30cm). **Flowers:** In clusters on upper ends of stem joints; wheel- or cup-shaped, rose-colored, 2″-2 1/2″ (5-7cm) long, perianth segments oval; fruit ovoid, spineless, but bearing many tiny barbed, stiff hairs in small circular or oval patches, grayish to brown. **Leaves:** Absent; stem composed of padlike joints, each 3″-8″ (7.5-20cm) long, flattened, spineless, gray-green. **In bloom:** March-June. **Habitat-Range:** Desert areas; California east to Utah.

Beavertail Cactus derives its name from the shape of its spineless pads or joints, which resemble a beaver tail. When in flower it is a conspicuous part of the desert flora. The absence of spines facilitates rapid identification in areas where many kinds of cacti are present.

197 BARREL CACTUS *(Ferocactus wislizeni)*   Cactus family *(Cactaceae)*

Height: Succulent perennial, up to 6′ (2m). **Flowers:** Borne around apex of stem; open bell-shaped, 2″-3″ (5-7.5cm) long, perianth segments numerous, lance-shaped, reddish yellow with purplish stripe; fruit ovoid, yellow. **Leaves:** Absent; stem cylindrical, up to 2′ (.6m) in diameter with 20-30 ribs bearing numerous spines up to 6″ (15cm) long, some with tips curved downward. **In bloom:** July-September. **Habitat-Range:** Desert flats, mesas from Arizona to Texas, south into Mexico.

This cactus, because of its huge stem, is a conspicuous part of much of the desert area of the Southwest. The juice obtained from pounding the pulp in the stem is credited with saving the lives of desert travelers who ran out of water. The pulp is also used to make a candy.

198 FIVESPOT MALLOW   Mallow family *(Malvaceae)*
(Malvastrum rotundifolium)

Height: Annual herb, 4″-16″ (10-40cm). **Flowers:** Terminal in corymbs; calyx 5-parted, lobes ovate, hairy; petals 5, 3/4″-1 1/2″ (2-4cm) long, rose-pink with large red-purple spot below middle; stamens many, united in tube surrounding single style; many thin black seed pods (carpels arranged in circle, around central axis of receptacle). **Leaves:** Heart-shaped, hairy, scalloped edges, 3/4″-2″ (2-5cm) wide. **In bloom:** March-May. **Habitat-Range:** Desert washes; southern California east to Nevada, Arizona.

The generic name means Mallow-like, referring to the large group of introduced plants that are sometimes called cheeses. This little Mallow with the five conspicuous spots belongs to a family that includes such well-known plants as Cotton, Hibiscus, Okra, Rose of Sharon, Hollyhock, and Abutilon.

199 OCOTILLO *(Fouquieria splendens)*   Ocotillo family *(Fouquieriaceae)*

Height: Spiny, erect, deciduous shrub, 6′-25′ (2-7m). **Flowers:** In terminal panicles; sepals 5, rounded, overlapping; corolla tubular, 5 short recurved lobes, scarlet. **Leaves:** In fascicles at joints of stems, ovate, 1/2″-1″ (1-2.5cm) long, fleshy; stems with rigid spines. **In bloom:** March-July. **Habitat-Range:** Deserts from California east to Texas, south into Mexico.

Ocotillo, like cacti, is a characteristic plant of the western deserts. Its tall, slender, thorny stems are leafless most of the year, the leaves appearing only in the wet season. The stems have long been used for fences; they will usually take root and continue growing when cut and placed in the ground. The powdered root is said to have medicinal value when applied to swellings, and a dressing for leather can be made from a waxy coating on the stems. The name Ocotillo is a diminutive of the Spanish *ocote*, a kind of pine. Its generic name honors Dr. P. E. Fouquier, a Parisian medical professor.

200 PURPLE MAT *(Nama demissum)*   Waterleaf family *(Hydrophyllaceae)*

Height: Prostrate annual herb, 1″-6″ (2.5-15cm). **Flowers:** In terminal clusters; calyx with 5 gray, hairy, linear lobes; petals 5, joined in tube about 1/2″ (1cm) long, red-purple; stamens 5 within corolla tube; styles 2, forming 10-16 seeded capsule. **Leaves:** Linear, about 3/4″ (2cm) long in terminal, compact clusters. **In bloom:** April-May. **Habitat-Range:** Dry desert slopes, 3000′-5500′ (900-1650m); southern California, Baja California, east to Arizona, Utah.

About 45 species of *Nama* occur in southwestern United States, Mexico, and South America, and one in Hawaii. Its generic name is Greek for a spring. This flat-growing desert plant is small but blooms in profusion in the spring when there has been some rain.

201 DESERT WILLOW *(Chilopsis linearis)*   Bignonia family *(Bignoniaceae)*

Height: Deciduous shrub, 8′-25′ (2.4-8m). **Flowers:** In terminal raceme; calyx inflated, 2-lipped, about 1/2″ (1cm) long; corolla funnel-shaped, 5-lobed, pink, lavender, or whitish; stamens 5, 1 without anther; style single, with 2 stigmas developing into woody, 2-valved capsule; seeds flattened, with hairy, silky tufts at either end. **Leaves:** Linear, 4″-6″ (10-15cm) long. **In bloom:** Intermittently April-September. **Habitat-Range:** Sandy washes from southern California to Texas.

This species is commonly cultivated in parts of Texas. It is also known as Flowering Willow, Flor de Mimbre, and Willow-leaved Catalpa.

202 BOUVARDIA *(Bouvardia glaberrima)*   Madder family *(Rubiaceae)*

Height: Perennial shrub, 3′ (1m). **Flowers:** Clustered at tips of branches; calyx 4-parted; petals 4, in narrow tube about 1″ (2.5cm) long, scarlet; stamens 4 within tube; style single. **Leaves:** Entire, some in circles of 3 or more. **In bloom:** May-October. **Habitat-Range:** Dry sandy deserts; southern New Mexico, Arizona, south into Mexico.

Only one species of this genus grows wild in the West, but several fragrant species are popular garden shrubs. The coffee tree is a member of the same family. Bouvardia is named for Dr. Bouvard, physician to Louis XIII and superintendent of the Royal Gardens in Paris.

203 CHUPAROSA *(Beloperone californica)*   Acanthus family *(Acanthaceae)*

Height: Deciduous shrub, spreading branches 1′-5′ (.3-2m). **Flowers:** Axillary; calyx deeply 5-parted; corolla tubular, 1″-1 1/2″ (2.5-4cm) long, 2-lipped with lower lip 3-lobed, spreading; dull red; stamens 2, extending beyond upper lip. **Leaves:** Ovate, 1/2″ (1cm) long, grayish green with fine hairs. **In bloom:** March-June. **Habitat-Range:** Desert washes, streamsides; southeastern California, Arizona, south into Mexico.

The nearly 2000 species of the Acanthus family are largely found in tropical parts of the world. The genus *Acanthus* itself is famous because the leaf shape of a Mediterranean species was used as the design of the ancient Corinthian column. Chuparosa, a Spanish word, refers to sucking because the red flowers, said to be edible, are sought after by hummingbirds.

204 HUMMINGBIRD FLOWER   Pea family *(Leguminosae)*
(Erythrina flabelliformis)

Height: Perennial shrub, up to 25′ (8m). **Flowers:** In long racemes; calyx tubular, about 3/8″ (9mm) long, reddish; petals pealike, with upper or banner up to 3″ (7.5cm) long, wings and keel petals much shorter; red. **Leaves:** Pinnate, leaflets up to 3″ (7.5cm) long, stems spiny. **In bloom:** March-May; September. **Habitat-Range:** Hillsides, rocky canyons; southern Arizona south to Mexico.

The Hummingbird Flower is so named because its long red flowers attract many species of hummingbirds seeking the nectar from the corolla.

205 SCARLET GLOBE MALLOW   Mallow family *(Malvaceae)*
(Sphaeralcea coccinea)

Height: Perennial herb, 1′ (.3m). **Flowers:** In loose raceme; calyx 5-lobed with 3 bracts below; petals 5, scarlet to yellowish-red, about 1/4″ (6mm) long; stamens numerous, joined in tube surrounding 5 or more styles. **Leaves:** Palmately 3-lobed. **In bloom:** June-September. **Habitat-Range:** Grassy prairies, foothills; New Mexico, Arizona east to Texas, north to Idaho, Canada.

This little plant of the Rocky Mountain area is one of the smallest of the Mallows. Typical of the family, the stamen tube encircles the pistil and is fused to the petals. Many cultivated plants belong to this group, such as Cotton, Hollyhock, Okra, and Hibiscus. The species name comes from the Latin *coccinea*, meaning "scarlet."

206 RED MAIDS *(Calandrinia ciliata)*   Purslane family *(Portulacaceae)*

Height: Annual herb, 4″-16″ (10-40cm). **Flowers:** In leafy racemes; sepals 2, ovate; petals 5, ovate, rose-red, less than 1/2″ (1cm) long; stamens 3-14, shorter than petals; style 3-branched. **Leaves:** Somewhat succulent, linear, 3/4″-3″ (2-7.5cm) long. **In bloom:** February-May. **Habitat-Range:** Grasslands, cultivated places below 6000′ (2000m); California north to British Columbia, south to Mexico, east to Arizona.

This bright little flower, which opens in the afternoon, is often abundant in great patches after a wet spring. The species and varieties are variable, one local common name being Kisses. The generic name honors an eighteenth-century Swiss botanist, J. L. Calandrini.

207 WINE CUPS *(Callirhoë involucrata)*   Mallow family *(Malvaceae)*

Height: Perennial herb, 1′-2′ (.3-.6m). **Flowers:** Single on long stalks; 3 linear bracts below flower; calyx 5-lobed; petals 5, red, 3/8″-5/8″ (7-13mm) long; stamens numerous, united into tube surrounding single style. **Leaves:** Mostly basal, palmately lobed, 1″-3″ (2.5-7.5cm) long, few on rough hairy stems. **In bloom:** April-August. **Habitat-Range:** Grassy prairies from New Mexico to Texas, north to Arkansas, Wyoming, North Dakota.

Wine Cups, or Poppy Mallows, are common in prairies and waste places of the western United States. As the species name describes, the plant has bracts at the base of the flower. The rough stems are vinelike and spreading. The Mallow family is a large one with some plants used as food, the leaves eaten raw or boiled, and others used for healing poultices made with boiled roots and leaves.

208 **WILD POINSETTIA** *(Euphorbia heterophylla)*   Spurge family *(Euphorbiaceae)*

Height: Perennial herb, up to 2′ (.6m). **Flowers:** Terminal in groups surrounded by red leaflike bracts; sepals, petals absent; flower cup containing clusters of single staminate or pistillate flowers, each cup bearing large gland on one side. **Leaves:** Diverse in shape; usually entire, irregularly toothed. **In bloom:** August-October. **Habitat-Range:** Waste places in grassland or streamsides; Arizona east to Florida, south to Tropical America.

This is a wild form of the cultivated Poinsettia so familiar in florist shops around Christmas. In parts of Mexico the hillsides are red with the showy bracts that surround the flowers. As in most Euphorbias, the juice is white.

209 **GIANT FOUR O'CLOCK**   Four O'clock family *(Nyctaginaceae)*
(Mirabilis multiflora)

Height: Perennial herb, about 18″ (45cm). **Flowers:** More than 3 in bell-shaped involucre; calyx red-purple, tubular, about 2″ (5cm) long, 5-lobed; petals absent; stamens 5, protruding, unequal length; single pistil forming achene. **Leaves:** Broad oval-shaped on long stalks, finely hairy. **In bloom:** April-September. **Habitat-Range:** Grassy mesas, hills, 2500′-6500′ (750-2000m); Arizona, New Mexico to Texas, north to Colorado, Utah.

As the species name suggests, this is the many-flowered Four O'clock, resembling the cultivated garden variety. The family name Nyctaginaceae derives from the Greek *nyx, nyktos,* "night," referring to their blooming late in the day. *Mirabilis* is Latin for wonderful. Hopi Indians are said to eat the root to induce visions; another use for the powdered root is to relieve stomachache.

210 **CHECKER BLOOM** *(Sidalcea malvaeflora)*   Mallow family *(Malvaceae)*

Height: Perennial herb, 1′-2′ (.3-.6m). **Flowers:** Of two types in loose racemes up to 12″ (30cm) long; petals 5, pink, perfect flowers 1/2″-1 1/4″ (1-3cm) long; pistillate flowers up to 1/2″ (1cm) long. **Leaves:** Palmately cleft, finely hairy. **In bloom:** March-May. **Habitat-Range:** Open hills throughout much of California apart from desert areas.

This is a common member of the family to which such well-known plants as the Hollyhock, Hibiscus, and Cotton Plant belong. Several species of *Sidalcea* are found in western North America. In the higher Rocky Mountains the White Checker Mallow *(S. candida)* grows in subalpine meadows.

211 **SUMMER'S DARLING**   Evening-primrose family *(Onagraceae)*
(Clarkia amoena)

Height: Annual herb, 1′-3′ (.3-1m). **Flowers:** Numerous on leafy spike; calyx 4-lobed, sepals lance-shaped, about 1″ (2.5cm) long, joined at tips turned to one side at blooming;

petals 4, fan-shaped, shades of pink, lavender, white, 3/4″-1 1/2″ (2-3.5cm) long; stamens 8, in 2 series; style 4-lobed at tip. **Leaves:** Lance-shaped, 1/2″-2 1/2″ (1-6cm) long, about 1/2″ (1cm) wide. **In bloom:** June-August. **Habitat-Range:** Coastal grasslands; northern California.

These lovely flowers, blooming in late spring, have been given charming popular names. The generic name honors Captain William Clark of the Lewis and Clark expedition, who crossed the Rocky Mountains in 1806. The seeds of some *Clarkias* were gathered and eaten by the Indians.

212 HORSE MINT *(Monarda punctata)*   Mint family *(Labiatae)*

Height: Aromatic annual herb, 1′-4′ (.3-1m). **Flowers:** In dense terminal clusters surrounded by pink to purplish or white bracts; calyx tubular with 5 triangular teeth; corolla tubular, 3/4″ (2cm) long, 2-lipped, lower 3-lobed with middle lobe much larger; pink, or yellow spotted with red; stamens 2. **Leaves:** Opposite, lance-shaped or oblong, up to 3″ (7cm) long, sometimes finely hairy. **In bloom:** June-September. **Habitat-Range:** Moist sandy situations, Arizona east to Texas, over much of East.

M. punctata, while often quite pink, may also be predominately yellow. The name Horse Mint for members of the genus *Monarda* refers to their coarse character. All are large and strongly aromatic. The genus is named for a sixteenth-century Spanish botanist, Monardes. Another species, Pink Horsemint *(M. fistulosa)*, found from Texas eastward, has a lavender-pink corolla. Another smaller species with a rose corolla, *M. menthaefolia*, grows in coniferous forests from Arizona north to Canada. It is known as Wild Bergamot or Beebalm. The leaves of Bergamot can be made into a spicy tea or used for flavoring like many other mints.

213 FAREWELL-TO-SPRING   Evening-primrose family *(Onagraceae)*
(Clarkia rubicunda)

Height: Annual herb, 1′-3′ (.3-1m). **Flowers:** Many on leafy spike; calyx 4-parted, lobes lance-shaped, 1/2″-1″ (1-2.5cm) long, united, turned to one side at blooming; petals roughly toothed, 1/2″-1 1/4″ (1-3cm) long, pinkish to lavender, showy red at base; stamens 8, red; style 4-lobed at tip. **Leaves:** Lance-shaped, 1/2″-2 1/2″ (1-6cm) long, about 3/8″ (8mm) broad. **In bloom:** May-July. **Habitat-Range:** Grassy places in woods of central California coast.

This species and *C. amoena* are hard to distinguish and some authors have included them in a separate genus, *Godetia*. They differ in distribution, and *C. rubicunda* has a red base to the petals. Many *Clarkias* are planted in gardens as showy annuals.

SHOOTING STAR   Primrose family *(Primulaceae)*
(Dodecatheon hendersonii)

Height: Perennial herb, 8″-14″ (20-35cm). **Flowers:** 1/2″-3/4″ (1-2cm) long in umbel at end of naked stem; each flower bent downward with petals projecting backward; stamens erect around extended style, forming bill-like projection; corolla pinkish purple with yellow band at base. **Leaves:** In basal rosette, round to elliptical; 1″-2″ (2.5-5cm) long; roots with bulblets like rice grains. **In bloom:** February-April. **Habitat-Range:** Grassy areas on lower mountain slopes of coastal California.

Many species of Shooting Stars are found over North America. The names Mosquito Bill and Bird's Bill are also used to describe some because of the shape of the flower. They are related to the Cyclamen, a well-known horticultural plant from Iran.

214 SHRUBBY RED SAGE *(Salvia greggii)*   Mint family *(Labiatae)*

Height: Perennial herb, 1 1/2'-2 1/2' (.5-.7m). **Flowers:** In terminal racemes; calyx tubular, 2-lipped; corolla red, tubular with tube enlarged basally, 1"-1 1/4" (2.5-3cm) long, 2-lipped, upper 2-lobed, concave, lower 3-lobed with cleft in middle lobe; stamens 2. **Leaves:** Opposite, ovate, 3/8"-3/4" (1-2cm) long, minutely hairy. **In bloom:** April-September. **Habitat-Range:** Grasslands of south-central and west Texas, south to Mexico.

This is one of more than 500 species in the genus *Salvia*. It is cultivated in much of Texas, where it is native. Like other sages it has a flower with an upper lip that protects the nectar in the tube from being diluted by rain, and a large lower lip on which pollinating insects that are attracted by the nectar, such as bees, may alight, thus insuring cross-pollination.

215 FIRECRACKER FLOWER *(Brodiaea ida-maia)*   Lily family *(Liliaceae)*

Height: Perennial herb, 1'-3' (.3-1m) high. **Flowers:** Pendulous, in umbels of 6-12 or more; corolla parts 6, joined in tube 1"-1 1/4" (2.5-3cm) long, scarlet, segments at tip greenish, turned back; stamens 3, within tube, fertile, extended; pistil single, forming capsule. **Leaves:** Linear, usually 3, 12"-20" (30-50cm) long. **In bloom:** May-July. **Habitat-Range:** Grassy slopes 1000'-4000' (300-1200m); northern California to Oregon.

This is a beautiful but strange plant, different from most of the Brodiaeas, which are blue or white with erect flowers. It has a peculiar structure with three sterile stamens whose tips appear outside the tube as white petals. The origin of the species name is uncertain; the generic name honors a Scotch botanist, James Brodie.

216 WINDMILL PINK *(Silene gallica)*   Pink family *(Caryophyllaceae)*

Height: Annual herb, 10"-15" (25-40cm). **Flowers:** In one-sided raceme; calyx tubular, 5-toothed, with 10 veins or ribs; corolla 3/8" (8mm) in diameter, with 5 oval-shaped petals; white or faintly pinkish; stamens 10. **Leaves:** Spade-shaped, 1"-1 1/2" (2.5-4cm) long, hairy. **In bloom:** February-June. **Habitat-Range:** Fields, wastelands at low elevations throughout much of North America.

This little member of the Pink family is a weed introduced from Europe but is so common that every wildflower observer will soon see it. The name is derived from the fact that each petal is turned at a slight angle, making the flower look like a miniature windmill.

217 SUGARBOWL *(Clematis hirsutissima)*   Buttercup family *(Ranunculaceae)*

Height: Perennial herb, 1'-2' (.3-.6m). **Flowers:** Nodding, single on end of stem; calyx 4-parted, purplish brown, thick with white, woolly edges; stamens numerous; pistils many, becoming achenes with feathery plumes up to 2 1/2" (6cm) long. **Leaves:** Opposite, pinnately divided twice into narrow leaflets. **In bloom:** April-July. **Habitat-Range:** Grassy plains, woods below 8000′ (2450m); New Mexico, Arizona north to Montana, Washington.

The shape of the flower, filled with feathery plumes, suggests the common name Sugarbowl. Other local names are Leather Flower, Old Man's Whiskers, Vase Vine, and Clematis. The species name means very hairy, a reference to the plumes. The wind easily picks up these seeds and aids in their distribution.

218 FOXGLOVE *(Digitalis purpurea)*   Figwort family *(Scrophulariaceae)*

Height: Biennial herb, 3′-6′ (1-2m). **Flowers:** In long terminal racemes; calyx 5-parted; corolla tube inflated, 1 1/2″ (4cm) long, pinkish purple to whitish; stamens 4. **Leaves:** Alternate, oblong-lanceolate, toothed, 3″-8″ (7.5-20cm) long. **In bloom:** June-September. **Habitat-Range:** Widespread near coast from northern California to British Columbia.

This European garden plant has become established in the wild along the Pacific coast. It is well known for the drug digitalis that it yields. Digitalis is a heart stimulant but because it accumulates in the body, it must be taken in small amounts as prescribed by a doctor.

219 STREAM ORCHID *(Epipactis gigantea)*   Orchid family *(Orchidaceae)*

Height: Perennial herb, 1′-5′ (.3-1.5m). **Flowers:** In racemes with leaflike bracts; sepals 3, reddish to greenish, concave, 1/2″- 3/4″ (1-2cm) long; petals 3 with lower one (lip) pouched at base, slightly shorter than sepals, pinkish veined with maroon. **Leaves:** Ovate below to lance-shaped above, 2″-6″ (5-15cm) long. **In bloom:** May-August. **Habitat-Range:** Widespread along stream banks below 7500′ (2300m); California north to British Columbia, east to South Dakota, Texas.

Stream Orchid is also known as Giant Helleborine because of the height to which it grows and its superficial resemblance to the Hellebore. It occurs in nearly every plant community within its range.

220 PINK SAND VERBENA   Four O'clock family *(Nyctaginaceae)*
(Abronia umbellata)

Height: Perennial prostrate herb, 1′-3′ (.3-1m) long. **Flowers:** 10-15 in heads on stalks 2″-6″ (5-15cm) long; involucre of 5-8 lance-shaped bracts; calyx rose-purple, tubular-salveriform; petals none. **Leaves:** Oval, 3/4″-2 1/2″ (2-6cm) long, succulent, often reddish, on petioles about as long. **In bloom:** Most of year. **Habitat-Range:** Sandy seashore; California, northern Baja California.

Sand dunes along the coast are often densely covered by this fragrant pink verbena. Like desert plants, the succulent leaves and stems conserve water. The generic name comes from the Greek *abros*, meaning "graceful."

Blue·Violet

Simplified Key

HABITAT	HERB	SHRUB
Regular **ALPINE**	225 Fringed Gentian 223 Sky Pilot 222 Alpine Lungwort 221 Forget-me-not	
Irregular	Beardtongue 224 Cusick's Speedwell	
Regular **CONIFEROUS**	241 Camas 231 Checker Lily 229 Blue Flax Mendocino Gentian Jacob's Ladder 233 Morning Glory Gilia 245 Stickseed 230 Lungwort 240 Spike Verbena 226/228 Bluebell 242 Wild Heliotrope	
Irregular	234 Slink Pod 235 Calypso Blue Monkshood 232 Blue Columbine 237 Delphinium 239 Blue Violet 236 Lupine 238 Elephant Head 244 Mountain Penstemon 243 Penstemon	
Composite	227 Cascade Aster 246 Wild Daisy	
Regular **WOODLAND**	250 Purple Milkweed 247 Hound's Tongue	
Irregular	249 Larkspur 248 Skullcap	
Regular **PINYON-JUNIPER-SAGE**	251 Hairy Verbena	
Irregular	253 Silvery Lupine 254 One-sided Penstemon	252 Great Basin Blue Sage
Regular **CHAPARRAL**	255 Canchalagua 257 Purple Nightshade	Jim Brush
Irregular	256 Sticky Phacelia 258 Chinese Houses	

	HABITAT	HERB	SHRUB
Regular	**DESERT**	259 Sand Verbena 261 Canterbury Bell Heliotrope Phacelia Wild Heliotrope	
Irregular		260 Broom Rape	Bladder Sage
Regular	**GRASS**	Blue Dicks 276 Mountain Iris 271 Blue-eyed Grass Spiderwort 268/269 Pasque Flower Jewel Flower 262 Desert Candle Purple Sanicle 270 Wild Geranium 272 Prairie Gentian 273 Blue Gilia 277 Ground Cherry 267 Lobelia	
Irregular		265 Western Larkspur 266 Locoweed 263 Bluebonnet 274 Prairie Violet Buffalo Burr 264 Owl's Clover Locoweed	
Composite		275 Townsendia	
Regular	**SEA COAST**	279 Cliff Spurge	
Composite		278 Seaside Daisy	
Regular	**WIDESPREAD**	281 Sickle-leaved Onion 282 Ithuriel's Spear 285 Stork's Bill 284 Baby Blue-Eyes	
Irregular		280 American Vetch Chia 283 Hedge Nettle Blue Toadflax Collinsia Foothill Penstemon	

221 FORGET-ME-NOT *(Mysotis alpestris)*   Borage family *(Boraginaceae)*

Height: Perennial herb, 4″-12″ (10-30cm). **Flowers:** In loose racemes; calyx 5-lobed; corolla wheel-shaped, about 1/4″ (6mm) across, 5 sky-blue lobes with prominent yellow crest at base of each; 5 stamens attached to tube, alternating with corolla lobes. **Leaves:** Lance-shaped to broadly linear, 2″-3″ (5-7.5cm) long, herbage covered with long, soft white hairs. **In bloom:** June-August. **Habitat-Range:** Moist alpine situations from Oregon and Colorado north to Alaska.

This alpine flower belongs to the same genus as our cultivated garden Forget-me-not *(M. sylvatica)*, which has become naturalized in certain areas. *Mysotis* means mouse ear from the Greek *mus*, "mouse," and *otis*, "ear," a reference to the shape of the leaves in some species.

222 ALPINE LUNGWORT *(Mertensia alpina)*   Borage family *(Boraginaceae)*

Height: Perennial herb, under 1′ (.3m). **Flowers:** In tight clusters on ends of stems; calyx 5-lobed; corolla regular, tubular, 1/4″-1/2″ (.6-1cm) long, 5-lobed, blue; stamens 5, attached to corolla tube; stigma single on threadlike style. **Leaves:** Alternate, smooth, narrow, with single vein, 3″ (7.5cm) long. **In bloom:** July-August. **Habitat-Range:** Alpine meadows above timberline; mountains of New Mexico to Idaho, Montana.

This alpine plant is common in the Rocky Mountains, differing from the closely related species *M. ciliata* in its small size and tightly clustered flowers. The blue tubular flowers of *Mertensia* are somewhat similar to the true Bluebells, which belong to another family. The common name Lungwort was first given to a European species with white-spotted leaves that resembled diseased liver; it was thought to be a cure. *Mertensia* is named for a German 18th-century botanist, F. K. Mertens.

223 SKY PILOT *(Polemonium viscosum)*   Phlox family *(Polemoniaceae)*

Height: Perennial herb, 2″-20″ (5-50cm). **Flowers:** Borne in cymes resembling head; calyx tubular, 5-parted; corolla funnel-shaped with 5 expanded lobes, 3/4″-1 1/2″ (2-3cm) across, purple. **Leaves:** Alternate, pinnate with numerous roundish leaflets less than 1/2″ (1cm) long, sticky, odorous. **In bloom:** June-August. **Habitat-Range:** Rocky crevices at arctic alpine heights, 9000′-12,000′ (2750-3650m); Rocky Mountains, Arizona north to Alberta.

Only those who venture above timberline see the Sky Pilot, aptly named for its preference for heights. The flowers are colorful but the herbage is sticky and has a somewhat skunklike odor that will adhere to shoes for some time.

224 CUSICK'S SPEEDWELL   Figwort family *(Scrophulariaceae)*
(Veronica cusickii)

Height: Perennial herb, 8″-9″ (20-22cm). **Flowers:** 3-9 in terminal racemes; calyx lobes 4, narrow, ovate; corolla somewhat wheel-shaped, 1/2″ (1cm) across, 4-lobed, upper lobe largest, lower smallest; 2 blue stamens. **Leaves:** Opposite, sessile, ovate to oblong, generally smooth. **In bloom:** July-August. **Habitat-Range:** Meadows or moist places in alpine or subalpine areas, 8500′-9200′ (2600-2800m); California north to Washington.

Members of the genus *Veronica*, named in honor of St. Veronica, have the lower leaves opposite and a corolla with 4 petals of unequal size. The uppermost petal is a fusion of two and therefore is the broadest. There are about 250 species, some of which are trees in the tropics. Speedwell refers to the use of some species to cure scurvy. The leaves may be cooked or used in salads.

BEARDTONGUE   Figwort family *(Scrophulariaceae)*
(Penstemon heterodoxus)

Height: Perennial herb, 4″-10″ (10-25cm). **Flowers:** In 2-4 clusters on stem; calyx 5-parted; corolla blue-purple, tubular, 1/2″ (1cm) long with equal upper, lower lips. **Leaves:** Opposite, largely basal; linear to spatulate, 1/2″-1″ (1-2.5cm) long. **In bloom:** July-August. **Habitat-Range:** Rocky slopes and alpine meadows up to 12,000′ (3650m); Sierra Nevada.

This colorful flower is seen, often in thick patches, at higher elevations in California during the summer months. A large blue penstemon *(P. cyanthus)* with flower clusters about 8″ (20cm) long is found in spring and summer in the mountains of Utah, Arizona, and Wyoming. These two species, unlike the Large Beardtongue *(P. glandulosa)* of Oregon, Washington, and Idaho, do not have sticky hairs on the outer part of the corolla. The generic name *Penstemon* means five stamens, but the fifth is sterile. In the group known as Beardtongues the tip of the sterile filament is hairy.

225 FRINGED GENTIAN   Gentian family *(Gentianaceae)*
(Gentiana thermalis)†

Height: Annual herb, 4″-16″ (10-40cm). **Flowers:** Single at end of stem; calyx tube 4-7 lobed; corolla 1″-2″ (2.5-5cm) long; 4-fringed lobes, blue-purple; stamens 4; style single within tube. **Leaves:** Basal, linear, short. **In bloom:** July-September. **Habitat-Range:** High alpine meadows, streams to 13,000′ (3950m); New Mexico, Arizona, north to Wyoming, Idaho, Canada.

Gentians are one of the most beautiful flowers found in the mountains of much of the world. This fringed species is especially lovely. It was named *thermalis* for the hot springs at Yellowstone Park and in 1926 was adopted as the park flower.

MENDOCINO GENTIAN   Gentian family *(Gentianaceae)*
(Gentiana setigera)

Height: Perennial herb, 10″-12″ (25-30cm). **Flowers:** One to few with 2 ovate bracts at end of stem; calyx tube up to 1/2″ (1cm) long, with 5 lobes half as long; corolla narrowly bell-shaped, blue, about 1 1/2″ (4cm) long, lobes about 1/2″ (1cm) long; stamens 5, inserted in corolla tube; style single, 2-branched. **Leaves:** Opposite, ovate, 1″-1 1/2″ (2.5-4cm) long, upper leaves enclosing base of flowers. **In bloom:** July-September. **Habitat-Range:** Wet coniferous forests, 4000′-6500′ (1200-2000m); northern California Coast Ranges to Oregon.

Flowers of the Gentian family are found in the high places of most of the world. The deep colors are usually blue to purple but may be pink, white, or yellow. It is named for King Gentius of Illyria, who is reported to have discovered medicinal value in the root of the yellow-flowered species, *G. lutea*. There are about 300 species of Gentians, with about 20 occurring in the Rocky Mountains.

226/228 **BLUEBELL** *(Campanula rotundifolia)*   Bellflower family *(Campanulaceae)*

Height: Perennial herb, 6″-24″ (15-60cm). **Flowers:** Nodding, 1-9 in loose panicle; calyx 5-lobed, spreading from short tube; corolla bell-shaped, purplish blue, 1/2″-3/4″ (1-2cm) long, 5 short lobes; stamens 5; style single with long, branched tip. **Leaves:** Mostly linear, entire, 1 1/2″-2 1/2″ (4-6cm) long, basal, round. **In bloom:** July-September. **Habitat-Range:** Coniferous forests, 4500′-8000′ (1350-2450m); California north to Alaska, east to Atlantic.

This is the Bluebell of Scotland, the Harebell, also called Bellflower. The generic name means "little bell." *C. rotundifolia* is strangely named for the inconspicuous basal leaves, which are round, rather than for the numerous and conspicuous stem leaves, which are linear. The delicate blue flowers bloom in late summer and early fall, bringing unexpected pleasure when other flowers have disappeared.

227 **CASCADE ASTER** *(Aster ledophyllus)*   Sunflower family *(Compositae)*

Height: Perennial herb, 1′-2′ (.3-.6m). **Flowers:** In one to several heads each, 1″-2″ (2.5-5cm), lavender-purple or bluish purple, disc yellow. **Leaves:** Extending length of stem, narrowly lance-shaped to elliptic, 1″-2 1/2″ (2.5-6cm) long, sessile, smooth above, woolly, grayish on underside. **In bloom:** July-September. **Habitat-Range:** Open woods, grassy places in coniferous forests, 5000′-7000′ (1500-2200); mountains of Pacific states, northern Rocky Mountains.

Asters are summer and fall flowers, blooming in mountain meadows when all the spring blossoms are gone. The star-shaped flower is responsible for the name "aster," which is the Greek for "star." The leaves of the Cascade Aster are known to be edible. A related species, the Alpine Aster *(A. alpigenus)*, is much shorter—4″-10″ (10-25cm)— and has only basal leaves; these are 4″-7″ (10-18cm) long.

229 **BLUE FLAX** *(Linum lewisii)*   Flax family *(Linaceae)*

Height: Perennial herb, 1 1/2′-3′ (.5-1m). **Flowers:** Open; in loose terminal clusters; sepals 5, ovate, 1/4″ (6mm) long; petals 5, 3/4″ (2cm) long; light lavender-blue; stamens 5, shorter than styles; styles 5. **Leaves:** Alternate; narrowly linear, about 1″ (2.5cm) long; gray-green. **In bloom:** May-September. **Habitat-Range:** Montane, open ridges, coniferous forests, 4000′-11,000′ (1200-3350m); in western North America.

This plant was named in honor of Captain Meriwether Lewis of the Lewis and Clark Expedition. It is closely related to the European species from whose fibers linen is made. The Indians used the fibrous stems to make fishing lines and cord.

230 **LUNGWORT** *(Mertensia ciliata)*   Borage family *(Boraginaceae)*

Height: Perennial herb, 2′-5′ (.6-1.5m). **Flowers:** In short, somewhat nodding racemes at ends of stems or branchlets; tubular; calyx lobes 5, 1/2″ (1cm) long, narrow, pointed; corolla up to 1″ (2.5cm) long, tubular with 5 lobes at mouth, blue; stamens 5, deep in corolla. **Leaves:** Alternate on short stem, or stem lacking; entire; ovate to lance-shaped; smooth, 2″-5″ (5-12cm) long. **In bloom:** June-August. **Habitat-Range:** 5000′-10,000′ (1500-3050m); mountains of western North America.

This shrublike herb with its soft green foliage is found most often along small streams and rivulets where individual bushes may produce an abundance of blue, tube-shaped, nodding flowers. The various species of *Mertensia* (a name that honors the German botanist F. K. Mertens) found over the Northern Hemisphere differ from most other members of the Borage family in their smooth rather than coarse, bristly foliage.

231 CHECKER LILY *(Fritillaria lanceolata)*†   Lily family *(Liliaceae)*

Height: Perennial herb, 1 1/2'-2 1/2' (.4-.8m). **Flowers:** In raceme, usually of 3 or 4, nodding; deeply bowl-shaped, about 1"-1 1/2" (2.5-4cm) long; perianth of 6 segments, deeply mottled with purple, green; style deeply 3-cleft. **Leaves:** In whorls on middle to upper part of stem; ovate-lanceolate, 2"-3" (5-8cm) long; grayish green. **In bloom:** March-May. **Habitat-Range:** Open wooded areas; Central California to British Columbia.

    Checker lilies are not uncommon, but the protective coloring of the flowers often makes them difficult to see. Other species in the genus *Fritillaria*, including the Yellow Fritillary *(F. pudica)*, occur in the mountains from Utah and California north to Canada. Yellow Fritillary flowers are smaller than those of the Checker Lily and are yellow to orange with the outsides tinged purple.

JACOB'S LADDER *(Polemonium caeruleum)*   Gilia family *(Polemoniaceae)*

Height: Perennial herb, 1'-3' (.3-1m). **Flowers:** In cymes; calyx campanulate; corolla broadly bell-shaped, 1/2" (1cm) long, 5 rounded lobes about twice length of tube, nearly 1" (2.5cm) across, blue. **Leaves:** Pinnate, 3"-10" (8-25cm) long, 19-27 lance-shaped segments 1/2"-1 1/2" (1-4cm) long. **In bloom:** June-August. **Habitat-Range:** Moist places, 3000'-11,000' (900-3350m); California north to Alaska, Rocky Mountains.

    Several species of *Polemonium* (named after Polemon, an Athenian philosopher), and especially *P. pulcherrimum*, which has a violet-blue corolla with a white or yellow tube, are known as Jacob's Ladder. The common name is derived from the shape of the leaves with the numerous leaflets looking like rungs of a ladder.

GILIA *(Gilia capitata)*   Gilia family *(Polemoniaceae)*

Height: Annual herb, 8"-36" (20-90cm). **Flowers:** In terminal head of 25-100 on bare stem; calyx with 5-pointed lobes; corolla about 1/4" (6mm) long, 5 lobes expanding from bell-shaped tube, pointed, light blue-violet, stamens 5, extending beyond corolla. **Leaves:** Alternate, bipinnately dissected, 1"-4" (2.5-10cm) long with linear lobes, smooth to hairy, glandular. **In bloom:** May-July. **Habitat-Range:** Open slopes in coniferous forests below 6000' (1800m); California north to British Columbia.

    Gilias are named after Felipe Luis Gil, a Spanish botanist of the late 18th-century. *G. capitata* is an easily recognized species because of its headlike inflorescence and blue to purplish lavender color.

232 BLUE COLUMBINE *(Aquilegia caerulea)*†   Buttercup family *(Ranunculaceae)*

Height: Perennial herb, 8"-24" (20-60cm). **Flowers:** Solitary on slender pedicels; sepals 5, petal-like, extending outward, 1"-1 1/4" (2.5-3cm) long, blue; petals 5, erect, white,

119

with blue spurs extending backward 1″-3″ (2.5-8cm) behind sepals. **Leaves:** Mostly basal on long stems, much divided as in Meadow Rue. **In bloom:** June-August. **Habitat-Range:** Moist situations, aspen groves in coniferous forests, 6000′-11,000′ (1800-3350m); Arizona, New Mexico north to Idaho, Montana.

Blue Columbine is the state flower of Colorado and one of the most striking members of a genus containing many beautiful species. There are many records of early uses of Columbine for medicinal purposes. The roots were boiled and made into a tea to stop diarrhea, or mashed and applied to inflamed joints. The Spanish are reported to have eaten the root on fast days. The common name comes from the Latin *columbinus*, "dovelike," out of a fancied resemblance of the inverted flower to a cluster of doves.

233 MORNING GLORY *(Ipomoea plummerae)* Morning-glory family *(Convolvulaceae)*

Height: Twining or spreading herb. **Flowers:** Calyx 5-parted, warty; corolla funnel-shaped, about 1″ (2.5cm) long, purplish. **Leaves:** Deeply cleft with narrow lobes, on very short petiole. **In bloom:** June-October. **Habitat-Range:** Coniferous forests; southern Arizona.

The Morning Glories of the genus *Ipomoea* (meaning wormlike) are plants of warm regions, especially the tropics where some grow into treelike form. One of the best known species is the Sweet Potato *(I. batatas)*, a native of Mexico now widely cultivated.

234 SLINK POD *(Scoliopus bigelovii)*   Lily family *(Liliaceae)*

Height: Perennial herb, 4″-9″ (10-23cm). **Flowers:** Like orchids, each on threadlike pedicel; perianth composed of 3 narrow erect petals, 3 broader-spreading sepals; greenish with reddish black veins; stamens 3, opposite petals; style with 3 long branches; odor foul. **Leaves:** 2, opposite, basal, elliptical, 4″-9″ (10-23cm) long, dark green splotched with purple. **In bloom:** February-March. **Habitat-Range:** Cool, shaded redwood forests; Coastal California, Oregon.

This beautiful little lily unfortunately has a most unpleasant odor and is often known as the Fetid Adder's Tongue. The name Slink Pod, by which it is better known, refers to the way the flower stalks sprawl when the 3-angled fruits mature.

235 CALYPSO *(Calypso bulbosa)*†   Orchid family *(Orchidaceae)*

Height: Perennial herb, 4″-10″ (10-25cm). **Flowers:** Solitary, terminal; sepals, petals alike, 6, about 1/2″ (1cm) long, purplish pink, lance-shaped except for lower lip that is inflated, sac-shaped, purple-mottled white with yellow hairs. **Leaves:** Solitary, basal, ovate, 1 1/2″-2 1/2″ (4-7cm). **In bloom:** March-July. **Habitat-Range:** Rich leaf mold in coniferous forests; California north to Alaska, east to Atlantic.

The Calypso Orchid or Fairy Slipper is one of the largest-flowered and most beautiful members of its family in the West, which may account for its being named after the Greek nymph. It is never common and usually very localized but generally occurs in patches. It grows from little bulbs or corms in the ground, as the name *bulbosa* implies.

236 LUPINE *(Lupinus latifolius)*   Pea family *(Leguminosae)*

Height: Perennial herb, 1′-4′ (.3-1m). **Flowers:** Scattered in racemes 6″-18″ (15-45cm) long; calyx 2-lipped, upper notched, lower entire; petals blue, fading brown, irregular with banner, wings, curved keel enclosing 10 stamens; seed pods dark brown, about 1″ (3cm) long. **Leaves:** Palmately compound, on stalks 2″-8″ (5-20cm) long; 5-12 leaflets, 1 1/2″-4″ (4-10cm) long, nearly smooth. **In bloom:** April-July. **Habitat-Range:** Open woods below 7000′ (2100m); mountains of California north to Washington, east to Arizona.

This lupine is common and widespread with several varieties from blue to purple, sometimes pink, white, or yellowish. The form is usually open and lax. *Latifolius*, meaning broad leaf, describes the shape of the leaflets.

237 DELPHINIUM *(Delphinium polycladon)* — Buttercup family *(Ranunculaceae)*

Height: Perennial herb, 20″-32″ (50-80cm). **Flowers:** Separated in loose racemes 4″-8″ (10-20cm) long; sepals 5, 1/2″ (1cm) long, blue-purple, upper sepal with long tubular spur into which spurs of 2 upper petals extend; petals 4, lateral pair small, upper petal paler blue, lower hairy, longer. **Leaves:** Mostly basal, kidney-shaped, dissected, up to 4″ (10cm) broad. **In bloom:** July-September. **Habitat-Range:** Meadows, streamsides, damp rocky ledges in coniferous forests to timberline, 7500′-11,000′ (2300-3350m); Sierra Nevada.

This is one of many western species of *Delphinium*, a name derived from the Latin *delphinus*, meaning "dolphin," a reference to the flowers that have, in some species, a dolphin-like shape. The seeds and herbage of Delphiniums possess an alkaloid poisonous to man and animals.

BLUE MONKSHOOD *(Aconitum columbianum)* — Buttercup family *(Ranunculaceae)*

Height: Perennial herb, 2′-5′ (.6-1.5m). **Flowers:** In showy raceme; each 1/2″-3/4″ (1-2cm) long; 5 sepals with uppermost forming hood, 2 lateral rounded, lower 2 narrow; petals 2-5 with upper 2 concealed in hood, 3 lower rudimentary or lacking; purplish blue. **Leaves:** Palmately lobed; 2″-3″ (5-8cm) across; distributed along stem. **In bloom:** July-August. **Habitat-Range:** Moist places around meadows or in willow thickets, 4000′-8000′ (1200-2450m); Rocky Mountains to Pacific coast.

Monkshood or Aconite is related to the Delphiniums but lacks the elongate spur at the base of the upper sepal. Instead, this element takes the form of a large hood, which gives the plant its common name. Some species of *Aconitum* have been a source of drugs and most species are poisonous. They are also cultivated as ornamental plants.

238 ELEPHANT HEAD *(Pedicularis groenlandica)* — Figwort family *(Scrophulariaceae)*

Height: Perennial herb, 6″-24″ (15-60cm). **Flowers:** In spikelike racemes; calyx 5-lobed, 1/4″ (6mm) long; corolla twice as long as calyx, red-purple, 2-lipped, upper developed into beak 1/4″ (6mm) long, curved upward; stamens 4, within corolla; style single, 2-lobed; pistil forming 2-celled capsule. **Leaves:** Lance-shaped, 1 1/2″-4″ (4-10cm) long, pinnately divided, lobed, toothed, fernlike. **In bloom:** June-August. **Habitat-Range:** Wet meadows in forests, 6000′-12,000′ (1800-3650m); California to New Mexico, north to Alaska, east to Labrador.

A flower of unique appearance, it often grows in great numbers, giving meadows a purple hue. Only on close examination does one notice the little flower with a face and trunk that suggest an elephant. Other members of the genus are the colorful Indian Warrior and Lousewort. The generic name is from the Latin for "louse," *pediculus*, but how it applies is uncertain. In the far north these plants have been used for food —the leaves for a tea and the roots, tasting like carrots, eaten boiled or raw.

239 BLUE VIOLET *(Viola adunca)* — Violet family *(Violaceae)*

Height: Perennial herb, 1"-6" (2.5-15cm). **Flowers:** Solitary, terminal, 1/4"-1/2" (6-12mm) long; sepals 5, narrow, pointed; petals 5, blue to violet, upper pair larger than lateral pair, bearded at base, lower petal with hollow sac or spur at base. **Leaves:** Ovate, entire, sometimes slightly toothed, 3/4"-1 1/2" (2-4cm) long. **In bloom:** March-July. **Habitat-Range:** Partly shaded margins of mountain meadows, stream banks in coniferous forests, sea level to 11,500' (3500m); California north to Alaska, east to Quebec.

There are over 300 species of *Viola* in the temperate zones. The name, an ancient one, was used by Virgil for these plants. Some are blue or violet, others yellow, yellow and blue, or yellow and maroon or brown. All are low-growing, usually perennial herbs. From the wild forms have come such garden flowers as pansies and violets.

240 SPIKE VERBENA *(Verbena macdougalii)* — Verbena family *(Verbenaceae)*

Height: Perennial herb, up to 2' (.6m). **Flowers:** Borne in long terminal spikes with short bracts; calyx tubular, 5-toothed; corolla small, 2-lipped with 2 erect lobes above, 3 partly reflexed lobes below, purple or blue. **Leaves:** Opposite, lance-shaped, 2"-4" (5-10cm), margin toothed; stems square. **In bloom:** June-September. **Habitat-Range:** Coniferous forests, 6500'-7000' (2000-2300m); Arizona east to Texas, and north to Wyoming.

This is a distinctive-looking plant with its long slender flower spikes. It is found commonly on both rims of the Grand Canyon and is frequent along roadsides.

241 CAMAS *(Camassia leichtlinii)* — Lily family *(Liliaceae)*

Height: Perennial herb, 1'-2 1/2' (.3-.75m). **Flowers:** Star-shaped, in simple raceme of 5-25 flowers; 6 perianth (sepals, petals) segments 1/2"-1" (1-2.5cm) long; dark blue, rarely white; stamens 6, with conspicuously yellow anthers. **Leaves:** Linear, basal, up to 24" (60cm) long. **In bloom:** May-August. **Habitat-Range:** Wet mountain meadows, 2000'-8000' (600-2400m).

Two rather closely related species of Camas occur in western North America, *C. leichtlinii* and *C. quamash*. The latter differs principally in having one of the perianth segments turned downward, and also in having many of the flowers on a raceme bloom at once rather than only 1 to 3 as in *C. leichtlinii*. The bulbs of both species were an important food for the Indians. The names Camas or Quamash refer to the Indians of the Northwest.

242 WILD HELIOTROPE *(Phacelia sericea)* — Waterleaf family *(Hydrophyllaceae)*

Height: Perennial herb, 4"-18" (10-45cm). **Flowers:** In dense spikes on upper half of stem; calyx linear, deeply 5-lobed; corolla open bell-shaped, bluish purple to whitish, about 1/4″ (6mm) long; stamens 5, nearly twice as long as corolla, showy; style purplish, branched. **Leaves:** Much dissected, silky, silvery-haired, 1″-5″ (2.5-12cm) long. **In bloom:** June-July. **Habitat-Range:** Rocky slopes, coniferous forests, 7000′-8500′ (2200-2600m); California north to British Columbia, east to New Mexico, Rocky Mountains.

This Phacelia can be recognized by its silvery-silky hair, long showy stamens, and low perennial growth. It is seen on many mountain trails and ridges. The generic name, from the Greek *phakelos*, "cluster," describes the arrangement of the flowers, and *sericea*, the species name, means "silky." Other common names describe the plant: Silky Phacelia, Scorpionweed, Purple Fringe.

243 PENSTEMON *(Penstemon procerus)* Figwort family *(Scrophulariaceae)*

Height: Perennial herb, up to 18″ (45cm). **Flowers:** Clustered in whorls at top of stem; calyx lobes 5; corolla tubular, blue, about 1/2″ (1cm) long, 2-lipped, upper with 2 lobes, lower 3 lobes, tiny; stamens 5, one with no anther; style single. **Leaves:** Deep green, smooth, ovate, basal ones about 1/2″ (1cm) long, in rosette. **In bloom:** July-August. **Habitat-Range:** Rocky or grassy areas in coniferous forests to 11,000′ (3350m); California north to Oregon, Washington.

Penstemons are numerous, with many species. All can be recognized by the 2-lipped tubular flower that has four fertile stamens and one sterile, often with hairs instead of anther. The Greek name *penta*, "five," and *stemon*, "stamen," describes this.

244 MOUNTAIN PENSTEMON Figwort family *(Scrophulariaceae)*
(Penstemon montanus)

Height: Perennial herb, less than 12″ (30cm). **Flowers:** Borne in racemes from woody stems; calyx short, 5-toothed; corolla blue-lavender, tube 1/2″ (1cm) broad, 1 1/2″ (4cm) long; stamens 5, one without pollen; style single. **Leaves:** Opposite, stiff, lance-shaped, edges toothed. **In bloom:** May-June. **Habitat-Range:** High dry coniferous forests, to 9000′ (2750m); Rocky Mountains.

This low-growing mountain Penstemon has large, brightly colored flowers. A similar Rocky Mountain species, *P. fruticosus*, is also shrublike in growth, but taller.

245 STICKSEED *(Hackelia longituba)* Borage family *(Boraginaceae)*

Height: Perennial herb, 1′-2′ (.3-.6m). **Flowers:** In elongate panicle; calyx 5-lobed, shorter than corolla tube, green; corolla tubular for 1/4″ (6mm), then expanded into 5 lobes, 3/4″ (2cm) in diameter; lobes blue, tube pink, conspicuous white crest at base of each lobe about mouth of tube. **Leaves:** Alternate, broadly lance-shaped, 1″-4″ (2.5-10cm) long, softly hairy. **In bloom:** June-July. **Habitat-Range:** Dry slopes or flat situations in coniferous forests of the Sierra Nevada of California from 6000′ to 7500′.

This is one of several kinds of mountain Forget-me-nots, better known as Stickseed because of the hooks on the nutlets that adhere to clothing when the plant goes to seed.

246 WILD DAISY *(Erigeron formosissimus)* Sunflower family *(Compositae)*

Height: Perennial herb, 4″-16″ (10-40cm). **Flowers:** Heads solitary to several on stem,

1″-1 1/2″ (2.5-4cm) across; involucres glandular, sticky, ray flowers narrow, asterlike, blue; disc yellow. **Leaves:** Simple, lanceolate, smooth to hairy, 1″-6″ (2.5-15cm) long, larger near base of stem, which is curved. **In bloom:** July-September. **Habitat-Range:** Mountain meadows, openings in coniferous forests, medium to high elevations; Arizona, New Mexico north to Wyoming, South Dakota, Alberta.

This lovely asterlike daisy is common in late summer and early autumn in high meadows throughout most of the Rocky Mountains. *Erigeron* means "soon becoming old" and refers to the worn-out appearance of some species when in bloom.

247 HOUND'S TONGUE *(Cynoglossum grande)*   Borage family *(Boraginaceae)*

Height: Perennial herb, 1′-3′ (.3-1m). **Flowers:** In loosely coiled clusters; calyx deeply 5-parted with lobes about 1/2″ (1cm) long; corolla funnel-shaped; up to 1″ (2.5cm) long; pinkish in bud, blue when open, with white ring in throat. **Leaves:** Mostly basal; oval to lance-shaped, up to 6″ (15cm) on petioles equally long; hairy beneath. **In bloom:** March-June. **Habitat-Range:** Moist, shaded woods, mostly below 4000′ (1200m); California to Washington.

The flowers resemble a larger version of the cultivated Forget-me-not. Like many native plants, it was used by the Indians as a medicine. The roots were believed to be good for treating ulcers and colic and served as a poultice for scalds and burns.

248 SKULLCAP *(Scutellaria tuberosa)*   Mint family *(Labiatae)*

Height: Perennial herb, 2″-8″ (5-20cm). **Flowers:** Solitary in axils, up to 3/4″ (2cm) long; calyx 2-lipped, both lips entire, upper with crestlike projection on top; corolla violet-purple, tubular, 2-lipped with middle lobe of lower lip expanded. **Leaves:** Opposite, oval, slightly toothed, 1/2″-3/4″ (1-2cm) long; stems square. **In bloom:** March-July. **Habitat-Range:** Woodlands below 5000′ (1500m); southwestern Oregon to Baja California.

The name Skullcap is applied to the nearly 100 species of *Scutellaria* because of the skull-like crest on the back of the upper lip of the calyx. All have aromatic herbage.

249 LARKSPUR   Buttercup family *(Ranunculaceae)*
(Delphinium tenuisectum)

Height: Perennial herb, up to 30″ (75cm). **Flowers:** In loose raceme with leaflike bracts; sepals 5, dark blue, uppermost with long tubular spur, up to 1 1/4″ (3cm) long; petals 4, upper 2 with spurs extending into spur of sepal; dark blue. **Leaves:** Divided twice into narrow lobes. **In bloom:** July-August. **Habitat-Range:** Open woodlands, mountains of Arizona, New Mexico.

This is a large and deep-blue member of the genus *Delphinium* that extends barely northward from Mexico into the southwestern states. The name Larkspur refers to the upper sepal, which has a clawlike spur as the spur or long claw of the lark.

250 PURPLE MILKWEED   Milkweed family *(Asclepiadaceae)*
(Asclepias cordifolia)

Height: Perennial herb, 1′-2 1/2′ (.3-.8m). **Flowers:** In loose, many-flowered umbels;

calyx 5-lobed, reflexed, purple; corolla 5-lobed, each reflexed with concavity or hood at top, 1/4″ (6mm) long, purplish; stamens 5. **Leaves:** Opposite, cordate, clasping stem, 2″-4″ (5-10cm) long, greenish blue or with purplish tinge; juice milky. **In bloom:** May-July. **Habitat-Range:** Open slopes in woodland, 500′-6000′ (150-1800m); California, Oregon, western Nevada.

Milkweeds are strange flowers with the corolla reflexed and a concavity or so-called hood at the crest of each lobe. Most have horns or crests on the hoods, but these are lacking in the Purple Milkweed. All have a white latex that exudes from cut leaves or stems, somewhat resembling the Euphorbias. Some species have medicinal uses but others are quite poisonous. The Indians used the tough inner bark of certain Milkweeds to make string and rope.

251 HAIRY VERBENA *(Verbena gooddingii)*   Verbena family *(Verbenaceae)*

Height: Perennial herb, 5″-18″ (12.5-45cm). **Flowers:** In headlike spike about 1/2″ (1cm) across; calyx tubular, 5-toothed; corolla tubular, purplish, with 5 spreading lobes, slightly irregular, about 1/4″ (6mm) across, purplish. **Leaves:** 1/2″-3/4″ (1-2cm) long, divided, lobed, hairy, more or less glandular. **In bloom:** April-June. **Habitat-Range:** Dry areas, especially in Pinyon-Juniper woodland, 4000′-6500′ (1200-1800m); eastern Mojave Desert east to Utah, Arizona.

This is a colorful native member of a genus better known in many parts of western North America for its weeds or cultivated species.

252 GREAT BASIN BLUE SAGE *(Salvia dorrii)*   Mint family *(Labiatae)*

Height: Low shrub, 1′-3′ (.3-1m). **Flowers:** In whorls with conspicuous purplish green bracts edged with hairs; calyx 2-lipped, lower deeply notched; corolla blue, 2-lipped, up to 1/2″ (1cm) long, stamen projecting. **Leaves:** Opposite, roundish to spade-shaped, up to 1/2″ (1cm) long, densely whitish; scurfy. **In bloom:** May-July. **Habitat-Range:** Principally Pinyon-Juniper woodlands, Sagebrush scrub, 2500′-10,000′ (750-3050m); southeastern California east to Arizona, north to eastern Washington, Idaho.

This colorful, much-branched shrub, also known as Blue Sage and Purple Sage, is widespread over the Great Basin region, extending to the north and south. Like all Sages, the herbage is aromatic.

253 SILVERY LUPINE *(Lupinus argenteus)*   Pea family *(Leguminosae)*

Height: Perennial herb, 1′-2′ (.3-.6m). **Flowers:** In dense racemes 2 1/2″-4 1/2″ (7-11cm) long; calyx 2-lipped, upper notched, lower entire; corolla blue to purple, 1/2″ (1cm) long, 5-parted, upper petal or banner broad, finely hairy on back, lateral wings smooth, keel of ventral petals with hairs on borders; pods up to 1″ (2.5cm) long, hairy. **Leaves:** Alternate, palmately compound, 1″-2″ (2.5-5cm) long, leaflets 5-9, silky. **In bloom:** June-October. **Habitat-Range:** Dry flats, principally in Pinyon- Juniper and Sagebrush scrub but also locally into Bristlecone Pine areas, 4000′-10,500′ (1200-3200m); California east to New Mexico, north to Oregon, Montana.

Most of the 200 or so species of Lupines in North America have colorful blossoms and are recognizable readily to genus but much less readily to species. Lupine *(Lupinus)* comes from the Latin *lupus*, "wolf," because the plants were believed to rob the soil of nourishment. Actually, Lupines benefit soil by the presence of bacteria in nodules on their roots, that take nitrogen from the air and turn it into compounds that fertilize the soil.

254 ONE-SIDED PENSTEMON
(Penstemon secundiflorus)

Figwort family *(Scrophulariaceae)*

Height: Perennial herb, 1'-2' (.3-.6m). **Flowers:** In showy, one-sided raceme; calyx short, with 5 parts, each terminating in slender, outcurved point; corolla 1"-1 1/2" (2.5-4cm) long; tubular, 2-lipped with 2 lobes above, 3 below; pinkish blue to magenta in bud, becoming pale blue when open; stamens 2 long, 2 short with anthers hairy. **Leaves:** Opposite, clasping stem, smooth, grayish green; fleshy; 2"-4" (5-10cm) long; ovate to lance-shaped. **In bloom:** May-July. **Habitat-Range:** Abundant on mesas and foothills of the Great Basin and Rocky Mountains.

This is frequently seen along roadsides in Rocky Mountain canyons of Nevada, Utah, and Colorado. Here it is classified as blue because the mature flowers are pale blue, but when young, the buds are often pink.

255 CANCHALAGUA
(Centaurium venustum)

Gentian family *(Gentianaceae)*

Height: Annual herb, 4"-12" (10-30cm). **Flowers:** Few to many in corymb; calyx lobes 5, deeply divided, about 1/2" (1cm) long; corolla tube as long as calyx, rose with red spots in white throat, or all white; lobes 5, ovate, about 3/4" (2cm) long; stamens 5, alternating with corolla lobes; style single with fan-shaped tip. **Leaves:** Opposite, simple, oblong, 1/2"-1" (1-2.5cm) long. **In bloom:** May-August. **Habitat-Range:** Chaparral, coniferous forests below 6000' (1800m); coastal southern California to Sierra Nevada.

This delicate little annual does not resemble the blue Gentians so common to this family. The generic name is supposed to refer to the mythical centaur because he introduced the medicinal use of the plant to heal a wound. The popular Spanish name derives from the language of Arauco, a district of Chile: *cachan* means "pain in the side," and *lahuen*, "medicinal herb."

256 STICKY PHACELIA
(Phacelia viscida)

Waterleaf family *(Hydrophyllaceae)*

Height: 1'-2' (.3-.6m). **Flowers:** Few to many in terminal raceme; calyx lobes linear to spatulate; corolla deeply saucer-shaped, up to 3/4" (2cm) in diameter, deep blue with whitish center; stamens not extending beyond corolla. **Leaves:** Roundish, slightly toothed, 1"-3" (2.5-7cm) long, with or without short petiole on simple or slightly branched stem; herbage hairy, glandular. **In bloom:** February-June. **Habitat-Range:** Open sandy situations in Coast Ranges of central and southern California and on the Channel Islands.

This colorful species of Phacelia has relatively large, deep blue flowers with white centers. It may be found in chaparral but grows best in disturbed land. *P. grandiflora* is a closely related species, more robust and taller, with leaves up to 6" (15cm) long. It occurs in coastal southern California and in northern Baja California.

257 PURPLE NIGHTSHADE   Nightshade family *(Solanaceae)*
(Solanum xanti)

Height: Perennial herb, 16″-36″ (.4-1m) tall or creeping. **Flowers:** Few in umbel; calyx tube about 1/4″ (6mm) long, 5 short lobes; corolla light blue, aging darker, 1/2″-1″ (1-2.5cm) broad, wheel-shaped, with 5 short teeth; stamens 5, attached to corolla; style short, fruit green berry. **Leaves:** Ovate, 3/4″-3″ (2-7cm) long, green or hairy gray. **In bloom:** February-June. **Habitat-Range:** Dry brushy places below 4000′ (1200m); California.

The name of this group of plants comes from the Latin *solamen,* "quieting," because of the narcotic in some species. The alkaloid poison solanine is present in the berries, tubers, and herbage. The Potato, which is made safe by cooking, belongs to this group. Most plants in this family possess poisonous or acrid qualities, and many have been cultivated: Pepper, Chilis, Tomato, Tobacco, Belladonna, and decorative Petunias and Bittersweet.

JIM BRUSH *(Ceanothus sorediatus)*   Buckthorn family *(Rhamnaceae)*

Height: Erect shrub, 4′-7′ (1-2m). **Flowers:** Small, in terminal or subterminal panicles, 1/2″-1 1/4″ (3cm) long, on branchlets; calyx 5-lobed; petals 5, blue or sometimes whitish with long slender bases, hooded or concave at apex; stamens 5. **Leaves:** Ovate, edged with glandular teeth, 1/2″-1″ (1-2.5cm) long, on numerous rigid branchlets. **In bloom:** February-May. **Habitat-Range:** Chaparral slopes below 3500′ (1050m); western California.

Jim Brush is another of the many kinds of so-called "Wild Lilac." Despite the fact that its branches are greatly divided into short, very rigid, almost spiny branchlets, it is a favorite food for deer. The leaves and flowers have been used for making tea.

258 CHINESE HOUSES *(Collinsia bicolor)*   Figwort family *(Scrophulariaceae)*

Height: Annual herb, 6″-18″ (15-45cm). **Flowers:** Several in whorl-like clusters with bracts; calyx bell-shaped, 5-lobed; petals in angled, expanded tube, blue-lavender, 2-lipped, upper about 1/2″ (1cm) long, lower 3-lobed, larger; stamens 4 in 2 pairs within middle lobe of lower lip; style single, enclosed. **Leaves:** Lance-shaped, opposite, smooth, 3/4″-2″ (2-5cm) long. **In bloom:** April-June. **Habitat-Range:** Chaparral below 5500′ (1650m); California.

These bright little flowers are common along the edges of bushy thickets, especially after good spring rains. The whorls of blooms suggest to the imagination oriental pagodas, hence the common name. The generic name honors a Philadelphia botanist of the late eighteenth century, Zaccheus Collins.

259 SAND VERBENA *(Abronia villosa)*   Four O'clock family *(Nyctaginaceae)*

Height: Annual herb, trailing 4″-20″ (10-50cm). **Flowers:** Borne in heads with involucre of 5-8 bracts; calyx tubular; corolla purplish rose, tubular, about 1/2″ (1cm) long, limb about as broad, 5-lobed; stamens 5; style single within tube. **Leaves:** Glandular, hairy, ovate, 1/2″-1 1/2″ (1-4cm) long, petioles almost as long. **In bloom:** February-July. **Habitat-Range:** Open sandy deserts below 3000′ (900m); southern California, Nevada east to Arizona, south to Baja California.

These flowers are fragrant and showy, blooming in the deserts especially after rain. The foliage is adapted by its glands and hairs to restrict evaporation of water. The generic name is from the Greek *abros*, "graceful," referring to the delicate flower heads.

HELIOTROPE PHACELIA   Waterleaf family *(Hydrophyllaceae)*
(Phacelia crenulata)

Height: Annual herb, 1'-2' (.3-.6m). **Flowers:** In dense scorpioid racemes; sepals 5, linear, glandular, hairy; corolla open-campanulate, approximately 1/2" (1cm) in diameter, lobes violet to purple-blue with throat white. **Leaves:** 1"-3 1/2" (2.5-8cm) long; undulately lobed or pinnate; thick, green with stems reddish, hairy, very glandular, strong-scented. **In bloom:** March-July. **Habitat-Range:** Desert valleys, mesas, generally below 5000' (1500m); southern California to Utah, Colorado.

This Phacelia is a common desert species, especially in washes, where its dense violet racemes, long stamens and glandular-hairy herbage provide clear details for field identification. Many persons are sensitive to its glandular secretion, which may cause a severe dermatitis.

WILD HELIOTROPE   Waterleaf family *(Hydrophyllaceae)*
(Phacelia tanacetifolia)

Height: Annual herb, 1'-3' (.3-1m). **Flower:** In coiled raceme on branched, hairy, glandular stem; calyx of 5 narrow, hairy sepals; corolla somewhat bell-shaped, blue to lavender; 5 stamens extending considerably beyond corolla. **Leaves:** Pinnately divided, fernlike, with scattered hairs. **In bloom:** February-May. **Habitat-Range:** In valleys, desert areas, usually below 4000' (1200m); Nevada, Arizona, California, as well as coastal southern California.

This species is often called Wild Heliotrope because of the appearance of its flower clusters, although it is not a member of the Borage family. It is common throughout much of the Southwest and is readily recognized by its divided, fernlike foliage and coiled inflorescence. In some areas it is one of the most conspicuous spring wildflowers. The genus is a large one with about 200 species, most of them in western North America.

260 BROOM RAPE   Broom-rape family *(Orobanchaceae)*
(Orobanche ludoviciana)†

Height: Parasitic herb, 4"-12" (10-30cm). **Flowers:** Many in spike with bracts; calyx in 5 unequal segments, 1/3 as long as corolla tube; petals purple, joined in curved tube about 1" (2.5cm) long, 5 lance-shaped lobes, erect from tube in 2 lips; stamens 4, in 2 pairs; style long, 2-lobed at tip. **Leaves:** Scalelike, lacking chlorophyll (green pigment). **In bloom:** January-May. **Habitat-Range:** Deserts below 4000' (1200m); southern California to Nevada, New Mexico, Texas, Mexico. Parasitic largely on the composite *Franseria dumosa* and cultivated tomato plants.

The parasitic plants in this genus are sometimes called Cancer Root because they obtain their nutrients from living material. The generic name, from the Greek *orobos*, "vetch," and *anchone*, "to choke," refers to this characteristic. Broom Rape is so called because the species lives on the Broom plant, which is related to the Vetch.

128

261 **CANTERBURY BELL**   Waterleaf family *(Hydrophyllaceae)*
(Phacelia campanularia)

Height: Annual herb, up to 2′ (.6m). **Flowers:** In elongate scorpioid racemes; pedicels 1/2″-1 1/2″ (1-4cm) long; sepals linear, glandular; corolla tubular, 5-lobed, 1″-1 1/2″ (2.5-4cm) long; deep blue; stamens barely extending beyond corolla. **Leaves:** Cordate, round, or slightly elongate with irregular edges; pubescent; glandular. **In bloom:** February-May. **Habitat-Range:** Mesas and deserts; southern California.

This Phacelia is known by several names including Canterbury Bell, California Bluebell and Desert Bluebell. It is probably the most striking member of a genus containing many beautiful species. The racemes are not closely coiled because of the large size of the deep blue corollas.

BLADDER SAGE *(Salazaria mexicana)*   Mint family *(Labiatae)*

Height: Deciduous shrub, 2′-3′ (.6-1m). **Flowers:** In loose, spikelike racemes; calyx 2-lipped, inflated at maturity into papery sac 1″ (2.5cm) across, tinged with rose; corolla 2-lipped, purple, upper lip arched, forming hood over stamens, 1/2″-3/4″ (1-2cm) long. **Leaves:** Lance-shaped, 1/2″-3/4″ (1-2cm) long, soon lost; stems weakly spiny. **In bloom:** March-June. **Habitat-Range:** Desert washes, foothills below 5000′ (1500m); southern California east to Texas, north to Utah.

Bladder Sage is often called Paper Bag Shrub because of the inflated papery calyx. It is the only member of the genus *Salazaria*, named in honor of Don José Salazar, a Mexican commissioner on the early boundary survey.

262 **DESERT CANDLE** *(Streptanthus inflatus)*   Mustard family *(Cruciferae)*

Height: Annual herb, 1′-2 1/2′ (.3-.75m). **Flowers:** In racemes arising from inflated stem; calyx 4-parted, about 1/4″ (6mm) long, purple in bud; petals 4, white, slightly longer than sepals. **Leaves:** Oblong, sessile, 1 1/2″-5″ (4-12cm) long, smooth. **In bloom:** March-May. **Habitat-Range:** Dry hills, grasslands, desert edges below 5000′ (1500m); interior valleys, Mojave Desert of southern California.

This unique member of the Mustard family has a stem that enlarges from the base to the middle, then tapers toward the top, where a small dense group of flowers may look like a purple flame. Although the petals are white, the purple sepals are more conspicuous. Because the seeds are not flattened it is sometimes placed in the genus *Caulanthus*.

JEWEL FLOWER   Mustard family *(Cruciferae)*
(Streptanthus glandulosus)

Height: Annual herb, 1′-2′ (.3-.6m). **Flowers:** In lax racemes, 2″-12″ (5-30cm) long; sepals 4, oval, purple; petals 4, about 1/2″ (1cm) long, recurved, purple or white with purple veins; pods 2″-4″ (5-10cm) long, slender. **Leaves:** Lance-shaped to linear, coarsely toothed, 1″-3″ (2.5-7.5cm) long, clasping stem. **In bloom:** April-May. **Habitat-Range:** Dry rocky ridges or disturbed soil, principally in grassy foothills or low ranges below 4000′ (1200m); Coast Ranges of central California.

Many of the approximately 25 species of *Streptanthus* in the West are difficult to segregate. Even *S. glandulosa* has a number of varieties. However, Jewel Flowers,

129

probably so named because of their small, richly purple-colored flowers, are commonly encountered. The 4-parted flowers and long linear seed pods readily identify them as members of the Mustard family.

263 BLUEBONNET *(Lupinus texensis)*   Pea family *(Leguminosae)*

Height: Annual herb, up to 2′ (.6m). **Flowers:** In dense terminal raceme 2″-6″ (5-15cm) long; calyx 2-lipped, 1/4″ (6mm) long; corolla pealike or butterfly-like with 5 deep blue petals, uppermost or banner broader than wings (lateral petals) with white spot dotted with yellow-green that turns red with age. **Leaves:** Palmately compound with 4-7 leaflets, hairy on both sides. **In bloom:** April-May. **Habitat-Range:** Widely distributed in calcareous soils, grasslands of central Texas.

The Bluebonnet is the state flower of Texas. It is readily distinguished from *L. subcarnosus*, also known as the Bluebonnet and the Big Bend Bluebonnet, which has a lemon-yellow spot on the banner and silvery hairs on the herbage.

264 OWL'S CLOVER (ESCOBITA)   Figwort family *(Scrophulariaceae)*
(Orthocarpus purpurascens)

Height: Annual herb, up to 1 1/4′ (.4m). **Flowers:** In terminal spikes; calyx tubular, lobed; corolla purple, 3/4″-1 1/4″ (2-3cm) long with 2 lips; lower lip tipped with white, dotted with yellow, purple; upper lip exceeding lower, with purple hairs on back; numerous narrowly divided purple bracts. **Leaves:** Divided into many narrow linear segments; pubescent. **In bloom:** March-May. **Habitat-Range:** Widespread in California, usually below 2000′ (600m); sea coast to the Mohave Desert.

In years of good winter and spring rains the valleys and hills of many parts of California may be tinted purple from masses of Owl's Clover in bloom. Its most common associates are Baby Blue-eyes, California Poppies, Goldfields, and Popcorn Flowers, all of which may provide much color. The Spanish name Escobita means "Little Broom," a reference to the shape of the inflorescence.

265 WESTERN LARKSPUR   Buttercup family *(Ranunculaceae)*
(Delphinium hesperium)

Height: Perennial herb, 1 1/2′-3′ (.5-1m). **Flowers:** In terminal racemes; commonly blue; sepals 5, 1/4″-1/2″ (6-12mm) long, pubescent on back, usually blue, uppermost with elongate spur at base; petals 4 in unequal pairs, shorter than sepals. **Leaves:** 2-3 times palmately cleft into linear segments; herbage finely pubescent. **In bloom:** April-July. **Habitat-Range:** Dry open ground at lower elevations throughout much of California.

This is one of the common western species of Larkspur. It occasionally has pink or white flowers. Members of the genus *Delphinium* can be recognized easily by the long spur on the base of the uppermost sepal.

266 LOCOWEED *(Astragalus amphioxys)*   Pea family *(Leguminosae)*

Height: Prostrate perennial herb. **Flowers:** In terminal racemes of 4-10; calyx 5-toothed; corolla purplish with pinkish tinge, pealike, upper petal or banner 1/2″-1″ (1-2.5cm) long; pod crescent-shaped, inflated. **Leaves:** Odd-pinnate, silvery haired on short, prostrate stems. **In bloom:** March-June. **Habitat-Range:** Grassy areas, northern Arizona, southern Nevada east to Colorado, New Mexico.

This is one of the small species of Locoweeds, but it has large beautiful flowers and silvery leaves and stems. It belongs to a group poisonous to stock because it extracts selenium from the soil. The generic name comes from the Greek *astragalos,* meaning ankle bone, which was used for some leguminous plants.

LOCOWEED *(Oxytropis sericea)*   Pea family *(Leguminosae)*

Height: Perennial herb, 6″-16″ (15-40cm). **Flowers:** In spikelike racemes, 10-25 flowered, each about 1″ (2.5cm) long; calyx 5-toothed; corolla long, narrow, with 5 petals, 2 lower joined to form keel, upper petal about 1/4″ (6mm) long; white or tinged lilac on keel; pod somewhat inflated, 1/2″ (1cm) long, 1/2″ (1cm) in diameter. **Leaves:** 2″-8″ (5-20cm) long; pinnate with 23-41 leaflets; silky. **In bloom:** May-August. **Habitat-Range:** Moist meadows from Alaska to California, east to Manitoba, northern New Mexico.

Locoweeds are legumes, mostly with inflated pods, that occur over the Northern Hemisphere, especially at high altitudes. They are disliked by stockmen because certain species are poisonous to sheep, cattle, and horses, causing death or derangement, which is responsible for the common name, "Locoweed."

267 LOBELIA *(Lobelia anatina)*   Bluebell family *(Campanulaceae)*

Height: Annual herb, 6″-28″ (15-70cm). **Flowers:** In loose raceme; calyx 5-lobed; corolla blue-purple, 2-lipped, 1/2″-1″ (1-2.5cm) long, united into short tube, 2 small lobes in upper lip, 3 in lower; stamens 5, united by anthers around single style emerging from slit in corolla tube. **Leaves:** Single, lance-shaped, up to 3″ (7.5cm) long. **In bloom:** July-October. **Habitat-Range:** Stream banks, marshes, grasslands; southern New Mexico, Arizona, into Mexico.

This flower has a very specialized structure and method of fertilization. It opens with the cylinder of stamens and style elongating outside a slit in the corolla tube. The style continues to elongate with the tips closed and picks up pollen but is not fertilized. Hummingbirds and bees collecting nectar pick up pollen and transfer it to another flower, which may be more developed and ready for fertilization. This genera is named for a sixteenth-century botanist from Flanders, Mathias de L'Obel. Many beautiful Lobelias are cultivated.

268/ /269 PASQUE FLOWER *(Anemone patens)*   Buttercup family *(Ranunculaceae)*

Height: Perennial herb, 2″-16″ (5-40cm). **Flowers:** Single at end of stems with leafy involucre; calyx with 6 lavender, purple, or white lobes about 1″ (2.5cm) long; petals none; stamens numerous, short; styles numerous, becoming long, feathery on ripening. **Leaves:** Basal, divided into narrow, linear lobes, silky with white hairs. **In bloom:** March-June. **Habitat-Range:** Texas, New Mexico north to Alaska, east to Illinois.

There are about 14 species of *Anemone* in the Rocky Mountains alone. This one, which is the state flower of South Dakota, is unique in its low-growing habit and being covered with fine white hair. The head of the flower is covered with featherlike plumes when the seeds ripen and might be confused with the Sugarbowl *(Clematis hirsutissima),* which, however, has opposite stem leaves. The common name Pasque refers to the early spring blooming of the flower. *Anemone* is from the Greek *anemos*, wind. Other common names are Windflower, Prairie Anemone, Blue Tulip, Wild Crows, and American Pulsatilla.

270 WILD GERANIUM *(Erodium texanum)*   Geranium family *(Geraniaceae)*

Height: Annual herb, stems prostrate, 4"-16" (10-40cm). **Flowers:** In clusters of 1-3; calyx 5-lobed, about 3/8" (8mm) long, silvery with purple veins; petals 5, purple, twice as long as calyx; stamens 5; styles 5, united on column about 2" (5cm) long. **Leaves:** Opposite, palmately 3-5 lobed, 1/2"-2" (1-5cm) long, ovate or triangular, basal, long-petioled. **In bloom:** March-May. **Habitat-Range:** Sandy-grassy places below 3500' (1050m); southern California east to Texas, south into Baja California.

This group of plants is called Stork's Bill because of the elongated fruit. The generic name comes from the Greek *eridios*, heron. Other common names are Cranesbill, Filaree, Pinkets, Alfilaria. The seeds with their long plumes are also called clocks because of the interesting way in which they twist and turn with changes in humidity, thus working into the ground. The plants germinate in late fall, waiting until spring to continue growth and bloom. The young plants are edible either raw or cooked.

271 BLUE-EYED GRASS *(Sisyrinchium bellum)*   Iris family *(Iridaceae)*

Height: Perennial herb, 4"-16" (10-40cm). **Flowers:** In umbels of 2-7; open, starlike; composed of 6 perianth (sepals, petals) segments, each with terminal toothlike projection; up to 1" (2.5cm) in diameter; blue to purple. **Leaves:** Grasslike; mostly basal; erect, shorter than stem. **In bloom:** March-May. **Habitat-Range:** Moist, grassy slopes, mostly below 3000' (900m); throughout California.

Several related species occur in western North America. *S. douglasii* has purplish red flowers and occurs from Nevada and California north to British Columbia. *S. idahoense*, which ranges from Washington and Idaho southward, has a simple, leafless stem. Yellow-eyed Grass *(S. elmeri)* differs in having bright yellow flowers and is a montane species found in wet situations above 4000' (1200m).

BLUE DICKS *(Brodiaea pulchella)*   Lily family *(Liliaceae)*

Height: 1/2'-3' (.2-1m). **Flowers:** In headlike umbel surrounded by 4 purplish bracts at apex of erect stem; perianth 3/4" (2cm) long, blue to dark purple. **Leaves:** Few; grasslike. **In bloom:** February-May. **Habitat-Range:** Hillsides, plains; Arizona, California to Washington.

This is one of the lilies most persons know well. Common throughout most of its range, it grows mostly in open grassy areas where its dense flower heads on tall, slender stems are usually conspicuous. The bulbs are edible but should be cooked to remove their mucilaginous quality. They are best roasted in ashes.

SPIDERWORT *(Tradescantia occidentalis)*   Spiderwort family *(Commelinaceae)*

Height: Perennial herb, 2' (.6m). **Flowers:** In terminal clusters with involucre of 2 long leaflike bracts; calyx 3-lobed; petals 3, about 1″ (2.5cm) long, blue to rose-violet; stamens 6, unequal length; style 3-branched; capsule 3-celled. **Leaves:** Alternate, long, narrow, grasslike. **In bloom:** March-June. **Habitat-Range:** Prairies, rocky places, Wisconsin, Manitoba south to Arizona, Texas, and Mexico.

The Spiderworts are hybridized and cultivated in much of the warmer parts of the Great Basin and Texas, requiring little care and offering an attractive border with delicate blue flowers. Because the blooms last only one day, another common name for them is Day Flower. *T. fluminensis*, a trailing variety, has long been grown as the house plant known as Wandering Jew. The genus is named for John Tradescant, botanical explorer of the seventeenth century, gardener to Queen Henrietta Maria of England, and founder of a museum of natural history in Lambeth.

272 PRAIRIE GENTIAN *(Eustoma grandiflorum)*   Gentian family *(Gentianaceae)*

Height: Perennial herb, 1′-2′ (.3-.6m). **Flowers:** Blue, showy, single on stem; calyx deeply 5-lobed; corolla bell-shaped, about 1″ (2.5cm) long, 5-6 lobes; stamens 5-6, attached to throat of corolla; style single, 2-lobed. **Leaves:** Smooth, 1″-2″ (2.5-5cm) long, in pairs on stem and in basal rosette. **In bloom:** June-August. **Habitat-Range:** Open grassland; New Mexico, Texas north to Nebraska.

A structural difference in the style separates this genus from the *Gentiana*. The appearance of the blue flowers is similar; a common name Bluebell is often used for it. The generic name, from the Greek, *eu*, good, and *stoma*, mouth, describes the large opening to the corolla throat.

273 BLUE GILIA *(Gilia rigidula)*   Phlox family *(Polemoniaceae)*

Height: Perennial herb, 4″-12″ (10-30cm). **Flowers:** Usually solitary on 1″ (2.5cm) long pedicels; calyx 5-lobed; corolla with 5 large lobes, almost lacking tube, bright blue; yellow rim at mouth of tube; stamens 5. **Leaves:** Alternate, pinnately divided into 3-7 narrow, stiff lobes. **In bloom:** April-September. **Habitat-Range:** Dry prairie lands from southern Arizona to central Texas, north to Kansas.

Blue Gilia is an elaborately branched perennial herb arising from a thick woody base. The leaves vary from smooth to sticky glandular.

274 PRAIRIE VIOLET *(Viola pedatifida)*   Violet family *(Violaceae)*

Height: Perennial herb, 4″-10″ (10-25cm). **Flowers:** Solitary, terminal, nodding, 3/4″-1″ (2-2.5cm) across; sepals 5; petals 5, pale violet with whitish bases, dark veins. **Leaves:** Twice or 3 times divided into linear lobes, 1 1/2″-2″ (4-5cm) long. **In bloom:** May-June. **Habitat-Range:** Prairie grasslands from central Arizona, New Mexico north to Alberta, east to Ohio, Missouri.

This violet of open prairies is distinguished by its large, pale violet flowers and leaves that are divided into narrow toelike lobes, which accounts for the species name.

275 TOWNSENDIA *(Townsendia incana)*   Sunflower family *(Compositae)*

Height: Perennial herb, up to 8″ (20cm). **Flowers:** In 1-3 aster-like heads; involucre less than 1/2″ (1cm), bracts in several series; rays about 13, 3/8″ (8mm) long, lilac to white, disc yellow. **Leaves:** Entire, small, spatula-shaped, stem covered with whitish down. **In bloom:** May-September. **Habitat-Range:** Prairies, mesas; Arizona, New Mexico north to Wyoming.

Townsendias, small asterlike composites with undivided leaves, occur mostly in the Rocky Mountain region in dry grassland. The genus is named after David Townsend, an amateur botanist from Pennsylvania.

PURPLE SANICLE *(Sanicula bipinnatifida)*   Parsley family *(Umbelliferae)*

Height: Perennial herb, 6"-18" (15-45cm). **Flowers:** Both perfect, staminate together in small umbels 3/8" (8mm) in diameter; reddish-purple. **Leaves:** Mostly toward base; pinnately divided; often purplish. **In bloom:** March-May. **Habitat-Range:** Grassy slopes from southern California to Canada.

This sanicle with small but conspicuous purple flower heads begins blooming about one month after its relative, Footsteps-of-spring *(S. arctopoides)*.

276 MOUNTAIN IRIS *(Iris douglasiana)*   Iris Family *(Iridaceae)*

Height: 1'-2' (.3-.6m). **Flowers:** In axils of bracts, large, composed of 6 petal-like elements arranged in 2 whorls; outer 3 large, recurved, inner 3 erect; 3 stamens attached to base of outer whorl; ovary inferior, 3-lobed; perianth elements usually bluish purple with purple veins, often striped with white, yellow; perianth pink, yellow, or white. **Leaves:** Narrow, swordlike, often exceeding stem in length; drying reddish brown. **In bloom:** February-June. **Habitat-Range:** Common in coastal California, Oregon, and northern Sierra Nevada.

Many kinds of iris grow in the Northern Hemisphere and some species have been cultivated. All are most distinctive because of the three erect petals, the three reflexed sepals, and the three petal-like branches of the style. One of the most widespread species is Western Blue Flag *(I. missouriensis)*, which ranges from the Dakotas west to the Pacific coast. It is less variable in color than Mountain Iris and has pale violet flowers. Fibers from the leaves of the Mountain Iris were used by Pacific coast Indians to make rope.

277 GROUND CHERRY *(Quincula lobata)*   Nightshade family *(Solanaceae)*

Height: Perennial spreading herb, stems up to 1' (.3m). **Flowers:** In axillary pairs; calyx bell-shaped, becoming enlarged to contain fruit; corolla of 5 petals united to form open, flat funnel, 3/4"-1" (2-2.5cm) across, bluish purple; stamens 5 with yellow anthers, tinged with purple. **Leaves:** Alternate, entire, oblong to spade-shaped, irregularly toothed, 1 1/2"-3" (4-7.5cm) long. **In bloom:** March-October. **Habitat-Range:** Plains, roadsides, Arizona east to Texas, north to Kansas.

This species is often placed with the other Ground Cherries in the genus *Physalis*. However, it has a purplish rather than yellow corolla. In some areas it is called Chinese Lantern-of-the-Plains because of the hanging bladder-like calyx that encases the fruit. It does well in cultivation and is very drought-resistant. The fruits of some kinds of Ground Cherries are edible, but caution is advised because this group contains such poisonous plants as Belladonna and Henbane as well as edible kinds like Potatoes, Tomatoes, and Peppers.

BUFFALO BURR *(Solanum heterodoxum)*   Nightshade family *(Solanaceae)*

Height: Annual herb, 6″-32″ (15-80cm). **Flowers:** In cymes; calyx large, bell-shaped, with 5 lobes; corolla 1/2″-1 1/2″ (1-4cm) across, 5-cleft, violet; stamens 5, yellow, with one much larger, darker than others. **Leaves:** Alternate, irregularly twice pinnate, 1″-5″ (2.5-12cm) long, hairy, prickly, glandular. **In bloom:** July-September. **Habitat-Range:** Dry areas; Colorado south to Arizona, east to Texas.

Though many species of *Solanum* are poisonous, others include edible plants such as the potato. *S. rostratum*, which ranges from California east to the Great Plains, has a yellow corolla; *S. elaeagnifolium* of the Great Plains has a blue-violet corolla.

278 SEASIDE DAISY *(Erigeron glaucus)*   Sunflower family *(Compositae)*

Height: Perennial herb, 6″-12″ (15-30cm). **Flowers:** Heads solitary to few on stem, 1 1/4″-1 1/2″ (3-4cm) across; involucre bell-shaped, up to 1/2″ (1cm) long; ray flowers about 100, 3/8″-1/2″ (8-12mm) long, pale violet to lavender; disc yellow. **Leaves:** Finely hairy, somewhat sticky, gray-green; alternate, mostly basal, spade-shaped, 1″-4″ (2.5-10cm) long, sometimes with teeth near tip. **In bloom:** March-August. **Habitat-Range:** Coastal bluffs, sand dunes; southern California to Oregon.

This is one of the typical seaside plants of California and Oregon. It was introduced into England early in the nineteenth century and cultivated as a garden plant.

279 CLIFF SPURGE *(Euphorbia misera)*   Spurge family *(Euphorbiaceae)*

Height: Much-branched shrub, 2′-3′ (.6-1m). **Flowers:** Few in solitary, terminal involucres; sepals, petals lacking; glands of involucre purple with white, toothed appendages. **Leaves:** Round to ovate, 1/4″-1/2″ (6-12mm) long. **In bloom:** January-August. **Habitat-Range:** Coastal bluffs, scrub; southern California, Baja California.

The Cliff Spurge, while a coastal species in most of southern California, ranges inland farther south, and is widely distributed in Baja California, both at and away from the coast. Like other members of the genus it has a milky juice.

280 AMERICAN VETCH *(Vicia americana)*   Pea family *(Leguminosae)*

Height: Perennial herb, trailing 2′-3′ (.6-1m). **Flowers:** 4-9 in racemes on stalks; calyx in 5 unequal, narrowly toothed parts; Petals 5, purplish blue, irregular, butterfly-like, 3/4″ (2cm) long; stamens 9 joined in tube around pistil, 1 enclosed in lower petal; style with tuft of hairs below tip; fruit, pea pod 1 1/4″-2″ (3-5cm) long. **Leaves:** Pinnate with 4-8 pairs of leaflets, ovate, 1/2″-1 3/4″ (1-4cm) long, terminal tendril. **In bloom:** April-June. **Habitat-Range:** Grassy places below 5000′ (1500m); California north to British Columbia, east to Idaho.

Like Sweet Peas, another member of the Pea family, Vetch supports its stems and climbs by means of tendrils. In the wild it often grows into long vines supported by shrubs and trees. The young seeds in the pea pods are edible and enjoyed by man and animals.

281 SICKLE-LEAVED ONION *(Allium falcifolium)*   Lily family *(Liliaceae)*

Height: Perennial herb, 2″-4″ (5-10cm). **Flowers:** In dense umbel of 20-30 on pedicels

1/2″ (1cm); perianth segments 6, lance-shaped, purple to rose, sometimes tinged green. **Leaves:** 2, sickle-shaped, narrow, longer than flower stem. **In bloom:** March-July. **Habitat-Range:** Rocky soil or outcrops, 500′-8000′ (150-2450m); Coast Ranges of central California to southern Oregon.

Allium is a very large genus containing about 500 species. It is the Latin name for garlic that, like onions, chives, and their relatives, was derived from a wild species of *Allium*. Sickle-leaved Onion is an attractive species with its rose-purple flowers and preference for rocky areas. Like all onions it grows from a tunicated or layered bulb that may be cooked in various ways or eaten raw.

282 ITHURIEL'S SPEAR *(Brodiaea laxa)*   Lily family *(Liliaceae)*

Height: Perennial herb, 1′-2 1/4′ (.3-.7m). **Flowers:** Borne in 8-48 flowered umbel on pedicels joined at stem; perianth tube violet-purple, rarely white, 1 1/4″-1 3/4″ (3-4cm) long, funnel-shaped, 6 lobes shorter than tube; stamens 6, high on tube; style slender. **Leaves:** Narrow, basal, 8″-16″ (20-40cm) long. **In bloom:** April-August. **Habitat-Range:** Mostly below 4600′ (1400m) in dry, heavy soils; California.

This is one of the tallest of many species of *Brodiaea* in western North America and South America. It is loose-flowered, as the name *laxa* indicates. The generic name honors James Brodie, a Scottish botanist. Ithuriel's Spear refers to the long thin leaves; other common names are Grass Nut and Wally Basket. The bulbs of most of the Brodiaeas have been used as food and are still recommended wherever they occur plentifully. They have a sweet nutlike flavor when boiled and can also be eaten raw.

283 HEDGE NETTLE *(Stachys bullata)*   Mint family *(Labiatae)*

Height: Perennial herb, 16″-32″ (40-80cm). **Flowers:** In whorls on stem, about 1″ (2.5cm) apart; calyx 5-toothed with spines in apex; petals purple, in 2-lipped tube, lower lip 1/2″ (1cm) long, upper shorter; stamens 4, extended beyond lips; style single; fruit separating into 4 small nutlets. **Leaves:** Ovate, 1 1/2″-7″ (4-18cm) long on stalks about 2 1/2″ (6cm) long, opposite, hairy, on square stems. **In bloom:** April-September. **Habitat-Range:** Widespread, below 4000′ (1200m); coastal California.

These Hedge Nettles grow abundantly on many slopes and in canyons, forming part of the coastal thickets. They are rather coarse, hairy plants, but not with stinging hairs as in the true Nettle, which belongs to the Urticaceae family. *Stachys* comes from the Greek *stachus*, "ear of corn," referring to the spikelike flower stalk.

BLUE TOADFLAX *(Linaria canadensis)*   Figwort family *(Scrophulariaceae)*

Height: Annual herb, 4″-24″ (10-60cm). **Flowers:** In loose, terminal racemes; calyx 5-parted; corolla 3/8″ (8mm) long, 2-lipped with upper larger than lower, short spur at base, blue-violet; stamens 4. **Leaves:** Alternate, mostly linear, 1/4″-1″ (.5-2.5cm) long. **In bloom:** April-June. **Habitat-Range:** Uncommon but widespread over North and South America with preference for sandy soil.

Linaria derives from the Latin for flax, *linum*, because the leaves of some species are flaxlike.

COLLINSIA *(Collinsia sparsiflora)*   Figwort family *(Scrophulariaceae)*

Height: Annual herb, 4″-18″ (10-45cm). **Flowers:** Borne singly on stalks 1/2″-1 1/4″ (1-3cm) long; calyx with 5 tiny lanceolate lobes; corolla 3/8″-1/2″ (8-12mm) long, purple, tubular with upper lip yellowish at base, purple-dotted, lower slightly longer, purple; stamens 4, enclosed with style in tube. **Leaves:** Smooth to slightly hairy, narrow-oblong, 1/2″-1 1/4″ (1-3cm) long, lower slightly toothed, on petioles 1/2″ (1cm) long. **In bloom:** March-May. **Habitat-Range:** Common in grassy places below 3000′ (900m); California, middle Coast Ranges, Sierra Nevada north to Washington.

This species belongs to the same genus as Chinese Houses *(C. bicolor)* but has a different appearance because of the more open, lax flower stalks. All but two of the 17 species are found on the Pacific coast. The generic name honors Zaccheus Collins, an 18th-century Philadelphia botanist.

284 BABY BLUE-EYES   Waterleaf family *(Hydrophyllaceae)*
(Nemophila menziesii)

Height: Branching annual herb up to 18″ (45cm). **Flowers:** Solitary in axils, to 1 1/2″ (4cm) wide; petals sky blue, lighter and dark-dotted toward base. **Leaves:** Opposite, pinnately divided; herbage with numerous hairs. **In bloom:** February-April in lowlands, April-July in higher mountains. **Habitat-Range:** Throughout most of California and western Oregon, occurring as well in Sagebrush and Creosote Bush desert.

This is one of the best-known spring wildflowers in California, growing in patches on hillsides and fields along with Shooting Stars and California Poppies. One of the most beautiful of the Nemophilas, it has been cultivated in England for more than a century. It was named for Archibald Menzies, a botanical explorer who visited the Pacific coast in the late eighteenth century.

285 STORK'S BILL *(Erodium cicutarium)*   Geranium family *(Geraniaceae)*

Height: Annual herb, 3″-12″ (7.5-30cm). **Flowers:** Borne in clusters on short stalks; calyx 5-toothed with bristle-like hairs; petals 5, purple, about 1/2″ (1cm) long; stamens 5; styles 5, united on column 1″-1 1/4″ (2.5-3cm) long. **Leaves:** Mostly in basal rosette, later on stems; pinnately, finely dissected, often with toothed lobes. **In bloom:** February through summer. **Habitat-Range:** Introduced from Mediterranean region, naturalized over most western areas.

This is similar to *E. texanum* but with smaller and finely divided leaves. It is a common forage plant because of its early germination in the fall, and spring growth. It has somewhat reddish stems, which account for the common name Red-stemmed Filaree —a short form of the Spanish name for the plant, *Alfileria*, meaning Pin Grass and referring to the long seed plumes.

CHIA *(Salvia columbariae)*   Mint family *(Labiatae)*

Height: Annual herb, 6″-24″ (15-60cm). **Flowers:** In 1 or 2 whorls or heads surrounded by bracts on stems arising from a basal rosette of leaves; heads about 1″ (2.5cm) in diameter; bracts purplish; calyx purplish red, irregular, with upper lobes curving over flower, terminating in 2-spined point; corolla small, irregular, blue with 2 darker blue spots on lower lips. **Leaves:** Pinnate, basal, some opposite on square stem; crinkly, green, slightly hairy. **In bloom:** March-June. **Habitat-Range:** Widespread in lower, dryer parts of California east to Utah, Arizona.

This species is often abundant and is easily recognized by its dark purple flower heads with numerous raylike points formed by the calyx. In the early days the Indians used the roasted seeds for meal and the mission padres made poultices from them to cure gunshot wounds. An infusion made from the seeds was used to treat fever. The seeds make a pleasant addition to cooked breakfast cereal.

FOOTHILL PENSTEMON   Figwort family *(Scrophulariaceae)*
(Penstemon heterophyllus)

Height: Perennial herb, up to 2′ (.6m). **Flowers:** In long racemes on short pedicels; tubular, markedly 2-lipped; 1″-1 1/2″ (2.5-4cm) long; calyx small, 5-parted with pointed lobes expanded, glandular; corolla with lips about 1/3 as long as tubular part; violet to rose with blue lips. **Leaves:** Narrow, linear; 1″-3″ (2.5-7.5cm) long. **In bloom:** May-June. **Habitat-Range:** Much of California below 5500′ (1650m) on open grassy or rocky hillsides or along creek bottoms.

Brown

Simplified Key

	HABITAT	HERB	SHRUB
Regular	**ALPINE**	286 Western Roseroot	
Regular	**CONIFEROUS**	287 Wild Ginger 290 Pinesap 291 Pinedrops	
Irregular		288 Boschniakia	
Regular	**GRASS**	289 Chocolate Lily	

286 **WESTERN ROSEROOT** *(Sedum rosea)*† Stonecrop family *(Crassulaceae)*

Height: Perennial herb, 3″-6″ (7.5-15cm). **Flowers:** Borne in dense cyme; calyx lobes 4, lanceolate, dark purple; petals 4, dark brownish purple, 1/8″ (3mm) long, slightly spread; stamens 8; styles 4, separate. **Leaves:** Flat, thin, ovate, about 1/2″ (1cm) long, equally spaced along stem. **In bloom:** May-August. **Habitat-Range:** Moist, rocky places, 7500′-12,500′ (2300-3800m); northern California east to Nevada, Colorado, New Mexico, north to Alaska, Siberia.

This tiny sedum is called Roseroot because the fleshy root has a rose fragrance. Its leafy stems and distribution in many alpine places of the Western Hemisphere make it a unique species. Some authors list it as a different genus, *Rhodiola rosea* var. *integrifolium*, or as *Sedum integrifolium*. Whatever its name, its dense flat heads of dark brownish flowers and light green leaves are beautiful. *Sedum*, from the Latin *sedere*, "to sit," describes this squat bush. The leaves and stems can be eaten raw or cooked if they are young and not too acid.

287 **WILD GINGER** *(Asarum caudatum)* Birthwort family *(Aristolochiaceae)*

Height: Perennial herb, 3″-7″ (7.5-18cm). **Flowers:** Single, from lower axils of creeping stem; calyx bell-shaped, dark red-brown, with 3 triangular lobes 1″-3 1/2″ (2.5-8.5cm) long, narrowing to tip; petals none; stamens 12, short; styles 6, united. **Leaves:** Heart-shaped, 2″-6″ (5-15cm) broad, on stalks 3″-7″ (7.5-18cm) long. **In bloom:** May-July. **Habitat-Range:** Deep shady Redwood forests of California, coastal coniferous forests north to British Columbia.

This plant forms a dark green ground cover. The flowers are easy to overlook because of their dark color and their being tucked under the leaves. A subtle, spicy odor gives the plant its common name. The creeping roots and stems can be cooked into a delicate preserve which is a favorite sweet. Dried roots ground to powder make a substitute for the commercial Ginger. Several North American species are more abundant than this Pacific-coast Ginger.

288 **BOSCHNIAKIA** *(Boschniakia tuberosa)*† Broom-rape family *(Orobanchaceae)*

Height: Parasitic herb, 6″-10″ (15-25cm). **Flowers:** Many in thick dense spike; calyx cup-shaped, 5-toothed; petals about 1/2″ (1cm) long, upper lip single, lower 3-lobed; stamens 4, extending outside floral tube; stigma 4-lobed. **Leaves:** Scalelike, overlapping. **In bloom:** June-July. **Habitat-Range:** Coniferous forests, 3000′-9000′ (700-2750m); California to British Columbia. Found on *Arctostaphyllos* or *Arbutus* roots.

The scalelike bracts on the thick stem almost hide the little irregular flowers. The plant has no chlorophyll (green matter) for manufacturing food, living as a parasite on the roots of host plants. The genus is named for Boschniaki, a Russian botanist. *Tuberosa* refers to the thick round tubers on the stem at the place of attachment to the host plant.

289 **CHOCOLATE LILY** *(Fritillaria biflora)*† Lily family *(Liliaceae)*

Height: Perennial herb, 6″-16″ (15-40cm). **Flowers:** 1-7, bell-shaped, nodding, dark brown or greenish purple, in terminal raceme; perianth segments 6, in 2 series, oblong,

3/4″-1 1/2″ (2-4cm) long; stamens 6, attached at base of segments; style single, 3-branched. **Leaves:** Oblong, 2″-5″ (5-12cm) long, alternate, often crowded at base. **In bloom:** February-June. **Habitat-Range:** Grassy slopes below 3000′ (900m), California Coast Ranges.

This is one of the most unusual Lilies with its dark brown, sometimes spotted coloration. The pendant flowers suggest its other names, Mission Bells and Bronze Bells. In some areas the Lilies have a disagreeable odor. *Fritillaria* is a large genus with yellow, pink, white, and red species. The bulbs of some were eaten by the Indians, but today these quite rare wildflowers should be enjoyed for their blooms rather than be eaten. The generic name comes from Latin *fritillus*, "dice box," a reference to the shape of the seed pod.

290 PINESAP *(Monotropa hypopithys)*   Heath family *(Ericaceae)*

A brown variant of the Pinesap (see No. 158).

291 PINEDROPS *(Pterospora andromedea)*†   Heath family *(Ericaceae)*

Height: Saprophytic herb, 1′-4′ (.3-1m). **Flowers:** In raceme on glandular stalk; calyx 5-lobed; petals 3/8″ (8mm) long, joined into rounded urn shape; 5 tiny lobes turned back; white to reddish, becoming brown; stamens 10; style with 5-lobed tip. **Leaves:** Scalelike, brown, with no chlorophyll. **In bloom:** June-August. **Habitat-Range:** Coniferous forests, 2600′-8500′ (760-2600m); California north to British Columbia, east to Atlantic coast.

This plant belongs to a group that lacks chlorophyll and obtains nutrients from organic material in the soil; they are therefore generally considered to be saprophytes. The stalks of Pinedrops are sticky and dry stiff and brown, often occurring in clusters in coniferous woods. They make attractive dry arrangements which last for years. The Greek name *Pterospora* means "wing-seeded"; *andromedea* refers to the Greek god with matted hair, which is descriptive of the roots of this plant. Common names are Giant Bird's Nest and Albany Beech Drops. Some botanists put this and related plants such as Sugar Stick, Indian Pipe, and Snow Plant in the Wintergreen family (Pyrolaceae).

Color
Illustrations

Note:

The following color illustrations have been divided into five color groups. Within each color group, they have been arranged by their habitat, and within each habitat, according to general visual similarities.

The plate number corresponds to the respective species description in the text.

1 Mountain Dryad

2 Western Pasque Flower

3 Marsh Marigold

4 White Heather✱   **5** Labrador Tea✱

6 Western Coltsfoot   **7** Spotted Coralroot

8 False Solomon's Seal

9 Solomon's Seal

10 Rein Orchid

12 Ground Iris

11 Alkali Grass

13 Mountain Misery

14 Leichtlin's Mariposa

15 Grass-of-Parnassus

16 Mariposa Lily

17 Inside-out Flower

18 Avalanche Lily

19 Tweedy's Lewisia

20 Indian Pipe

21 Lady's Slipper

22 Southern Lewisia

23 Bride's Bonnet

24 Syringa

25 Bitter Cherry

26 Bitter Cherry

27 Bear Grass*

28 Anemone*

29 Mountain Dogwood

30 Pussy Ears

31 Deer Brush

32 White Globe Lily

33 Salal

34 Vanilla Leaf

35 Woodland Star

36 Western Azalea

38 Apache Plume

37 Jimson Weed

39 Milkmaids *

40 Sego Lily

41 Evening Primrose

42 Sand Corn

44 Western Morning Glory

43 Our Lord's Candle

45 Nolina

46 Parry Manzanita

47 Matilija Poppy

48 Pitcher Sage

49 Desert Evening Primrose

50 Sand Blazing Star

51 Desert Star

52 Chicalote

53 Pincushion Cactus

54 Fleabane

55 Desert Lily

56 Desert Chicory

57 Milkweed

58 Desert Lily

60 Lace Pod

59 Wild Onion

61 Cream Cups

62 Meadow Sidalcea

63 Beach Strawberry*

64 Ice Plant*

65 Canadian Dogwood*

66 Mouse Ear

67 Cow Parsnip

68 Alpine Sunflower

69 Alpine Gold

70 Subalpine Buttercup

71 Evening Primrose

72 Cinquefoil

73 Alpine Lily

74 Glacier Lily

75 Yellow Lady's Slipper

76 Ground Iris

77 Wood Violet

78 Golden Columbine

79 California Pitcher Plant

80 Balsam Root

82 Pale Agoseris

81 Heartleaf Arnica

83 Mountain Dandelion

84 St. Johnswort

85 Mule Ears

86 Golden Pea

87 Oregon Grape

88 Stonecrop

89 Broom Rape

90 False Lupine

91 Hooker Evening Primrose*   **92** Yellow Mariposa*

93 Rabbit Brush   **94** Sulphur Flower

95 Sagebrush Buttercup

96 Sunflower

97 Prince's Plume

99 Bush Penstemon

98 Bush Monkey Flower

100 Humboldt Lily

101 Globe Lily*

102 Engelmann Prickly Pear

103 Prickly Pear

105 Ghost Flower

104 Century Plant

106 Sicklepod Rushweed

107 Bladder Pod

108 Desert Trumpet

109 Lesser Mohavea

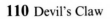
110 Devil's Claw   **111** Desert Mariposa

112 Panamint Daisy   **113** Creosote Bush

114 Yellow Elder

115 Ground Cherry

116 Desert Senna

117 Coneflower

118 Cutleaf Coneflower

119 Wild Gourd

120 California Poppy

122 Tidy Tips

123 Butterfly Weed

124 Fiddleneck

125 Great Mullein

126 Yellow Sand Verbena

127 Live Forever

128 Salt Marsh Gum Plant

129 Skunk Cabbage

130 Pond Lily

131 Common Madia*

132 Blazing Star

133 Common Dandelion

134 Salsify

136 Common Monkey Flower

135 Western Wallflower

137 Sticky Cinquefoil

138 Rose Epilobium

139 Parry's Primrose   **140** Red Mountain Heather

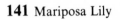

141 Mariposa Lily

142 Redwood Sorrel

143 Hedge Nettle

144 Gilia spp.

145 Mountain Pride

146 Western Corydalis   **147** Indian Warrior

148 Western Peony

149 Old Man's Whiskers

150 Red Columbine

151 Shooting Star

152 Grassleaf Peavine

153 Bleeding Heart

155 Skyrocket Gilia

154 Barbey Penstemon

156 Wintergreen

157 Fringe Cups

158 Pinesap

159 Fireweed

160 Sugar Stick

162 Bitterroot

163 Lewisia

164 Indian Pink

165 Pussy Paws

167 Coast Trillium

166 Rock Penstemon

168 Pink Monkey Flower

169 Common Trillium

170 Star Flower

171 Dogbane   **172** Thistle

173 Scarlet Paint Brush   **174** Scarlet Paint Brush

175 Fuchsia-flowered Gooseberry

176 Red Larkspur

177 Lewisia

178 Sweetbrier*   **179** Lupine*

180 Pink Phlox   **181** Fairy Duster

182 Rocky Mountain Bee Plant

183 Scarlet Locoweed   **184** Strawberry Cactus

185 Desert Monkey Flower*   **186** Catchfly

187 Chaparral Pea   **188** Cardinal Flower

189 Crimson Sage

190 Western Redbud

191 Snapdragon

192 Coast Morning Glory

193 Dutchman's Pipe

194 Hedgehog Cactus*

195 Fishhook Cactus

196 Beavertail Cactus

197 Barrel Cactus

198 Fivespot Mallow

199 Ocotillo

200 Purple Mat

201 Desert Willow

202 Bouvardia

203 Chuparosa

204 Hummingbird Flower

205 Scarlet Globe Mallow

206 Red Maids

207 Wine Cups

208 Wild Poinsettia

209 Giant Four O'clock

210 Checkerbloom

211 Summer's Darling

212 Horse Mint

213 Farewell-to-Spring

214 Shrubby Red Sage

215 Firecracker Flower

216 Windmill Pink*

217 Sugarbowl

219 Stream Orchid

218 Foxglove

220 Pink Sand Verbena*

221 Forget-me-not

222 Alpine Lungwort

223 Sky Pilot

225 Fringed Gentian

224 Cusick's Speedwell

226 Bluebell*

227 Cascade Aster

228 Bluebell

229 Blue Flax

230 Lungwort

231 Checker Lily

232 Blue Columbine

233 Morning Glory

234 Slink Pod

235 Calypso

236 Lupine

237 Delphinium

238 Elephant Head

239 Blue Violet

240 Spike Verbena

241 Camas

242 Wild Heliotrope

243 Penstemon

244 Mountain Penstemon

245 Stickseed

246 Wild Daisy

247 Hound's Tongue*

248 Skullcap

249 Larkspur

250 Purple Milkweed

252 Great Basin Blue Sage

251 Hairy Verbena

253 Silvery Lupine

254 One-sided Penstemon*

255 Canchalagua

256 Sticky Phacelia

257 Purple Nightshade   **258** Chinese Houses

259 Sand Verbena

260 Broom Rape

261 Canterbury Bell

262 Desert Candle

263 Bluebonnet

264 Owl's Clover

265 Western Larkspur

266 Locoweed   **267** Lobelia

268 Pasque Flower

269 Pasque Flower   **270** Wild Geranium

271 Blue-eyed Grass

272 Prairie Gentian

273 Blue Gilia

274 Prairie Violet

275 Townsendia

276 Mountain Iris

277 Ground Cherry

278 Seaside Daisy

279 Cliff Spurge

280 American Vetch*

281 Sickle-leaved Onion

282 Ithuriel's Spear

283 Hedge Nettle

284 Baby Blue-eyes

285 Stork's Bill

286 Western Roseroot*

287 Wild Ginger

288 Boschniakia

289 Chocolate Lily*

290 Pinesap

291 Pinedrops

Families of Western Flowers

Acanthus family *(Acanthaceae)*. Herbs or shrubs; leaves opposite, simple; flowers complete; calyx 5-parted with 2 bractlets; corolla 2-lipped, upper 2-lobed, lower 3-lobed; stamens 2 or 4; ovary superior, 2-celled; fruit 2-celled capsule; seeds few; distributed throughout tropics except one species, *Beloperone*, which occurs in deserts of southwest North America; about 250 genera, 2500 spp. The Mediterranean Acanthus was the motif of Greek and Roman art of the Corinthian order.

Arum family *(Araceae)*. Herbs; terrestrial or rarely aquatic; leaves mostly basal, simple or compound, base of leaf sheathing; flowers small, usually imperfect, often crowded on fleshy stalk that is usually surrounded by colored bract; corolla reduced to 4-6 scalelike parts; stamens 1, 2, 4, or 8; ovary superior, single style; fruit berry; seeds 1-many; family largely tropical, subtropical, several genera occurring in temperate areas; about 100 genera, 1500 spp. Well-known North American members are Calla, Jack-in-the-Pulpit, Water Lettuce and Skunk Cabbage. Many have foul-smelling parts, attracting carrion insects that transport the pollen. The garden Calla is characteristic of the family with its large white sheath surrounding the flower stalk.

Barberry family *(Berberidaceae)*. Shrubs or herbs; leaves alternate, compound; flowers perfect; sepals 6, in 2 circles; petals 6, in 2 circles; stamens opposite petals; ovary superior; a berry fruit, capsule or dry and leathery; temperate parts of Northern Hemisphere; about 4 genera, 575 spp. Many plants are cultivated as ornamentals.

Bellflower family *(Campanulaceae)*. Slender or small herbs with bitter or milky juice; leaves alternate; flowers perfect, parts usually in 5s, corolla united, bell-shaped; fruit capsule with remains of calyx at tip, seeds released by small holes on sides; temperate, tropical regions; about 60-70 genera, 2000 spp. Lobelias belong to a sub-family of the Campanulaceae with the flower structure in a 2-lipped corolla and stamens joined.

Bignonia family *(Bignoniaceae)*. Trees, shrubs, or woody vines; leaves usually opposite, simple; flowers complete; calyx lobes joined in 2 lips; corolla 2-lipped, often large, showy; stamens 4, in 2 sets; ovary superior, style single; fruit 2-valved capsule, splitting open from central partition; large family, tropical, semitropical, especially in South America; about 100 genera, 600 spp. The family was named for Abbé Bignon, librarian to Louis XIV. Some of the showy species are cultivated, such as Catalpa, Tecoma, and Trumpet Vine.

Birthwort family *(Aristolochiaceae)*. Twining shrubs or low herbs; leaves simple, alternate, heart-shaped; flower form varying, perfect, with or without petals; calyx 3 or 6 lobes or irregular; stamens 6-12, partly united; ovary partly inferior; fruit many-seeded capsule; widely distributed, chiefly warm climates; 7 genera, about 400 spp. The family is named for the interesting plant *Aristolochia*, known as Dutchman's Pipe.

Bleeding-heart family *(Fumariaceae)*. Herbs, perennial, smooth; leaves alternate, compoundly dissected; flowers perfect, irregular; sepals 2, scalelike; petals 4, inner pair narrower, united by tips over stamens, style; stamens in 2 sets of 3, filaments usually united; ovary superior; fruit long, dry, 1-celled capsule with many seeds; North Temperate Zone and South Africa; about 16 genera, 450 spp.

Borage family *(Boraginaceae)*. Herbs; foliage usually coarse, hairy with leaves alternate, generally simple, entire; flowers perfect in cymes or racemes; corolla 5-lobed; calyx 5-lobed; stamens 5, alternating with corolla lobes; ovary superior, forming 4 one-seeded nutlets; worldwide; about 100 genera, 2000 spp.

Broom-rape family *(Orobanchaceae)*. Herbs, root-parasitic, lacking chlorophyll; leaves replaced by alternate bracts; flowers complete in axil of bract; corolla tubular with upper, lower lip; stamens 4 in 2 pairs; calyx persistent; fruit a capsule; common in temperate, north temperate regions; about 14 genera, 180 spp. This family is also called Squaw-Root or Cancer-Root.

Buckthorn family *(Rhamnaceae)*. Shrubs or small trees; leaves simple, mostly alternate; flowers small, regular, perfect, usually in showy clusters; calyx 4-5 lobed, tubular at base, forming disk as base for flower; petals 4-5, usually with claws, sometimes lacking; stamens alternate with sepals, opposite petals; ovary partly inferior in disk; fruit berry or capsule. Temperate and tropical regions; about 58 genera, 900 spp. The dried bark *Rhamnus purshiana* is used as a stimulant and cathartic.

Buckwheat family *(Polygonaceae)*. Herbs or low bushes; leaves simple, toothless, often sheathing swollen joints of stem; flowers with no petals; calyx usually 3-6 divisions, resembling corolla; stamens 4-9; ovary superior; styles 2-3; fruit dry, one-seeded, usually brown or black; widely distributed; about 40 genera, 800 spp. Sour juice is a characteristic of this family; rhubarb and buckwheat are cultivated as food plants.

Buttercup family *(Ranunculaceae)*. Herbs or slightly woody vines; leaves many shapes, usually lobed; flowers with parts usually all present, free; sepals in different shapes, spurs or hoods or colored like petals; petals sometimes lacking; stamens numerous; pistils several or many, superior, 1-celled with single style; flower parts separate from each other, borne on receptacle; fruit an achene (dry, nonsplitting, one-seeded fruit), pod, or berry; widespread in North Temperate and Arctic regions; about 50 genera, 800 spp. Cultivated members of this family include Clematis, Palonia, Anemone, and Delphinium.

Cacao family *(Sterculiaceae)*. Trees, shrubs, or herbs, mostly with hairs in starlike arrangement; leaves alternate, simple, or rarely compound; flowers perfect, regular or nearly so; calyx usually 5-lobed; petals 5 or none; fertile stamens 5, with filaments united up to middle; ovary superior, fruit with 1-5 cells in capsule; warmer regions; about 60 genera, 700 spp. Seeds of tropical cacaos are used for chocolate, and the West African cola nut is the source of cola drinks. The single genus, *Fremontia*, is named for General John C. Frémont, explorer.

Cactus family *(Cactaceae)*. Large, fleshy, leafless stems; spines in clusters; flowers showy with numerous sepals, petals intergraded on funnel-shaped receptacle; stamens numerous, lining receptacle; ovary inferior; style single with several stigmas; fruit usually pulpy berry with many seeds; chiefly in desert areas of Mexico, southwestern U.S.; about 50 genera, 150 spp.

Caltrop family *(Zygophyllaceae)*. Herbs or shrubs, often jointed at nodes; leaves opposite or alternate, pinnate or 2-3 parts; stipules paired, often spinelike; flowers perfect, regular; sepals, petals usually 5; stamens 10, inserted with petals on receptacle; ovary mostly superior; style simple; fruit various forms; widespread in tropical to warm temperate regions; about 25 genera, 240 spp. Caltrop is known as Puncture-vine because of its spiny nutlets.

Candlewood family *(Fouquieriaceae)*. Spiny, branched shrubs or small trees; flowers in terminal clusters; petals 5, united into tube; sepals 5, not united; stamens 10-15; ovary superior; styles 3, united to middle; fruit capsule; seeds with long fringe of hair; deserts of Southwest, into Mexico; 2 genera, about 11 spp. The Boogum Tree of Baja California, sometimes cultivated, has a curious upside-down appearance.

Caper family *(Capparidaceae)*. Herbs or shrubs, heavy-scented; leaves alternate, 3 or more leaflets with stalks; flowers perfect; sepals 4; petals 4; stamens 4 or more; ovary superior, 1-celled; fruit 2-valved capsule, often on threadlike stalk; seeds 1-many, kidney-shaped; warm temperate, tropical regions; about 30 genera, 650 spp. These plants supply the capers used in cooking and the ornamental buds cultivated in southern Europe.

Carpetweed family *(Aizoaceae)*. Herbs or, rarely, low shrubs; leaves simple, often scalelike or succulent, opposite; flowers perfect, symmetrical; sepals 5-8, joined; petals none; stamens 5, appearing numerous because of many divisions; ovary 1-10 chambers, many seeds; fruit capsule or berry-like; distribution centered in South Africa; also called Ice Plant and found along the California coast; about 130 genera, 1200 spp.

Daffodil family *(Amaryllidaceae)*. Perennial herbs from bulbs or rootstalks; leaves straight-veined from base to tip; flowers perfect, regular; flower cup in 6 divisions; calyx, petals alike; stamens 6; ovary inferior, otherwise similar to Lily Family; widespread in warm and temperate regions; about 85 genera, 1100 spp. The Agave or Century Plant contains fibers used in making sisal and its fermented juice is made into the popular Mexican drink, *pulque*.

Devil's-claw family *(Martyniaceae)*. Herbs with speading stems, sticky, hairy; leaves simple, upper ones opposite; flowers perfect, irregular with 2 lips; lobed; calyx 4-5 lobes; stamens 4; ovary superior, single-celled; fruit capsule with elongated beak, splitting in 2-3 parts resembling cattle horns; chiefly tropics of Western Hemisphere; about 3 genera, 13 spp. Members of this family are also called Unicorn Plants. When the edges of pods are split they yield fibers which are woven as black designs into Indian baskets.

Dogbane family *(Apocynaceae)*. Perennial herbs with milky juice; stems fibrous from horizontal rootstocks; leaves simple, usually opposite; flower parts 5; petals joined, funnel-shaped, twisted in bud; calyx free, deeply lobed; stamens attached at base of corolla, alternate with lobes; ovaries 2 with single style; fruit 2 narrow follicles; seeds numerous; family closely related to Milkweeds, worldwide; about 180 genera, 1500 species. Most species are tropical, acrid, and poisonous. Periwinkle is well known, often escaping to moist places.

Dogwood family *(Cornaceae)*. Herbs, trees or shrubs; leaves entire; flowers small, borne in loose clusters or close heads; flower heads surrounded by showy petal-like

243

bracts in several species; petals 4-5; calyx 4-5 parts; stamens 4-5; ovary inferior, developing stony fruit; mostly Northern Hemisphere; about 12 genera, 100 spp.

Evening-primrose family *(Onagraceae)*. Herbs, shrubs or trees; leaves simple, alternate or opposite; flowers perfect, showy, mostly symmetric, parts usually in fours; calyx tubular; 4-lobed sepals attached to inferior ovary; stamens 4 or 8 attached to petals on calyx tube; style single; stigma 4-lobed; fruit 4-celled capsule with many seeds; wide distribution, especially western North America; about 21 genera, 640 spp. Fuchsias are a spectacular and varied part of this showy family.

Figwort family *(Scrophulariaceae)*. Herbs, with few exceptions; leaves simple, toothed or rarely parted; flowers usually irregular, generally 2-lipped, upper lip 2-lobed, sometimes hooded, lower 3-lobed, often with 3 sacks; stamens often 4, in 2 pairs, 1 shorter; fifth stamen present in some, usually sterile; calyx lobes usually more or less united; fruit 2-celled capsule from superior ovary; widespread; about 220 genera, 3000 spp.

Flax family *(Linaceae)*. Herbs or shrubs; leaves simple; flowers complete, regular; petals usually 5; sepals 5, alternate with petals; stamens 5, united at base; ovary superior; fruit a capsule, 2-5 cells; seeds 8-10, oily; widely distributed; about 12 genera, 290 spp. Flax plants supply fibers for linen, and seeds for linseed oil.

Four-o'clock family *(Nyctaginaceae)*. Herbs or low shrubs, often succulent; leaves opposite, entire; joints commonly swollen; flowers perfect, without petals; calyx colored like corolla with 4-5 lobes, more or less funnel-shaped; stamens 3-7; style single; fruit small, 1-seeded, nutlike achene with tough outer skin; warm temperate and tropical regions; about 30 genera, 290 spp.

Gentian family *(Gentianaceae)*. Mostly herbs with colorless, bitter juice; leaves usually opposite, simple, sometimes 3-parted; flower parts in fours or fives, perfect, regular; calyx free from ovary; petals joined; stamens inserted on corolla tube, alternate with lobes; ovary superior, single-celled; fruit capsule, many seeds; widely distributed in temperate zones; about 80 genera, 900 spp.

Geranium family *(Geraniaceae)*. Annual or perennial herbs; leaves opposite or alternate, simple or compound; flowers perfect, 5 parts, lobes usually overlapping in bud; calyx 5 parts, remaining as base of flower; petals 5, often alternate with 5 glands at attachment; stamens in circles of 5, 10 or 15; pistil 3-5 parts; ovary superior, forming fruit splitting into several parts, detaching and coiling or curving upward from bottom; temperate, subtropic regions; about 5 genera, 750 spp. Geraniums and Pelargoniums are cultivated for their large, colorful flowers.

Gourd family *(Cucurbitaceae)*. Herbs, annual or perennial; often climbing vines with tendrils; leaves simple, alternate, usually lobed; flowers unisexual; petals, calyx 5-lobed; stamens 5, 2 pairs united, appearing 3; ovary inferior; fruit berrylike, fleshy interior, leathery exterior; tropics, warmer temperate zones; about 110 genera, 640 spp. Family members include melons, squash, and pumpkins.

Heath family *(Ericaceae)*. Herbs, shrubs, or trees; leaves alternate, simple, often thick, tough; flowers perfect, regular; calyx with 4-5 divisions; petals usually united in bell shape, 4-5 lobes; stamens as many or twice numer of petal lobes; anther 2-celled opening by terminal pores; ovary superior or inferior; fruit capsule, berry, or drupe (fleshy, with hard inner core); cooler regions, acid soil, or bogs; about 50 genera, 1350 spp.

244

Heather, cranberries, blueberries, huckleberries are some of the smaller-flowered species. Both the wild and cultivated varieties of rhododendrons and azaleas are prized.

Honeysuckle family *(Caprifoliaceae)*. Shrubs, twining vines or small trees; leaves opposite, usually simple, sometimes compound; flowers regular or irregular; radially or bilaterally symmetrical; corolla usually composed of 5 petals, tubular or spreading, and lobed; stamens usually 5, attached to base of lobe; calyx remaining attached to fruit, a fleshy berry; widely distributed in Northern Hemisphere with some representatives in South America and New Zealand; about 12 genera, 450 spp. Many species are grown as ornamentals. Elderberries produce a fruit used for wine and preserves.

Iris family *(Iridaceae)*. Perennial herbs; leaves long, narrow, toothless, folded sheathlike; flowers showy, perfect, regular, 3 and 6 parts; stamens 3 at base of sepals; anthers turning outward; style single, 3-branched; ovary inferior, becoming 3-celled, usually 3-angled, many-seeded capsule; widespread; about 60 genera, 800 spp. The variegated flower tints explain its derivation from the Greek word for "rainbow."

Leadwort family *(Plumbaginaceae)*. Perennial herbs, shrubs, or woody vines; leaves simple, often in basal rosettes; flowers perfect, regular, in 5 parts often in heads on long stalk; calyx tubular, often folded, fanlike; petals somewhat joined at base, folded over in bud; stamens opposite center of petals; pistil with 5 styles; ovary superior, single seed; arid regions, often sea coasts; about 10 genera, 500 spp.

Lily family *(Liliaceae)*. Perennial herbs from bulbs or root-stalks; leaves toothless, usually straight-veined from base to tip; flowers perfect, symmetrical, flower cup in 6 divisions; calyx, petals often termed "tepals"; stamens 6, opposite tepal divisions, 3 sometimes without anthers; style or stigmas 3; ovary superior; fruit 3-celled capsule or berry with few to many seeds; widely distributed; about 250 genera, 3700 species. This large family includes many garden flowers such as tulips and hyacinths and food plants such as onions and asparagus.

Loasa family *(Loasaceae)*. Erect herbs, often with barbed, stinging hairs; leaves alternate or opposite; flowers in racemes or cymes, regular, perfect; sepals 4-5, folded; petals 4-5 or 10, yellow or red; stamens 5; ovary inferior, 1-celled; fruit a capsule; mostly North America; about 15 genera, 250 spp.

Madder family *(Rubiaceae)*. Herbs, shrubs, trees, or woody vines; leaves simple, usually entire, opposite or whorled; flowers usually perfect; corolla funnel-shaped; 4-5 parts of calyx attached to ovary; stamens as many as corolla lobes, inserted on tube; ovary inferior 2-4 chambers; fruit capsule or berry; distributed throughout tropics and subtropics; about 500 genera, 6000 spp. Many members of this family are grown as ornamentals (e.g., Bouvardia and Gardenia) or have economic importance (e.g., coffee and quinine).

Mallow family *(Malvaceae)*. Herbs, soft, woody shrubs, usually with stellate pubescence; leaves alternate, usually lobed or palmately ribbed; flowers regular, perfect, or sometimes pistil, stamens on different plants; calyx with 5 sepals, often surrounded by several bracts; petals 5, bases united with stamen tube; stamens numerous, united, forming tube enclosing pistils; ovary superior; fruit a capsule, often breaking into several 1-seeded parts; widely distributed in temperate, tropic regions; about 75 genera, 1000 spp. Garden Hollyhock and Hibiscus are attractive species. Okra is the fruit of a variety of Hibiscus.

Meadow-foam family *(Limnanthaceae)*. Herbs; annual; leaves pinnately divided, alternate; flowers complete, from axils on long pedicels; calyx parts 3 or 5, persisting on fruit; petals 3 or 5, equal; stamens 6-10 in two series, outer alternate with petals; ovary superior, 5-celled with common style; fruit in 5 separated nutlets. Two North American genera; all species low-growing herbs densely covering moist, flat meadows. The family name derives from the Greek *limne*, meaning "marsh," and *anthos* for "flower."

Milkweed family *(Asclepiadaceae)*. Perennial herbs, vines or shrubs with milky juice; leaves usually large, toothless, opposite; flowers perfect, regular in roundish clusters; calyx, corolla 5-lobed; stamens 5 on base of petals, more or less united around disclike stigma; ovary superior; fruit 2 conspicuous pods opening at side, filled with numerous seeds with silky tufts; widely distributed, mostly in warmer regions; about 130 genera, 2000 spp. Many genera contain commercially useful latex.

Mint family *(Labiatae)*. Herbs or low shrubs, annual or perennial; leaves opposite, simple; stems square; flowers perfect; corolla tubular, 2-lipped; usually 2 lobes to upper, 3 to lower lip; calyx 5-toothed, often 2-lipped; stamens 4, in 2 pairs; fruit composed of 4 nutlets enclosed in calyx; worldwide, most abundant in Mediterranean region; about 180 genera, 3500 spp. Many species are used medicinally and in seasonings.

Morning-glory family *(Convolvulaceae)*. Annual or perennial herbs, sometimes woody, twining; leaves alternate; flower perfect; calyx 4-5 parts more or less folded over; petals 4-5 lobed, joined in folded funnel or tube; stamens 5 at base of flower tube; styles 1-3; ovary superior; fruit usually capsule with 1-4 seeds; warmer regions; about 55 genera, 1650 spp. The sweet potato is in this family.

Mustard family *(Cruciferae)*. Herbs, with alternate leaves; flowers in terminal racemes; sepals 4; petals 4; stamens 6 (2 short, 4 longer); ovary superior with 2 chambers; fruit with 2 valves; widespread with many species, mostly in north temperate, arctic regions; about 375 genera, 3200 spp. The family name "cross-bearer" refers to the petals, which form a cross. The watery juice of the plants is mustard-like.

Nightshade family *(Solanaceae)*. Herbs, shrubs or vines; leaves alternate, mostly entire; flowers perfect, regular with 5 united lobes, folded lengthwise in bud, usually in clusters on short stems; stamens 5, on throat of flower; ovary superior, 2-celled; fruit berry or capsule; widely distributed, abundant in tropics; about 90 genera, more than 2000 spp. Many species are poisonous or have a strong odor. Important as cultivated plants are chilies, cayenne pepper, tomato, potato, belladonna, petunia.

Orchid family *(Orchidaceae)*. Perennial herbs from various kinds of roots; leaves usually alternate, toothless, sheathing stem; flowers perfect, irregular, 6 divisions; sepals 3 alike, colored; petals 2 alike, central differing as lip; stamens, pistil joined in column with anther at tip, stigma below; ovary inferior, becoming 3-valved capsule with many seeds; exotic members widespread in tropics, smaller members in temperate areas of North America; about 735 genera, 20,000 spp. Many tropical orchids cling as epiphytes to branches of trees but take no nourishment from the host.

Oxalis family *(Oxalidaceae)*. Herbs, shrubs or trees, acid sap; leaves usually compound, alternate, or basal opposite; flowers perfect, regular; sepals 5; petals 5; stamens 10; styles 5, separate; ovary superior, 5-celled; fruit capsule or berry-like; widespread, temperate and tropic regions; about 3 genera, 875 spp.

Parsley family *(Umbelliferae)*. Herbs, usually strong-smelling, hollow, grooved stems; leaves alternate, compound, generally deeply cut; flowers tiny, borne in flat-topped clusters or umbels; sepals 5; petals 5; stamens 5; styles 2; ovary inferior; fruit 2 oval pods, usually ribbed; wide distribution in temperate regions; about 275 genera, 2850 spp. This economically important family includes celery, dill, anise, parsnip, parsley, and carrot. The hemlock of Socrates is one of several poisonous species.

Pea family *(Leguminosae)*. Herbs, shrubs or small trees; leaves alternate, usually compound; flowers perfect, some regular, mostly with lower petals forming "keel" enclosing stamens, pistil; calyx 5-toothed; petals 5, distinct or 1 erect, 2 wings, 2 joined in keel; stamens commonly 10, sometimes many; pistil 1; ovary superior, becoming 2-valved pod in fruit; seeds solitary to numerous; widespread; about 600 genera, 12,000 spp. Next to the Sunflower family this is the largest plant family and includes edible beans and peas.

Phlox family *(Polemoniaceae)*. Annual or perennial herbs, shrubs, or vines; leaves simple or divided; flowers regular, often in flat-topped cluster; calyx usually 5 narrow sepals; petals usually united, rolled up in bud, opening into tube with flared top; stamens generally 5, partly joined with petals; stigma slender, 3-lobed; ovary superior; fruit pod with 3 compartments, many seeds; numerous in western North America; about 15 genera, 300 spp.

Pink family *(Caryophyllaceae)*. Herbs; leaves mostly opposite, entire, stems usually swollen at joints; flowers regular, mostly perfect; sepals 4-5; petals usually 4-5; stamens same or twice numer of petals; ovary superior; fruit dry capsule, opening by valves at top; widely distributed in temperate zones; about 70 genera, 1750 spp. Carnations and Chickweed are well-known members.

Pitcher-plant family *(Sarraceniaceae)*. Insectivorous herbs; leaves basal with pitcher-like petioles, lidlike blades containing liquid with digestive properties; flowers on leafless stems; petals, sepals 5; stamens many; ovary superior, 3-5 celled; fruit a capsule splitting lengthwise, seeds numerous; found in swamps, bogs; about 3 genera, 17 spp.

Poppy family *(Papaveraceae)*. Herbs or shrubs with milky or colorless juice; leaves alternate or opposite; calyx with 2-3 sepals, falling off before other parts; flowers regular, complete; petals twice as many as sepals; stamens often many; ovary superior; pistil single; fruit capsule, usually many seeds released at pores or valves in tip; widely distributed, most abundant in western North America; about 26 genera, 200 spp. Opium and morphine are from this family.

Primrose family *(Primulaceae)*. Annual or perennial herbs; leaves simple, opposite or alternate; flowers perfect, regular, 5 parts; calyx deeply lobed; corolla deeply lobed, spreading or reflexed; stamens attached opposite center of petals; ovary superior, 1-celled; fruit a capsule; widely distributed, chiefly in Northern Hemisphere; about 20 genera, 1000 spp. Primulas and Cyclamen are cultivated varieties.

Purslane family *(Portulacaceae)*. Herbs; leaves usually thick, succulent; flowers perfect; sepals 2; petals 2-5 or more; stamens sometimes numerous; ovary superior, 1-celled; fruit many-seeded capsule; Northern Hemisphere; about 19 genera, 350 spp. The Purslane Tree or Spek-boom is the chief food of elephants in South Africa. Other well-known members are Purslane (a common weed) and cultivated Portulaca.

Rock-rose family *(Cistaceae)*. Herbs or shrubs; leaves simple, entire, usually alternate; flowers complete, regular, all parts borne on receptacle; sepals 5, two outer are smaller, often bractlike; petals 3-5, lasting one day or less; stamens many; ovary superior; fruit a capsule with many seeds; mostly Northern Hemisphere; about 8 genera, 200 spp.

Rose family *(Rosaceae)*. Herbs, shrubs or trees; leaves alternate, simple or pinnate; flowers regular, perfect, in clusters or solitary; petals 5; stamens 10 to numerous; ovary nearly or completely inferior; fruit a pod, achene, drupe (cluster as blackberry) or pome (plum); about 100 genera, 2000 species. This large family includes roses, hawthorns, strawberries, blackberries, raspberries, cherries, plums, peaches, and almonds.

St. Johnswort family *(Hypericaceae)*. Herbaceous or somewhat woody plants; leaves opposite, entire, with dark glands or clear dots; flowers perfect, regular; sepals 5 or 4, herbaceous and persistent; petals 5 or 4, usually yellow; stamens generally numerous, separate or united into 3-5 clusters; ovary superior; fruit a capsule; temperate and warmer regions.

Saxifrage family *(Saxifragaceae)*. Herbs or shrubs; leaves simple or compound, alternate or opposite, commonly deciduous; flowers perfect, borne often in clusters; calyx, petals commonly in fives; ovary partly inferior to superior; fruit capsule to berry; widespread in North Temperate and Arctic regions; about 30 genera, 580 spp. Sweet-smelling Mock-orange or *Philadelphus* is an early spring favorite. Other members are Hydrangeas, Gooseberries, and Currants.

Silk-tassel family *(Garryaceae)*. Evergreen shrubs; leaves opposite, simple, leathery; flowers small, without petals, imperfect, borne in striking pendulous clusters on different plants; staminate flowers in groups of 3; calyx 4-parted; stamens 4; pistillate flowers borne single amidst bracts; ovary inferior; fruit berry with bitter pulp, dark purple to black; western North America; 1 genus, about 18 spp.

Spiderwort family *(Commelinaceae)*. Herbs; leaves thick, alternate, succulent, sharply folded with leaf base sheathing stem; flowers radial or bilaterally symmetric; calyx 3 green lobes; corolla blue, purplish, or white, 3 lobes, opening singly in morning; stamens 3 or 6; ovary superior; style single, 3-branched; fruit 3-celled capsule; seeds few; family mainly tropic, semi-tropic in southern United States, Mexico; about 34 genera, 500 species. Two well-known species occur in the Southwest: Dayflower *(Commelina)* and Spiderwort *(Tradescantia)*. Wandering Jew *(Zabrina)* and Oyster Plant *(Rhoeo)* were introduced from Mexico. The family is named for famous Dutch botanists of the 17th and 18th centuries, Jan and Kaspar Commelin.

Spurge family *(Euphorbiaceae)*. Herbs, shrubs, or trees, usually with milky juice; some succulent, cactus-like; leaves simple, some with glands at base; flowers with stamens or pistils, with or without petals, sepals; some flowers reduced to single stamen or pistil, grouped together with bracts resembling petals; ovary superior; fruit usually 3-lobed capsule; widely distributed; about 300 genera, 5000 species. Many cultivated as ornamentals (e.g., Poinsettia and Crown-of-thorns) or used for castor and tung oil and rubber.

Stonecrop family *(Crassulaceae)*. Fleshy, succulent herbs; flowers usually in cymes, regular, usually perfect; calyx free from ovary, in 4-5 parts; petals same number; stamens, pistils same number as petals, or stamens twice as many; fruit, 1-celled follicles;

widely distributed; about 35 genera, 1500 spp. Familiar plants are Live-forever and Hen-and-chickens.

Sunflower family *(Compositae)*. Usually herbs, sometimes trees; leaves opposite, alternate or basal; flowers crowded into heads on top of stalk; surrounded by bracts, scales or bristles; individual flowers in head of 2 types: outer ray flowers with petals united into strap, or disc flowers with 5 petals united to form small tube; anthers united into tube around pistil, extending above petals only in disc flowers; ovary inferior; worldwide, most common in warmer regions; largest plant family with about 900 genera, more than 13,000 spp. Members are varied in appearance and specialized in insect pollination and seed dispersal. They include the Common Thistle, Daisy, Sunflower, and Dandelion.

Sweet-shrub family *(Calycanthaceae)*. Aromatic shrubs; opposite entire leaves, no stipules; flowers large, solitary at ends of branches; bracts, sepals, petals similar, crowded in series attached to enlarged cuplike base; stamens, pistils numerous, nearly enclosed in hollow cup; seeds 1-seeded achenes, many enclosed in cup; North America and East Asia; 2 genera, about 7 spp.

Verbena family *(Verbenaceae)*. Herbs or shrubs; leaves opposite or in whorls; flowers perfect, sometimes somewhat irregular, in terminal spikes; calyx lobed; petals united in tube, 4-5 lobes; stamens usually 4, in 2 sets on petals; ovary superior; style 1; stigmas 1-2; fruit when dry separating into 2-4 bony nutlets; widely distributed, mostly in warmer regions; about 75 genera, 3000 spp.

Violet family *(Violaceae)*. Herbs, shrubs or rarely trees; leaves alternate or basal, simple, entire to laciniate; flowers irregular, axillary, nodding; sepals 5, persistent; petals 5, unequal, lower one larger than lateral and upper pair; stamens 5, alternating with petals; ovary superior; fruit a 3-valved capsule; worldwide; about 22 genera, 900 spp.

Waterleaf family *(Hydrophyllaceae)*. Herbs or shrubs; leaves often hairy, mainly alternate or from base; flowers regular, usually blue or white, often in coiled clusters; calyx 5 united sepals; petals 5, united; stamens 5 on base of petals; style with 2 stigmas; ovary superior; fruit capsule containing many seeds; largely western North America; about 18 genera, 250 spp. American Indians and pioneers used some species as herbs in cooking.

Water-lily family *(Nymphaeaceae)*. Herbs, perennial, aquatic; rootstalks thick, horizontal, or tubers; leaves large, floating from long stalks; flowers solitary on long stalks; sepals 3-12; petals 3-many; stamens 6-numerous; ovary superior; stigmas distinct or united into disk; fruit a firm-rind berry; widely distributed; about 2 genera, 75 spp.

Wildflower Recipes

Many native plants in North America were used by the Indians for food thousands of years before Europeans discovered this continent. Some species, like maize, beans, and squash, were cultivated. Today we either buy or raise our fruits and vegetables, yet there are many edible wild species that are ours for the gathering. It is interesting to try some of these, especially when camping or backpacking in remote areas.

It is not our purpose to encourage the eating of rare or protected species no matter how good they may taste. Common plants, however, are not likely to suffer from nature enthusiasts. Their principal enemies are the plow and the bulldozer.

Care must be exerted in experimenting with wild species because some are very toxic, including poison hemlock, digitalis, locoweed, and those that contain alkaloids.

To supplement our comments on edibility in our species descriptions, we add here a group of recipes using common native plants. They will serve to introduce the reader to the pleasures of eating such plants.

SOUPS

Bistort Soup
Boil young leaves of Smartweed *(Polygonum bistortoides)* until tender; chop, add seasoning to taste, milk or soup stock, and serve hot.

Imitating the Indians, we can also eat the roots. Boil the washed roots about 20 minutes, eat as a starchy vegetable, chopped, or fry in butter.

Violet Leaf Soup
Make a clear broth or bouillon and add a few fresh chopped violet leaves just before serving. Violet blossoms may be floated on top.

Nettle Brotchän *(Urtica* spp.*)*
This thick, tasty soup comes from Ireland. Take tops of young nettle, wash and cut into 1-inch pieces to make 4 cups. Add 2 tablespoons of quick-cooking oatmeal and simmer for 45 minutes. Finally, add 1 tablespoon butter, 2 tablespoons chopped parsley, 4 cups milk or soup stock, salt and pepper to taste. Just before serving, add a bit of cream if desired. This makes about 6 cups of soup.

Sorrel Soup *(Oxalis oregana)*
Several plants are called sorrel. The new, basal leaves of *Rumex acetosella* or Sheep Sorrel (introduced from Europe and considered a weed) can be cooked as greens or in soup. Redwood Sorrel *(Oxalis oregana)*, found in shaded woods, makes the following delicious soup:

> 1 cup fresh leaves
> 1 tablespoon butter
> 1 cup cooked potato, mashed or puréed
> 2 cups milk
> salt, pepper to taste

Melt butter in saucepan; add well washed leaves, without stalks; brown lightly; add cooked potato and seasoning. Mix in milk slowly and heat, being careful not to boil.

POTPOURRI

Chia *(Salvia columbariae)*
The seeds of this sage plant were used by Indians and early settlers in many ways. They were highly prized and sold for $6-$8 a pound as late as 1894 in Los Angeles. A popular drink in Mexico today is made by soaking 1/4 pound of Chia in 1 1/2 quarts of water. In 5 minutes the seeds swell and become gelatinous. Adding lemon or lime juice and sugar to taste makes this a nutritious, refreshing drink. Add 1 teaspoon dried Chia seeds to cooked cereal, baked breads or muffins for the nutty flavor. They have such high food value that 1 teaspoonful was said to be enough to keep an Indian traveling on foot for 24 hours.

Yellow Pond Lily *(Nuphar polysepalum)*
This lily grows in such profusion in many small ponds and lakes that using it for food would help clear the waterways. Gather large seed pods that develop after the yellow flowers wither, shake out the seeds, and dry them. Like popcorn they can be popped in a small amount of salad oil in a heavy frying pan or ground into a meal to be used in baking or for thickening soups. The root cores can also be dried and ground into a flour. Young tuberous roots, rich in starch, can be used in soup or stews.

ENTREES

Fireweed Eggs *(Epilobium angustifolium)*
Gather a quart of young shoots and leaves. Wash, cut into 1-inch pieces, and sauté in 2 tablespoons of oil or butter in heavy frying pan. When greens are limp add 1 cup water, cover, and simmer several minutes until shoots are tender. These may be eaten as a vegetable or, to make them into a main dish, add 6 well-beaten eggs, salt and pepper to taste, and stir until set. Serve over toast or biscuits, garnished with paprika and parsley. Fireweed shoots are called Wild Asparagus by the French Canadians. The older flower stalks can be peeled and eaten raw or cooked into a thick soup.

Milkweed Shoots *(Asclepias speciosa)*
All parts of the Milkweed are edible, but in this recipe we use the young shoots in spring. Collect sprouts about 8 inches tall. The plant contains a bitter milky latex which is soluble in water.

> 16 young Milkweed shoots
> 2 tablespoons butter
> 2 tablespoons flour
> salt and pepper to taste
> 2 hard-boiled eggs
> 1 cup rich milk

Cover Milkweed shoots with boiling water in saucepan and boil about half an hour or until tender. Change water twice during cooking to remove latex. Drain and set aside. Melt butter, add flour, seasonings, and, gradually, milk; stir until thickened and cook on low heat about five minutes. Pour mixture over cooked Milkweed shoots and garnish with sliced hard-boiled eggs. Serve on buttered toast or cooked rice.

Dandelion or Mustard Soufflé

Frances Welch, an excellent cook and teacher who grew up in Oregon, used to gather young Dandelion or Mustard greens for this delicious dish. Make a sauce by cooking 1 tablespoon butter, 1 tablespoon flour, and 1 cup milk until thick.

Separate 3 eggs and beat whites until stiff; beat yolks and add one cup finely chopped greens. Combine sauce and yolk mixture and fold in beaten egg whites. Pour into straight-sided baking dish, place in flat pan of water in 375° oven, and bake 40-50 minutes. Serve at once.

Maggie Cavagnero's Nettle and Cheese Pie

Collect 2 pounds of tender tips of Nettle, *Urtica*. Be sure to wear gloves and cut with scissors.

> 1 pound Italian filo dough
> 1/4 pound butter
> 1 pound feta cheese (or ricotta or Parmesan)
> 7 eggs
> 1 medium onion
> salt, pepper to taste

Steam nettles; wring out in clean towel until dry; chop fine. Beat eggs and add cheese broken into bits. Sauté onion and add to eggs and nettles. Season to taste. Place 6-8 layers of filo dough in greased 12 x 18-inch pan, brushing each layer with butter and spreading with nettle mixture, ending with layer of filo. Bake at 350° for 1 hour. Cut in squares to serve. If filo dough is unobtainable use a rich pie dough layer on bottom and top.

Mint Sauce

> 1 cup chopped mint leaves
> 2 tablespoons sugar
> 1/4 teaspoon salt
> 3/4 cup white vinegar
> 1/4 cup lemon juice

Place over slow heat until the sugar is dissolved and the leaves limp. This is especially good over cooked carrots or as a meat sauce.

VEGETABLES

Milkweed Flower Buds *(Asclepias speciosa)*

Boil young, well-washed flower-bud clusters in salted water until tender; change water once (the milky substance, which is bitter, is soluble in water). Season with salt and pepper and serve as a vegetable with melted butter.

Milkweed Pods *(Asclepias speciosa)*

Gather young seed pods when they are light green and about 1 1/2 inches in length. Wash well, add to boiling salted water, and boil for about 10 minutes until tender. Strain and season with salt, pepper, grated cheese, and butter.

Dandelion Greens

Young Dandelion leaves can be cooked until tender in a small amount of water, seasoned, and eaten as greens.

Salsify Roots *(Tragopon dubius)*
This is called Oyster Plant in the market. The roots can be cooked as a vegetable by boiling until tender and removing the outer skin. Dice and season with salt, pepper, and butter.

BREADS AND PIES

Ground-Cherry Coffee Cake *(Physalis pubescens)*
This delicious coffee cake has ripe, husked ground-cherries baked on top. These berries belong to the Nightshade family which has some poisonous species; these, however, are edible.

Sift and mix 2 cups flour, 3 teaspoons baking powder, 1/2 teaspoon salt, 2 tablespoons sugar; cut in 1/3 cup shortening; add 1/3 cup milk with 1 beaten egg. Mix and place in greased 9-inch square pan. Cover with 3/4 cup brown sugar and 1 teaspoon cinnamon. Top with husked Ground Cherries. Bake at 450° about 20 minutes. Serve warm.

Huckleberry Muffins *(Vaccinium ovatum)*
Picking Huckleberries is a time-consuming but rewarding experience when one can enjoy fresh muffins filled with the purple berries. A good basic recipe:

> 2 cups sifted flour
> 3 teaspoons baking powder
> 1/2 teaspoon salt
> 3 tablespoons sugar
> 1 egg, well beaten
> 1 cup milk
> 3 tablespoons shortening, melted

Sift dry ingredients together. Combine egg, milk, and melted shortening, add to dry ingredients, mix until just moistened. Add 1 cup or more of washed Huckleberries coated with 1/2 cup sugar; a few stems remaining in the berries disappear in the cooking. Bake in greased muffin pans 20-30 minutes at 425° F.

The tiny berries add a uniquely pleasing flavor to pies and pancakes and are delicious when made into jam and jelly.

Serviceberry Pie *(Amelanchier pallida)*
The ripe berries are juicy and sweet during the summer months. Add sugar and a dash of lemon juice to make a fruit pie filling. These purple-black berries can be dried and used in winter. The Indians made a nourishing dry fruit and meat mix called pemmican which sustained them on long trips.

Fruit Cobbler
A favorite dessert over the campfire or at home can be made from Serviceberries, Huckleberries, or any of the wild berries, as follows: melt 2 tablespoons butter in a heavy iron frying pan; add about 1 cup white or brown sugar; mix well. Add 2 cups berries and enough water to cover. Cook until hot and bubbly, stirring to prevent burning. Cover surface with drop biscuit dough, one tablespoonful at a time about 2 inches apart. Remove to cooler part of the fire, cover, and cook slowly until dough is cooked through. Serve warm.

CONFECTIONS

Mint Leaf Candy(*Monardella* spp. and *Mentha* spp.)
Use dried or fresh, washed mint leaves. Beat 2 egg whites until stiff, brush on both sides of leaves, dip in fine granulated sugar. Dry on waxed paper. These are good with fruit cocktails, cold drinks, and desserts.

Cactus Candy
Remove outside layer from any large cactus fruit. Cut pulp into half-inch slices and soak overnight in cold water. Make syrup of 3 cups sugar, 1/2 cup water, 2 tablespoons orange juice, 1 tablespoon lemon juice. Add cactus pieces, cook slowly until syrup is nearly absorbed. Drain pieces on cake rack and dry.

Wild Ginger Candy *(Asarum caudatum)*
Any species of Wild Ginger may be used. Gather several feet of the roots (which lie along the ground), wash, and cut into 2-inch pieces. Cover with water and boil for 5 minutes. Change water and boil twice again. Cool and rub off outer skin. Dissolve 2 cups sugar in 1 cup water, add ginger root pieces, bring to boil, and simmer 10 minutes. Set aside and repeat the following day, simmering until the syrup is nearly absorbed. The ginger pieces may be stored in jars in the syrup or removed, dried, and rolled in sugar. The syrup is good over ice cream.

Uncooked ginger root can be dried and powdered to use as a substitute for commercial ginger.

Wild Rose-Hip Jam
The red seed capsules of the Wild Rose are useful as a source of vitamin C. Gather 3 cups of fully ripened rose hips, remove hairs from the calyx end, split, and remove seeds. Wash and measure 1 1/2 cups of capsules. Cut peel from 1 orange and 1 lemon and slice in thin slivers; boil in 1 cup water for 5 minutes. Add 1 1/2 cups sugar; stir to dissolve. Add rose hips and juice of orange and lemon. Cover and cook slowly for 15 minutes. Uncover and cook until fruit is clear and syrup thick. Pour into sterilized jar and seal.

A jelly can be made instead of jam by straining the fruit and cooking as for any fruit jelly.

Other delicious jams can be made from Huckleberries *(Vaccinium ovatum)*, Serviceberries *(Amelanchier pallida)*, Manzanita *(Arctostaphylos* spp.*)*, Gooseberries *(Ribes* spp.*)*, Currants *(Ribes* spp.*)*, and Ground Cherries *(Physalis pubescens)*.

Ground-Cherry Jam *(Physalis pubescens)*
This fruit belongs to the Nightshade family, which has some poisonous species. *Physalis* berries, however, are tásty and useful raw or cooked. They may be gathered ripe, dried in their husks, and stored. They are delicious made into a preserve or dessert. Poha is a Hawaiian jam made from Ground Cherries:

> 3 cups sugar
> 1 cup water
> 1 lemon, sliced thin
> 1 stick cinnamon

Bring these ingredients to a boil and add 1 quart husked, ripe Ground Cherries. Cook until thickened.

BEVERAGES

Manzanita Nectar *(Arctostaphylos* spp.*)*
The berries or "little apples" can be eaten fresh from the plant or cooked as a dessert or preserve. A favorite early western drink is as follows: One quart ripe berries, scalded with 1 cup boiling water. Mash into pulp, add 1 quart cold water, allow to settle for at least an hour, strain and cool. It may be sweetened.

Dandelion Wine I *(Agoseris* spp. or *Taraxacum* spp.*)*
Gather 1 quart of fresh, clean Dandelion flowers. Pour 1 quart of boiling water over them and allow to stand three days. Strain out flowers and add 1/2 pound chopped raisins, the peel and juice of 2 oranges and 1 lemon. Boil for half an hour, cool to lukewarm; add 1 pound sugar, 1/2 yeast cake. Keep in warm place three days; strain. Cover for 2-3 weeks until fermentation stops. Bottle and age at least a year.

Dandelion Wine II
Put 3 pints Dandelion flowers in 4 pints water. Let stand 6 days. Strain through cloth and boil liquid 1/2 hour with 1 lemon, 2 oranges, and 2 pounds sugar. Store in large containers 6 months, then bottle.

Dandelion Beer
Wash and boil 1/2 pound young plants, including tap root, in 2 cups water. When tender, cool and add 1 pound sugar, 1 tablespoon crushed fresh ginger root, juice of 2 lemons, 1 teaspoon yeast, enough water to make 1 gallon. Ferment until sugar has gone and then bottle.

Nettle Beer *(Urtica* spp.*)*
Young nettles can be used in the same way to make beer. Strain the nettles after cooking and proceed as above.

Tea
Many wild plants rich in vitamin C can be used to make refreshing teas. The method of preparation and strength of the brew are matters of personal taste, so experiment with some of the following, using fresh leaves or drying them for later use.

Yerba Buena *(Satureja douglasii)* is also called Oregon Tea. The Spanish named it Good Herb because of its pleasing odor and taste. The dried leaves steeped for a few minutes in hot water make a good tea.

Yerba Santa *(Eriodictyon californicum)* makes a bitter but refreshing tea with a soothing effect on throat congestion.

Yarrow *(Achillea millefolium)* dried and boiled makes a nourishing brew, but should be used sparingly because of its stimulant effect.

Labrador Tea *(Ledum glandulosum)* has dry, leathery leaves that make a refreshing drink when added to boiling water for a few minutes.

Fireweed *(Epilobium angustifolium)* leaves, fresh or dried, make a flavorful drink when steeped in hot water.

Mint *(Mentha* spp. or *Monarda* spp.) comes in many fragrant species in these genera, any of which are a good source of tea leaves. Try them for strength and blend some for variety.

Wild Lilac *(Ceanothus* spp.*)* shrubs with aromatic, often leathery leaves are useful for making refreshing drinks. An eastern variety called New Jersey Tea was a favorite during the early days of our country as a substitute for the tea sent from England.

Select Bibliography

Abrams, L.R., 1940-1960, *Illustrated Flora of the Pacific States*, Stanford University Press, California, 4 vols.

Armstrong, M., 1915, *Field Book of Western Wild Flowers*, G.P. Putnam's Sons, New York.

Arnberger, L.P., 1952, *Flowers of the Southwest Mountains*, Southwestern Monuments Association, Globe, Arizona.

Balls, E.K., 1962, *Early Uses of California Plants*, California Natural History Guides, University of California Press, Berkeley.

Barkley, T.M., 1968, *A Manual of the Flowering Plants of Kansas*, Kansas State University Endowment Association, Manhattan, Kansas.

Boorman, S., 1962, *Wild Plums in Brandy*, McGraw-Hill, New York.

Craighead, J.J., Craighead, F.C., Jr., and Davis, R.J., 1963, *A Field Guide to Rocky Mountain Wildflowers*, Houghton Mifflin Co., Boston.

Davis, R.J., 1952, *Flora of Idaho*, William C. Brown Co., Dubuque, Iowa.

Dodge, N.N., 1967, *One Hundred Roadside Wildflowers of Southwest Uplands in Natural Color*, Southwest Parks and Monuments Association, Globe, Arizona.

Hitchcock, C. Leo, et al., 1955-1969, *Vascular Plants of the Pacific Northwest*, University of Washington Press, Seattle, 5 vols.

Horn, E.L., 1972, *Wildflowers: The Cascades*, Touchstone Press, Beaverton, Oregon.

Irwin, H.S., 1961, *Roadside Flowers of Texas*, University of Texas Press, Austin.

Jepson, W.L., 1925, *A Manual of the Flowering Plants of California*, Associated Students Store, University of California, Berkeley.

Kearney, T.H., and Peebles, R.H., 1960, *Arizona Flora*, 2nd ed., University of California Press, Berkeley.

Kirk, D.R., 1970, *Wild Edible Plants of the Western United States*, Naturegraph Publishers, Healdsburg, California.

Munz, P.A., 1972, *California Mountain Wildflowers*, University of California Press, Berkeley.

——— 1962, *California Desert Wildflowers*, University of California Press, Berkeley.

——— 1961, *California Spring Wildflowers*, University of California Press, Berkeley.

——— 1959, *A California Flora*, University of California Press, Berkeley.

Murphey, E. Van A., 1959, *Indian Uses of Native Plants*, Mendocino County Historical Society, Fort Bragg, California.

Patraw, P.M., 1951, *Flowers of the Southwest Mesas*, Southwestern Monuments Association, Globe, Arizona.

Rickett, H.W., 1966—, *Wild Flowers of the United States*; Vol. 3, *Texas*; Vol. 4, *The Southwestern States*; Vol. 5, *The Northwestern States*, New York Botanical Garden, McGraw-Hill, New York.

Shreve, F., and Wiggins, I.L., 1964, *Vegetation and Flora of the Sonoran Desert*, Stanford University Press, California, 2 vols.

Sweet, M., 1962, *Common Edible and Useful Plants of the West*, Naturegraph Co., Healdsburg, California.

Stevens, O.A., 1950, *Handbook of North Dakota Plants*, North Dakota Agricultural College, Fargo.

Thompson, S., and Thompson, M., 1972, *Wild Food Plants of the Sierra*, Dragtooth Press, Felton, California.

Weber, W.A., 1967, *Rocky Mountain Flora*, University of Colorado Press, Boulder.

257

Index of Common Names

Index of Scientific Names

Numbers in boldface refer to color plates and corresponding species descriptions.

Credits

All photographs are by Robert T. Orr, except where otherwise noted.

(The work of certain photographers has come to us through the courtesy of the California Academy of Sciences, abbreviated CAS)

1, Jack Dermid; 2,3 Paul Jarrett; 4, Ed Cooper; 5, Margaret Orr; 6, Donald Myrick; 7, Paul Jarrett; 8, Glenn Baum; 10, Margaret Orr; 11, Robert & Ira Spring; 12, Margaret Orr; 13, Ed Degginger; 14, P.R. Ferguson; 15, Robert & Ira Spring; 16, Paul Jarrett; 17, Margaret Orr; 18, Paul Jarrett; 19, 20 Robert & Ira Spring; 21, Charles Johnson; 22, Betty Mackintosh; 23, Robert & Ira Spring; 27, Roger & Joy Spurr; 28, Charles Johnson; 30, Roger & Joy Spurr; 32, Robert Potts; 33, 34 Robert & Ira Spring; 35, Betty Mackintosh; 36, Charles Johnson; 37, Betty Randall; 38, Elizabeth Henze; 40, Sherry Ballard: CAS; 41, 42 Bill Ratcliffe; 43, Bill Stackhouse; 45, Charles Webber: CAS; 47, Ed Ross; 49, Jack Dermid; 50, Bill Ratcliffe; 51, Charles Johnson; 52, Paul Jarrett; 53, George Lindsay; 54, Al Hesselberg; 55, Bill Ratcliffe; 56, Ed Cooper; 57, 58 Paul Jarrett; 60, Margaret Orr; 61, Sherry Ballard: CAS; 62, 63 Paul Jarrett; 64, Betty Mackintosh; 65, Robert & Ira Spring; 66, Roger & Joy Spurr; 67, Paul Jarrett; 68, Jack Dermid; 69, Glenn Baum; 70, Paul Jarrett; 71, Betty Randall; 72, Ed Degginger; 75, Paul Jarrett; 76, Charles Johnson; 77, Bill Ratcliffe; 78, Paul Jarrett; 79, Charles Johnson; 80, Ed Cooper; 81, Jack Dermid; 82, Bill Ratcliffe; 83, Paul Jarrett; 84, Al Hesselberg; 86, Paul Jarrett; 88, Roger & Joy Spurr; 91, Anna Cole; 92, 93 Bill Ratcliffe; 95, Ed Ross; 96, Paul Jarrett; 97, 98 Bill Ratcliffe; 99, Paul Jarrett; 100, Robert & Ira Spring; 101, Margaret Orr; 102, Paul Jarrett; 103, George Lindsay; 105, 106 Paul Jarrett; 107, Werner Schulz; 108, P.R. Ferguson; 109, Sally Myers; 110, Elizabeth Henze; 111, Dorothy Richards; 112, Emil Muench; 113, 115, 116, 117, 118 Paul Jarrett; 119, Charles Johnson; 120, Ed Cooper; 121, Robert Potts; 122, Margaret Orr; 123, Werner Schulz; 125, Ed Degginger; 126, Bonnie & Ed McClellan; 127, Robert Potts; 128, Paul Jarrett; 129, Ed Cooper; 130, Paul Jarrett; 131, Robert Potts; 132, P.R. Ferguson; 135, Jack Dermid; 136, Charles Johnson; 138, P.R. Ferguson; 139, Jack Dermid; 140, 141 Paul Jarrett; 143, Ed Degginger; 144, Robert Potts; 146, 149, 150, 151, 152 Paul Jarrett; 153, Charles Johnson; 154, Paul Jarrett; 156, Robert & Ira Spring; 157, Margaret Orr; 158, Charles Johnson; 159, Ed Cooper; 160, Charles Johnson; 161, Betty Randall; 162, Robert & Ira Spring; 163, Robert Potts; 164, Ed Ross; 165, P.R. Ferguson; 166, Ed Cooper; 168, Paul Jarrett; 169, Charles Johnson; 171, 172 Paul Jarrett; 173, Bill Stackhouse; 174, Robert Potts; 178, Margaret Orr; 179, Charles Johnson; 180, Betty Mackintosh; 181, Paul Jarrett; 182, Bill Ratcliffe; 183, Betty Randall; 184, Bill Ratcliffe; 185, Betty Randall; 186, 188 Paul Jarrett; 189, Betty Randall; 190, Joan Stockert; 192, Bill Ratcliffe; 193, Glenn Baum; 194, Emil Muench; 195, Bill Ratcliffe; 196, Emil Muench; 197, George Lindsay; 198, P.R. Ferguson; 199, Bill Stackhouse; 200, Ed Cooper; 201, Charles Johnson; 202, Al Hesselberg; 203, Robert Potts; 204, Ed Ross; 205, Bill Ratcliffe; 206, Ed Ross; 207, Peter Koch; 208, Charles Johnson; 209, Joan Stockert; 210, Sally Myers; 212, Werner Schulz; 213, Anna Cole; 214, Werner Schulz; 215, Ed Ross; 216, Margaret Orr; 217,

Schulz; 218, Ed Cooper; 219, Betty Mackintosh; 221, Carlyn Galati; 223, Jack Dermid; 224, Ed Cooper; 225, 226, 227 Robert & Ira Spring; 228, Ed Cooper; 229, Paul Jarrett; 230, Robert & Ira Spring; 231, Margaret Orr; 232, Dorothy Richards; 233, Paul Jarrett; 236, Margaret Orr; 238, Ed Cooper; 239, Robert Potts; 240, 242 Paul Jarrett; 243, Robert & Ira Spring; 244, Ed Cooper; 246, Paul Jarrett; 247, Margaret Orr; 248, Charles Johnson; 249, 251 Paul Jarrett; 252, Joan Stockert; 253, Paul Jarrett; 255, Betty Mackintosh; 257, Evan Davis; 259, Betty Randall; 260, Paul Jarrett; 261, Margaret Orr; 262, Emil Muench; 263, Werner Schulz; 266, Bill Ratcliffe; 267, Paul Jarrett; 268, Roger & Joy Spurr; 269, Robert Potts; 270, Paul Jarrett; 271, Charles Johnson; 272, Elizabeth Henze; 273, Al Hesselberg; 274, Charles Johnson; 275, Bill Ratcliffe; 277, Paul Jarrett; 278, Bill Ratcliffe; 279, Betty Mackintosh; 282, P.R. Ferguson; 285, Bill Ratcliffe; 286, Betty Randall; 287, Roger & Joy Spurr; 288, Charles Johnson; 289, Betty Mackintosh; 290, Ed Degginger; 291, Paul Jarrett.

All drawings of flower parts and types of leaves were supplied by Rachel Speiser, formerly illustrator for the New York Botanical Garden.

Symbols for chapter openings were drawn by Irva Mandelbaum.

This book was planned and produced by Chanticleer Press, Inc., New York
Publisher: Paul Steiner
Editor: Milton Rugoff
Associate Editor: Celeste Targum
Art Director: Ulrich Ruchti
Color layout: Irva Mandelbaum
Production: Gudrun Buettner, Helga Lose
Printed by Amilcare Pizzi, S.p.A., Milan, Italy